THE ART DEALERS

Betty Parsons   Irving Blum   Holly Solomon
Sidney Janis   Joseph Helman   Charles Cowles
Tibor de Nagy   Arnold Glimcher   Brooke Alexander
Alexandre Iolas   Marian Goodman   Patricia Hamilton
André Emmerich   Xavier Fourcade   Miani Johnson
Joan Washburn   Paula Cooper   Mary Boone
Lawrence Rubin   John Weber   Annina Nosei
Leo Castelli   John Gibson   Helene Winer
Ileana Sonnabend   Ronald Feldman   Janelle Reiring
Richard Bellamy   Daniel Wolf   Tony Shafrazi
Ivan Karp   Max Protetch

Clarkson N. Potter, Inc./Publishers

NEW YORK

DISTRIBUTED BY CROWN PUBLISHERS, INC.

The Powers
Behind the Scene
Tell How the Art World
Really Works

THE  DEALERS

Laura
de Coppet

Alan
Jones

Published by Clarkson N. Potter, Inc., One Park Avenue, New York,
New York 10016 and simultaneously in Canada by General Publishing
Company Limited

Manufactured in the United States of America

Library of Congress Cataloging in Publication Data

Jones, Alan, 1950–
    Art dealers.
    Includes index.
    1. Art dealers—United States—Interviews.
I. de Coppet, Laura.   II. Title.
N8659.J66   1984   380.1'457   83-10923

ISBN 0-517-54648-5
Design by: Two Twelve Associates
10 9 8 7 6 5 4 3 2 1
First Edition

TO

Maurice Girodias

CONTENTS

Acknowledgments   9

Introduction   11

Betty Parsons   **20**

Sidney Janis   **32**

Tibor de Nagy   **42**

Alexandre Iolas   **48**

André Emmerich   **56**

Joan Washburn   **64**

Lawrence Rubin   **72**

Leo Castelli   **80**

Ileana Sonnabend   **110**

Richard Bellamy   **120**

Ivan Karp   **134**

Irving Blum   **150**

Joseph Helman   **159**

Arnold Glimcher   **164**

Marian Goodman   **174**

Xavier Fourcade   **180**

Paula Cooper   **186**

John Weber	196
John Gibson	204
Ronald Feldman	214
Daniel Wolf	220
Max Protetch	227
Holly Solomon	234
Charles Cowles	242
Brooke Alexander	250
Patricia Hamilton	258
Miani Johnson	266
Mary Boone	272
Annina Nosei	282
Helene Winer	290
Janelle Reiring	291
Tony Shafrazi	298
List of Illustrations	306
Index	313
Photo Credits	320

ACKNOWLEDGMENTS

We would like to express our appreciation to the art dealers to whom this book is devoted, and to their gallery staffs, for the courtesy and cooperation they have granted us.

We particularly want to thank our editors, Carol Southern and Kathy Powell, for their judicious guidance, patience, and high spirits, and our agent, Harvey Klinger, for his confidence. We would also like to extend our gratitude to Henry Geldzahler and to Calvin Tomkins for their help from the beginning of our task. And for their encouragement, supportiveness, friendship, and insightful observations, many thanks to: John Anderson, Bill Beckley, Olivier Bernier, Dianne Blell, Coby Britton, Ugo Carrega, Saint Clair Cemin, Colette, Michael Cusick, Diane de Coppet, Suzan Etkin, Richard Hennessy, Howard Hussey, Gary Indiana, Jeff Koons, Andrew MacNair, Mark Upton, Jeffrey Wasserman, and Nancy Wilson.

INTRODUCTION

"**A**sk anything you like. I'll answer if I can, and if I don't want to, I won't." The tape recorder took in a long pause of traffic noise coming up from Fifty-seventh Street as Betty Parsons pondered a moment longer. "A book on dealers. Well, I'm very scared of *that*. You writers are always trying to dig secrets out of us we don't like to tell!"

The hour and a half that followed on that rainy afternoon in February, as we listened to this grand woman speak passionately about the artists and the art she loved, contained all the reasons for writing a book about dealers. Here was the unique eye that seizes upon what few others see, then singles those artists out and gives them their earliest support; here was the dealer who leads rather than follows public taste.

What then is this profession that centers on rooms without shadows, starkly lit spaces dedicated month after month to exhibiting works of art? If you are willing to accept the factual with the mythical, art dealers easily represent the greatest wellspring of lore about the art scene from the present day back to the dawn of Modernism itself. Next to the artists themselves, here are the people to go to if you take your art history straight. But will they tell their stories? Outspoken opinions do not encourage sales. And what of that old Italian proverb, "Those who know the rules do not teach them"?

The autobiography of the late Julien Levy, *Memoir of an Art Dealer*, admirably broke the dealer's vow of silence and served as a great inspiration to the undertaking of the present book. Yet few gallery owners in the United States have ever written about their careers, even though their life stories are often interesting. Love of scandal, the bravado of single-handedly defending an unpopular art movement — such pleasures must play a part in the motives of any contemporary impresario. "My greatest pleasure," the French dealer Kahnweiler once revealed, "was to applaud a piece of music I liked in the face of hissing adversaries. The same is true of painting: I adore defending what I love."

But how to convince members of a tightly knit profession to reveal their feelings about the dealer's craft? The only thing to do was to force their hand, just slightly, and let each tale unfold in its own way. And in the end, the art dealers who appear in these pages simply could not resist talking about art, about artists – and, like everyone else, about themselves.

The "one-sided" conversations that follow, edited from taped interviews that were conducted in 1980–1982, best permitted each dealer to tell his story in his own words. Together they create a collective ideogram of some of the deep themes and dramatic moments in contemporary art. We open right after the end of the Second World War and follow the evolution of the gallery world up to the eighties, witnessing the quest to tear down the barrier between life and art, the perennial swing of the pendulum from representation to abstraction and back again. Whether confronting Mondrian's formulation of passionate yet immaculate compositions or Pollock's revolutionary gesture, Rauschenberg's introduction of whole new realms of content, or the return to figurative painting today, an art dealer has been among the first to register an early impression of each shock wave.

Dealing art requires an engaging personality as well as instinct, and we found personality in abundance: the flamboyant Alexandre Iolas in his hotel suite, relating one anecdote after another about everything from Cairo to Joseph Cornell, demonstrating ballet acrobatics from his bed; a circumspect Sidney Janis in his office on Fifty-seventh Street, positioning himself in a chair for a clear view of a favorite painting, warming as he spoke of Brancusi and Duchamp; the astute André Emmerich lucidly placing one idea beside another, speaking in a small room rich with pre-Columbian gold; courtly Leo Castelli standing before a new work by Jasper Johns, "a painting that critics will still be discussing many years from now . . ."; and regal Ileana Sonnabend, supremely calm and soft-spoken, all the while relating her involvement with the most radical of contemporary artists. Every dealer, whether in conducting business or discussing art, seems to insist on a style and outlook as distinctive as a painter's brush stoke.

It can be said that the art gallery is one of best-preserved examples of capitalism still existing; the dealer's business is clear-cut and individual; his service extends in two basic directions, to those who make art and those who collect it. But what are the origins of the dealer's profession? Its earliest form can be detected in the commercial movement of art from Greece to Rome, where we find Cicero thinking aloud about the pros and cons of the resale of certain commemorative sculpture to the art dealer Damasippus. In the Middle Ages "corporations" such as the Guild of Saint Luke, organized in 1391 in Antwerp, carefully guided artists through distinct career phases – apprentice, journeyman, master – finally granting them the privilege of opening shops and engaging in business as independent artisans.

It took an idea emanating from Italy in the sixteenth century, the new Humanist concept of the artist as creator, to bring about new methods for the exchange of art. The shift from artisan to artist brought about the first separation between art-maker and art-consumer; as stone carvers became sculptors and painters became unapproachable geniuses, the gulf that keeps audience from creator was already growing. Dealers like the Florentine Giovanni della Palla began serving as go-betweens for artist and patron. Speculation was the rule; Vasari tells how a Madonna commissioned from Andrea del Sarto by François I of France "fetched for the merchants four times as much as they had paid for it."

While Raphael could boast to his uncle, "I am paid for my work whatever sum I deem fitting," most often artists' fees were established by the size of the work, the number of figures depicted, the amount of apprentice help involved, and the cost of precious materials like gold leaf. According to Vasari, Bernardino de Rossi made payment of 100 florins to the painter Perugino for a picture of Saint Sebastian and promptly turned the work around for 400 ducats, a considerable profit. Della Palla could name his own price when sending the French king works like the Hercules he acquired from the studio of Michelangelo.

In Paris during the seventeenth century, artists signed contracts for set periods of time, sometimes exclusive arrangements committing them to surrender all their output to one dealer, such as the early *marchand de tableaux* Lazare Duvaux, who counted Madame de Pompadour among his clients. Academies had taken on the task of regulating artists' careers in both France and England. The Académie Royale de la Peinture, founded in 1648, forbade members to engage personally in the commerce of their own works; they were, nonetheless, permitted to maintain contacts with collectors, thus keeping open the way for the intermediary. Diderot expressed little fondness for art merchants. "It is these people," wrote the philosopher in 1767, "who interpose themselves between the man of wealth and the indigent artist; who make the man of talent pay for protection they provide him; who open and close doors for him; who snatch the best of his products from him. . . ." The commercial middleman was from then on to play a central role in every artist's career, as history shows us by the circumstances of Watteau's death – in the arms of his dealer, Gersaint.

While the art gallery in the nineteenth century retained a strong resemblance to its antique- and curiosity-shop forerunners, the dealer's mission continued to evolve. Some of the famous names of the time – Georges Petit, Wildenstein, Knoedler, Colnaghi, Seligmann, Agnew – retain their importance today. But elevating the dealer's position from merchant to that of a new type of patron was the accomplishment of one man. The art dealer as we know him today was first seen in the Frenchman Paul Durand-Ruel, son of a paper-and-art-supply dealer who came to sell the work of his customers. Paul Durand-Ruel, born in 1831, looked beyond, to an enlightened dealer prepared when necessary "to sacrifice his apparent immediate interests to his artistic convictions and prefer a fight against speculators to an association with them." Emile Zola cast him in somewhat less idealistic terms in the novel *L'Oeuvre*, where Durand-Ruel appears under the name Naudet, "a dealer who for some years had been revolutionizing the picture trade. . . . He was changing the market completely by forcing out of it the collector of taste and dealing only with monied clients who knew nothing about art and bought pictures as shares of stock either out of vanity or in the hope that they would appreciate. . . ."

Artists' complaints about dealers are nothing new; Camille Pissarro, one of many Impressionists championed by Durand-Ruel, laments in a letter to his son, "The lower the prices the better for him. He can leave our canvases to his children. He behaves like a modern speculator for all his angelic sweetness." In another letter he declares, "It is disgusting to be part of such a degenerate business."

Still, the dealer was often rescuing unconventional artists who otherwise would have had to give up hope for patronage if rejected by the Salon, while official artists, like respectable functionaries of the state, settled in for comfortable careers revolving around the Academy. In a letter of 1881, we find Renoir reminding Durand-Ruel that Paris contained "barely fifteen *amateurs* capable of loving a work of art that hasn't been shown at the Salon." Thus the support of an art dealer was indispensable to counteract the drawbacks of artistic independence, if experimentation was to find encouragement. Theo Van Gogh, an art dealer himself, saw the perils of neglect in his own brother as well as in artists like Gauguin, Lautrec, and Redon, whom he also promoted. "The crux of the matter, you see, is that my work depends on the sale of my paintings," Vincent once wrote to Theo. "Not selling, when one has not other resources, one is faced with the impossibility of making any progress, while such progress would go on by itself if the opposite were true."

One of the most interesting art dealers of the period was Père Tanguy, an aging color-grinder and vendor of art supplies. Nonetheless, he was the proprietor of a shop that showed Monet, Renoir, Pissarro, Van Gogh, Gauguin, and Seurat; his was also the only place where the work of Paul Cézanne, whom Durand-Ruel had passed over, was on public view. The death of Père Tanguy in 1893 coincided, however, with the arrival of the legendary art dealer Ambroise Vollard.

Pissarro reported to his son in 1894 about a young man who had opened a *petite boutique* on the rue Laffitte, intent on showing only paintings by young artists, including some very beautiful canvases by Gauguin that Pissarro was quick to admire. "I think this little merchant will make a go of it," Pissarro concluded. Indeed, the high-hearted Vollard did gather up the most exciting artists of his time, a young Spaniard named Picasso among them. With an odd mixture of idealism and cunning, a duality not uncommon in the profession even today, Vollard did much to formulate the mechanics of speculation on avant-garde art. He would watch, wait, then suddenly sell, at prices set by the artificial scarcity he had created.

Vincent Van Gogh looked back into Dutch history for an apt comparison to speculation in art. "It is no use trying to get me out of my pessimism about picture-dealing," he wrote Theo. "I see this peculiar interference with prices in painting more and more as a sort of traffic rather like the one in tulips."

While Durand-Ruel had already consolidated all the

roles that the métier of art dealing can include – publicist, father figure, banker, merchant, patron, advisor to artist and collector alike – it was Daniel-Henry Kahnweiler who perfected the practice, demonstrating just how far art dealing could be lifted from the commercial plane. His manner of doing business, in the words of a contemporary, kept something of a "sportive quality" at all times. Kahnweiler went into business in 1906 and came to represent many notable artists, including Braque, Derain, Vlaminck, Miró, Léger. Throughout his career he saw the moral justification of his profession in the plethora of material cares a dealer could eliminate from artists' lives.

The following three-year "contract" of 1912 between Picasso and Kahnweiler is an example of artist-dealer relations during this time:

> I agree to sell nothing to anyone except you. The only exceptions to this agreement are the old paintings and drawings that I still have. I shall have the right to accept commissions for portraits and large decorations intended for a particular occasion. . . . I promise to sell to you at fixed prices my entire production of paintings, keeping for myself a maximum of five paintings a year. In addition, I shall have the right to keep that number of drawings I shall judge necessary for my work. You will leave it to me to decide whether a painting is finished. It is understood that during these three years I shall not have the right to sell the paintings that I keep for myself.

America was long considered an untapped market by European dealers. The French dealer Goupil had a representative named Michel Knoedler based in New York since 1846; Durand-Ruel opened a New York gallery in 1886. But from the beginning of this century it took the pioneering efforts of people like Alfred Stieglitz, who, as early as 1908, was showing Lautrec, Rousseau, Cézanne, Matisse, and Picasso in his gallery at 291 Fifth Avenue.

The gallery of Surrealist dealer Julien Levy, beginning in 1931, offered a more adventurous spirit – Dali, Tchelitchew, Cornell, Leonor Fini – than the cautious blue-chip operations of Mortimer Brandt or Curt Valentin. Sam Kootz and Charles Egan both showed their own daring, Kootz by exhibiting artists like Gottlieb, Rothko, and Picasso (to whom he made the famous gift of a brand-new Cadillac), and Egan by putting on early shows of de Kooning and Barnett Newman. The Hugo Gallery, started by Jean and Maria

Hugo, provided a great showcase for the European vanguard, from Victor Brauner to de Chirico, and gave Alexandre Iolas his first gallery adventure.

Like Levy, Peggy Guggenheim provided a great haven for innovation in the New York of the forties. Well served by her advisor Marcel Duchamp, she managed to recruit the best Americans and Europeans, from Max Ernst to Jackson Pollock, for her Art of This Century Gallery. Guggenheim remained an active presence until she moved permanently to Venice in the early fifties. Levy retired in 1949.

The years following the Second World War prepared the New York art world for the drastic changes to come. As principals like Levy and Guggenheim departed, the curtain rose on a different cast – and these new figures are the subject of this book. Within two decades, newspaper headlines could proclaim, "Paris – Dethroned Queen of Arts," while American contemporary art was transformed from a poor-but-proud elite into a prospering industry and New York gained its undisputed title of art capital.

The dealers who tell their stories in the pages that follow are in large part responsible for the international status of American artists in our time. Just as the goal of every gallery is to represent as many as possible of the great artists of its era, so too had we hoped to include each outstanding dealer in this book – a desire obviously impossible to achieve in a single volume. Left with a choice of hundreds of dealers and galleries, we looked for those whose unique contributions represent their time; since New York's place in avant-garde chronicles – as well as the intensity of its art market – is unrivaled, we have concentrated fully on the rich resources of this one city. To include European or regional dealers and do them justice would have required an undertaking of a totally different nature. Also, the format best suited to our task, that of focusing on dealers with galleries currently in operation, likewise prevented inclusion of such vital presences as Eleanor Ward, Virginia Dwan, or Klaus Kertess, whose contributions as art dealers were made in galleries no longer in operation. But most of all we greatly regret being unable to include so many others, several of whom had graciously granted us interviews, yet were omitted due to the limitations of space alone: Grace Borgenicht, Rosa Esman, the late Robert Elkon, Allan Frumkin, Barbara Gladstone, Max Hutchinson, Nancy Hoffman, Phyllis Kind, Jill Kornblee, David McKee, Robert Stefan-

otti, Allan Stone, Angela Westwater, and Virginia Zabriskie, to name but a few.

The art world is the most volatile and unpredictable of
all possible worlds. John Russell wrote in the *New York
Times* in 1982, "Contrary to what is sometimes thought, the
New York galleries are not all standardized. The better they
are, the more individual they are." In many respects, the
risks are akin to the perils that artists themselves must face.
The merchant needs the dedication and self-confidence of
an art maker, in addition to a solid business sense and a
unique before-and-after-the-fact talent for seeing the direction individual artists and public taste will take. But behind
the glamour and fanfare of opening nights, the services of a
dealer often relieve the artist from the burden of everyday
bookkeeping: accounting, shipping, insuring, archiving.
More often than not, the business of art is business.

A manager, to paraphrase Saul Hurok, cannot invent an
artist; he can only provide the audience. The art world rises
or falls on the artist alone, not on the merits of the support
system that takes its lead from him. If artists in the past
have challenged the "gallery system" as a corrupt anachro-
nism, today we have seen artists rally to revitalize it. The
community of interests, cultural and monetary, that centers
on the artist in our time can sometimes resemble the Dar-
winian jungle, and it is increasingly difficult to distinguish
predator from prey in the ecology of contemporary art.

In the end, we get the kind of art world we deserve —
artist, dealer, collector, curator, and critic are all part of the
process. Each must look to make a world in which grand
appetites are never sated at what the Italian art dealer
Arturo Schwarz once called "the feast to free us once again
from habit, and to set out in search of the extraordinary."

Alan Jones
December, 1983

THE ART
DEALERS

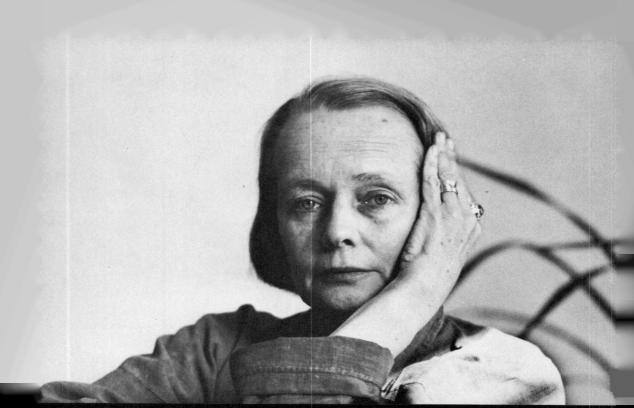

Betty **Parsons**

Betty Parsons (born 1900, New York City, died 1982) studied sculpture with Antoine Bourdelle at the Académie de la Grande Chaumière in Paris, and later with Ossip Zadkine and Alexander Archipenko. An artist in her own right, she was director of the Wakefield Gallery and Mortimer Brandt Contemporary Gallery before opening the Betty Parsons Gallery in 1946, where she showed the early work of the Abstract Expressionists

I remember Paul Mellon once asking me, "How do you do it?" I didn't know what to tell him. I think I was born with a love of the unfamiliar. How else can you describe it? I had no idea that I had this talent — an "eye" — even though I was as well educated as anyone else. Everyone has instincts, but having faith in them is something you have to work for.

A good eye is a very mysterious thing; nobody can teach it to you. It's a talent you're born with. When you study the history of the selection of talent, you find not very many people on those pages. There was that amazing man in Paris, Vollard, two or three others in Paris, and there are two or three alive in the world today. But if it weren't for that eye, if there weren't those people, the artist would be lost. For a long time I used to think that Clyfford Still was going to be lost. No one wanted him. He was still having a hell of a time after years of painting. They all would have been lost, those artists of the forties and fifties, if someone hadn't realized what life and what energy they had.

Of course, I fell in love with all those artists; I thought they were just terrific. I never had the slightest doubt that they were terrific.

In a sense it was all destiny. As a young woman, I was in Europe just after the First World War studying very hard to be a sculptor. I was over there for about eleven years working with the masters: Bourdelle, Zadkine, Archipenko. I went broke in 1929 and came back to America and went to California, wondering what I would do to make a living. Hollywood was not such a bad place to be at the time. I taught a little art class out there, played tennis, did some portraits, and took odd jobs.

I knew that New York would draw me back eventually. Alan Gruskin gave a little exhibition of my watercolors at his Midtown Gallery in 1938. I told him I had to earn a living and asked if he had any ideas. He suggested that I work at the gallery, on a commission basis. So I did — not realizing that it was the beginning of what I was to do for the rest of my life.

Soon Mrs. Cornelius J. Sullivan, one of the founders of The Museum of Modern Art, offered me a job in her Park Avenue gallery. Working with her was fascinating: she had a marvelous collection, from nineteenth-century French to Modigliani. Again, I worked on a commission basis, and by this time I was hooked.

21

In 1940, the Wakefield Bookshop asked me to run a gallery for them in their cellar, and it was there, actually on my own, where I began to realize that I had the ability to pick out talent. I showed Hedda Stern, Walter Birch, Saul Steinberg, Ad Reinhardt, and many others, and I began to see that this was the thing I should do to make a living, that I should be a dealer. I stayed on at the Wakefield two or three years and did fairly well, struggling along.

Mortimer Brandt had an old-masters gallery in New York and asked me to run a contemporary section for him after the War. I agreed and began by showing a lot of people who have since become famous, like Gorky and Reinhardt. Mortimer Brandt never had much faith in the new art and came to the conclusion, premature as it turned out, that there wasn't enough money to be made in the contemporary field. After the War, he wanted to go to England anyway, so he offered me his whole space. I decided to take half of it, and rented the rest to the art dealer Sam Kootz, who represented Picasso and other European moderns.

Here was my chance. It was 1946, and I opened my gallery intent on showing all those people nobody had really wanted up to then. I met the artists through one another gradually, in particular through Ad Reinhardt and Adolph Gottlieb. Gottlieb invited me for dinner one night, and there was a very imposing gentleman at the table: "I'd like you to meet Barnett Newman." It was a revelation! Barney in turn introduced me to Jackson Pollock, who was on the lookout for a new gallery at the time since Peggy Guggenheim was headed off for Europe again. Peggy took me to Pollock's studio on Long Island. With her gallery in New York she had started a great many things, but she was more interested in collecting paintings than in selling them, and had very little talent for business. Her gallery wasn't much of a financial success. The artists needed sales, and they were never altogether happy in her gallery for that reason. She used to have awful fights with all of them. When I took on Pollock, she was still subsidizing him. So for the first year whenever I sold anything, I would give the money to Peggy.

I gave Pollock his first one-man show, in 1947, then Rothko, Still, Reinhardt, Tomlin. I met with a lot of hostility, but I did have a handful of loyal clients who liked what I showed, people like Edward Root, the English car manufacturer, who was quite a famous collector at the time. Root used to buy from me and keep me going. Mrs. Gates Lloyd

Adolph Gottlieb

Untitled

1 9 4 2

Barnett Newman

Concord

1 9 4 9

also kept me going; Mrs. Millikin kept me going. Without a small nucleus of supporters, no gallery can make it, and I had about five very good clients who saved me from debt.

When I started there were about fifteen galleries in New York. Now there must be 515. All the same, there were only about three or four galleries concentrating on the very contemporary area in 1946. There was Marian Willard, who was before me; there was Charlie Egan, a great friend of mine who showed de Kooning and Franz Kline. Egan had those two famous painters; I had most of the rest. Stieglitz, at the American Place, represented Marin, O'Keeffe, Arthur Dove, and all those. Peggy Guggenheim had exhibited Pollock, Rothko, and Still before I did in her Art of This Century gallery, all in group shows.

I was the first to put up plain white walls in a gallery. Why? Well, showing these great big pictures of the Abstract Expressionists, I got to thinking about the look of the gallery itself. In those days galleries mostly had velvet walls and very Victorian decoration. I decided to hell with all that, and the artists agreed. When you're showing a large painting by Jackson Pollock, the last thing the work needs is a plush velvet wall behind it. The white was very severe; I wanted nothing else in the gallery, no furniture, except maybe one chair or bench. That was the idea, to have it as simple as possible, and it did catch on.

Jackson Pollock

No. 2

1 9 5 1

Ellsworth Kelly

Cowboy

1 9 5 8

From the very start, I had no intention of being an "American" gallery; I wanted an international scope. I still don't believe in nationalism, in the arts or anything else. It only makes wars. But in Paris I couldn't find anybody as good as the Americans I was already showing. Once, I was about to leave my hotel for the trip back to New York when the telephone rang: someone was calling me to say there were two marvelous artists in Paris who I must see. They were Americans! I groaned, but promised I'd go. The next day I found myself looking at the work of Ellsworth Kelly for the first time. I took him on immediately, he was so marvelous. Then I went to see the other artist, Jack Youngerman. I took him right on, too. The early things of theirs that I bought are still in my apartment in New York.

I knew a lot of New York dealers. One day I was talking with Curt Valentin, the great specialist in artists like Juan Gris, Paul Klee and Miró, all that sort of thing. He asked me, "What do you think of Pollock? What do you think of Rothko? What do you think of Newman?" I told him that I thought they were marvelous. "Then I'm going to get right out of the business," he said, "because I wouldn't touch any of them."

Of course, all of these artists would have much rather shown with Valentin; he was the established, older gallery. I was quite young, and I was fortunate to have come along when I did, because galleries like Valentin's were not interested in tackling the new art. And no wonder: it was so difficult in those days to convince people to buy the work of the rising American artists; it was hard enough just to get people to look. I had to do a lot of talking, and it wasn't easy to get collectors to come around. But soon there were the first few converts, people who began having faith in the American creative ability. It was a terrific creative period then, the years right after the War.

Clyfford Still

Untitled

1 9 4 5

I had, as I said, four or five collectors who were very interested in what was really going on in art. But nineteenth-century French was in its ascendancy, and everybody was buying nineteenth-century French. Galleries showing American art, even from the generation before mine, were also very irritated that no one would buy. It had to be French, and it had to be nineteenth century. I kept saying, "Don't scotch it. Art has nothing to do with what you sell or don't sell." I have always believed that art has something to do with the very best you can find, and the nineteenth-century French painters are marvelous, and it is right that they should have come into this country. But finally, thank God, it was bought out and there was nothing left. We could move on.

Still, I braced myself against a lot of negative reactions from what I call the heavy artillery. There were the elderly, people who'd been buying only the French. One lady was so rude to me that I finally told her, "The elevator is over there. It goes down every minute." The worst thing was vandalism. People would come in, and when they left I would notice four-letter words scribbled across Pollock pictures, Newman pictures. They would try to cut the paintings, too.

When I first opened my gallery there weren't very many critics around, but I had a hard enough time with the few there were. Once, Stuart Preston, a critic for the *New York Times*, came off the elevator, took one look at the Clyfford Still show and started back into the elevator. I told him, "Please do me a favor." (We were friends, you know.) "Would you mind going into that room with a Clyfford Still and staying there for five minutes? I'll close the door and let you out afterwards." So he went in and sat there. When the five minutes were up, Preston walked out and reluctantly admitted that maybe, after all, I did have something.

Art critics still seem always to want to find historical associations instead of *creativity*. That remains my one great complaint. They are all historians, they know their art history backwards, and all are beautiful writers. But when looking at something new they immediately feel the need to put it in its place, to make a new page in the art books like reporters with an exclusive for the tabloids. But you can't put something that's just been done into history; you've got to talk about its creative impact for the moment. A new work by a new artist is not history, it's the present. Leave it alone, at least for a while, let it come to life fully before you put it into this or that category.

One great saving grace of those early days was the good relation I had with the marvelous Alfred Barr and Dorothy Miller of The Museum of Modern Art. Alfred Barr loved

Jan Groth

Sign

1 9 8 1 – 8 2

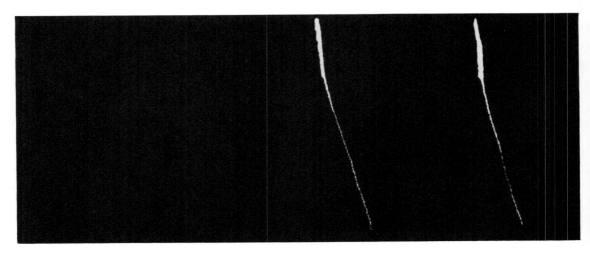

everything I did; to him, I could do no wrong. But he used
to have a rough time himself. I remember once Alfred
bought a big Rothko from me. He convinced Philip Johnson
to buy it for the museum, and it was put up for approval
before the next meeting of the trustees. They were outraged. Half of them rose to their feet and said, "If you show
that picture you can get out, out of the museum." Barr had
to put it in the closet. Four years later he put it on the wall:
the board of directors applauded.

No one caught on to artists like Rothko faster than
Alfred Barr and Dorothy Miller. They accomplished mira-
cles, though it was never easy going. Without them, I would
never have survived. I would have starved, and the artists
along with me. They were always helping and showed all my
painters at the museum. You're not going to see that happening today. Museums have relinquished their responsibility to keep up with what's going on. Lack of money is the
universal complaint of museums, and I think that's probably
true. And they still have to get trustees to back them when
they go out on a limb with a show. But still, The Museum of
Modern Art hasn't done anything in *years*, since Alfred Barr
got sick. They have no new ideas. The Whitney Museum
doesn't do much, and the Guggenheim doesn't do much better. And few acquisitions. Very, very little.

If someone wants to see what's going on in art, he has to
go to the galleries. An artist like Jan Groth is an example: I
have given him two shows, his marvelous black tapestries.
The Art Institute of Chicago bought one, but it's wicked
that there isn't any of his work in New York. The Met
should have bought one. But where can this artist be seen?
In a gallery.

My favorite clients have always been the ones who collect out of love, just as children collect postage stamps: you
fall in love with things that delight you, that you can't resist.
One of the most marvelous collectors I loved selling to was
Duncan Phillips of the Phillips Gallery in Washington.
There was such an intensity in the way he would study the
paintings in a show, the attention he gave to each work. His
curiosity for art was inexhaustible.

Then there is the collector who comes in and wants art
for investment, or wants something to put over the sofa;
there are those who buy for status, for some vague goal of
attaining a higher social position. We hear more and more
talk about art as investment, art as a store of value. It is.

Art and real estate are the two things that have paid off the most handsomely today. They have both held their values, and they will keep going up.

After all, what is left in terms of a society's history, of the history of the world? It is only art that is left. All else goes. Without art, would we have any idea what the past was like? The Greeks and the Jews knew that. The past would have been lost and destroyed, all of it. Art is the record of mankind, what man felt about his world. We are in such an industrialized, technological society that it is all in the head, instead of the heart. I have the greatest belief in what art embodies; it's what you *feel* that will save the world, not the brain, which is so cruel, so rational.

Being both an art dealer and an artist is a rather special situation to be in. When I was eighty, I had the biggest year of my life: six shows of my own stuff, three of which sold out. But sculpting is a compulsive thing with me; I've never cared whether I showed my own work or not, whether I sold it or whether anyone liked it. I just have to do it. It keeps me going.

I'm fascinated by the creative world in every direction: dance, music, literature, painting, and sculpture. It's all submerged beneath the scientific world we live in. Where is the hand of man? You used to be able to buy the most beautiful toys made by hand. Everything is machine-made today, but it is the hand of man that is conducive to beauty. When I buy something for myself, like a piece of Congolese sculpture from the Pace Gallery, it's a perfect example of the creative world to me. That's what I'm always trying to explain, my interest as a dealer in the creative world.

I've always looked for the tremendous wallop. There is a lack of it around these days, and it's strange that there should be, with the political and economic situation, the world on the brink of disaster. Such times are bound to produce powerful art, but so often I see so many nice, very attractive things that lack that great significance, that grandness, I've always looked for.

Today I think it is sculptors who have the chance to project a powerful vision, and there are some very good ones around. Architects would be wise to involve themselves with sculpture more than they do, and I also like seeing so many galleries putting on exhibitions of architecture, which has long been a passion of mine. Tony Smith built my studio and guest house at my place down on Long

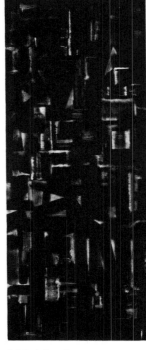

Ad Reinhardt

#38

1 9 4 9

Island, and he was a marvelous architect; that was before his wings were clipped, and he went totally into sculpture. He was one of the very great sculptors, and it was terrible that he died.

I'm not attracted to the cliché or to the repetitive image; all along I've been interested in finding the great artist: the drama of it, the thing that really moves you. As time went by, well up into the fifties, interest in the creative world was increasing, and since I had a reputation for showing the new, more young collectors kept coming to me, people who were looking for the unfamiliar, not something easily categorized.

Isms. I have never liked isms. I believe in the differences, not the similarities, and I have always said, "*Vive la différence.*" I can't stand fashions, all those terms like Pop, Op, and so forth. I was never interested in Pop, while at the same time I appreciate the individuals in that group. Its humorous angle came as a relief from the seriousness and the drama that had been going on for so long before; I respected it but never was interested in showing it. Richard Lindner, whom I did show, was never really considered Pop, at least by me. And before Pop became popular, nobody wanted his work. That changed quite rapidly for Lindner.

I don't think there is too much friendship among dealers. It's a fact, for example, that I took Sidney Janis to court over a disagreement about our gallery space, but I've forgiven him finally, although I still think he's too commercial. Leo Castelli, by far my favorite dealer, knows how to take care of his artists and knows how to promote them. I have great respect for that. In the end, I think art dealers do their best to get along with each other. We have to.

When I started my gallery, nearly all art dealers were women: people like Marian Willard and Martha Jackson. It's surprising how many women there were giving the creative push to contemporary art, the pioneering and promoting. And there still are: Virginia Zabriskie is terrific; Paula Cooper has a beautiful gallery full of good artists. I think women are more creatively oriented than the male dealers, who are all money, money, money. That's the first male consideration. My first thought: Is the artist any good? If he's good and doesn't sell, that doesn't change my faith in him.

Many pictures have gone up in value so fast that it's

Saul Steinberg

Drawing of Betty Parsons

1 9 5 8

hard to keep track of the market; therefore, auctions have become a sort of barometer for pricing art. For instance, twelve years ago I bought a painting by Kitaj from his studio for $500; recently I called another dealer to find out its current value. Fifty-five thousand. That's quite a jump, and it has been established by auction prices. There are people who decide they want something and they're going to get it come hell or high water. They'll pay anything for it. Dealers have to keep track of these price increases, to protect their artists. Sometimes it's a false value; if a dealer has one of his artist's paintings up for auction and he's afraid the price will drop, then he'll go and protect its value by buying it back. I've done that, and so has every dealer. It might be a wet, rainy day the afternoon of the sale – so many factors enter in at auctions, it's beyond predicting.

If a painter becomes famous when he's forty, he doesn't want to see his prices starting to go down when he turns sixty. It has happened in quite a few cases, with good painters, too. They don't hold their interest and fade out of the picture. But they can come back, be rediscovered and regain their former value. It's a fluctuating market. Some, like Jasper Johns, keep going up and up.

It is regrettable that this great interest in the arts today caught on more with investors than with politicians. Nobody in Washington really gives a damn about the arts. We have

a terrible time getting a penny from them, and it's going to get worse. Public funding should be carefully supervised by someone who knows a little something about art; politicians don't. You have to really teach them, if you can – and good luck trying.

I once spoke to a large group of Democratic Party leaders in Washington. I asked the chairman beforehand, "Do these people know what I'm going to talk about? Would it be insulting to define what I mean by abstract art?" She told me to go ahead and try it on them. I did. I put a painting up in front of them, and by the end of my little talk they were all still squinting painfully, looking for a hand, a mouth, a foot. They couldn't find these in the painting I showed them; they weren't there. They just couldn't look at it in terms of the abstract.

Education can help, and I think it already has. Every public school should have an art teacher, in my opinion; why shouldn't the butcher, the baker, and the candlestick-maker take part in the experience of art? That's where I'd be putting my money if I were in the government. But again, art education should be careful to take the creative as its point of departure, not the historical. Too often in the schools, art is treated on the historical basis: impose, impose, impose. The opposite of what art is about.

If only the political world could be more creative, could see what artists have to contribute to current society. It is a common misconception to think of the process of making art as something impractical and beyond it all; contrary to that myth, the artists I know are all extremely competent people: sculptors are the best carpenters, for example, and there's nothing dreamlike about hammers and nails. But everyone thinks of the artist as a *rêveur*. It isn't true. Artists have great creative resources to offer the world.

The buying and selling, all of that, is in the end only the expedient for something else, permitting things to happen, to come into the world, to be created; the paintings and sculpture that result are valuable in the true sense. For an art dealer, discovering a young artist and giving him his first show is the most exciting thing in the world. When out of nowhere I find someone who really *has it*, whose work delivers that tremendous wallop, at that moment I feel I'm doing the job I set out to do. That's the thing: I know of no greater thrill.

Betty Parsons

Eyes of the Sea

1 9 8 1

Betty Parsons

Village Shop

1 9 8 1

31

Sidney Janis

Sidney Janis (born 1896, Buffalo, New York) was already a well-known art collector and the author of *They Taught Themselves, Abstract and Surrealist Art,* and *Picasso: The Recent Years* before he opened his gallery in September 1948, exhibiting the leading Abstract Expressionists alongside the early-twentieth-century European masters.

T

here was a very beautiful museum in Buffalo, where I grew up, called the Albright Art Gallery overlooking Park Lake, where we used to skate as youngsters. Many times after skating I'd visit the museum with my skates over my shoulders. It was free, it was interesting, and I felt it was a privilege to go there and look at the pictures.

When I married and moved to New York in 1924, I spent a great deal of time on Fifty-seventh Street. There were very few galleries then – Knoedler, Valentine Dudensing, and perhaps half a dozen others. I felt it a gift to be able to walk in, without admission, stay as long as you liked and enjoy great pictures. In those days it was quite easy to cover the art world and see all the exhibitions in any given week. Today, with two or three hundred new shows opening each month, you *might* be able to cover the scene with half a dozen lieutenants to help you. The great enthusiasm today is all to the good. But then the public was very antagonistic toward vanguard art. Miró's large blue pictures of 1926–27 were offered for a couple of hundred dollars, and found no takers. Cubism was only a dozen years old and had been neither visually digested nor accepted. The very few collectors who were interested bought primarily Picasso and Matisse.

Mrs. Janis and I began collecting in 1926. The first picture we bought was a Matisse. We had been looking, shopping around, for quite some time. It was a painting that intrigued us, and although having possessions was against our principles, we felt the painting was something we had to experience at first hand.

Constantin Brancusi

Fish

circa 1 9 2 6

We began meeting artists. We visited Brancusi in 1926. His studio was so cold; I remember a girl once boasting that she had gone to bed with him, and he had kept on his long underwear! His sculpture was all set in place, each carefully wrapped in the sort of quilted material that you see the girls wearing on the streets today. When we asked to see a *Bird in Space*, he took a long pole with a hook at the end and attached it to the metal ring at the top of the cloth shield. When he gently lifted the covering from the sculpture, it was so erotic – like undressing a beautiful woman. I wanted to buy one of his pieces, but he said, "Oh, that would break up my arrangement."

The arrival of so many European artists here after the fall of Paris in 1939 had quite an impact on painting in New

York. The artists in exile were among the best: Léger, Mondrian, Breton, Duchamp, Ernst, Matta. They were gregarious, interested in what was happening in America, and they stimulated the younger Americans whom they were eager to encounter. Motherwell, Pollock, Kline, Gorky, and de Kooning had already been meeting at The Club on Eighth Street, batting out their ideas and in the process sharpening their perceptions. Their meetings and the exchange of ideas with the European exiles meant a great deal, and it was really this stimulation that helped create the New York School.

I had already known Marcel Duchamp in Paris, and we spent many wonderful evenings together exchanging opinions. He was very fond of my wife. She and I did an article in 1946 for *View* magazine entitled "Duchamp, Anti-artist." He liked the title. He was probably the only artist, with the exception of Dali, who kept abreast with what the young artists were doing. He was a great catalyst, and his talent for inspiring people was evident years later in his influence on the new realist ideas of Johns and Rauschenberg. Like a good actor on the stage who knows how to throw away a line, Duchamp's one liners, always terse and meaningful, registered on minds ready to accept his pronouncements.

Mondrian spent four years in New York and painted but four pictures during that entire time. He was very fond of jazz and always had records spinning while he painted. One day I mentioned that Stuart Davis was having a show at the Downtown Gallery and that James P. Johnson would be there with his boogie-woogie piano. We visited the show together; he looked at all the pictures, but I think he really went for the music. He began adding little touches to his paintings that seemingly had been finished in Europe. One day I found him working on a picture that was ostensibly finished – it was dated 1935 – and here it was back on the easel in 1942. He said, "Yes, now I'm adding boogie-woogie." I still have one of these canvases to which small color squares have been added along certain edges.

Mondrian, because of his catholic tastes, liked art that was very different from his own. He admired Hirschfield, the primitive artist, who he described as the "master of two dimensions." At the opening of the Hirschfield exhibition at the Museum of Modern Art, accompanied by a coterie of less interested abstract painters, he studied every work.

Mondrian died in New York in 1944 at the age of sev-

Matta

To Cover the Earth with a

New Dew

1 9 5 3

Piet Mondrian

New York City, New York

circa **1 9 4 2**

enty-four, before he could finish his *Victory Boogie-Woogie*. The highest price he ever received was $600 for *Broadway Boogie-Woogie*. The dynamics of New York were a great stimulus to him, just as they were to Léger, who had been in a slump abroad for years. It was in New York that Léger painted some of his best pictures.

My book *Abstract and Surrealist Art* was finally published in 1944. It included many artists who had not yet reached their image – works that might be termed Pollock before Pollock, Hofmann before Hofmann, Rothko before Rothko. When I visited Rothko at his studio in 1943, I selected a picture for my book that was quite unlike those of his later years. At the end of the evening, Rothko asked me, "What section do you think you'll put me in? I would like to be in the Surrealist section." So at that time, many of the artists had *not* yet arrived. In hindsight, it seems I selected many of the artists before their time.

I met Pollock in 1942. Lee Krasner, who later became his wife, took me to his West Eighth Street studio – a visit that left me greatly impressed. On a second visit a few months later I chose *She Wolf* for my book. Pollock had not gone into drip painting, a technique not unrelated to the uncensored Surrealist image, until 1946. But the scale of Pollock's image was monumental, rather than of the easel dimensions of the Surrealists. As a result of the action of the whole arm and body, his paintings were bolder and not easily accepted.

Because of his silent nature Pollock was considered

Fernand Léger

Deux Plongeurs

1 9 4 2

Jackson Pollock

The She-Wolf

1 9 4 3

inarticulate by many. This was not so; when he had something to say it was original and to the point. His artist
friends respected his comments as they did his art. After
my first visit, I dropped in on Hans Hofmann, who lived
next door. When I mentioned that I had just been to see
Pollock, Hofmann asked, "Who's that?"

Pollock was greatly influenced by André Masson, a
brilliant spontaneous painter. Nevertheless, when the first
Pollock exhibition took place in Europe in the late fifties,
Masson went to Switzerland especially to see it, and when
asked by a friend, "What are you doing so far from home?"
he replied, "I come to pay homage to the master."

Writing books on art wasn't very profitable, and in the
late forties I decided to come out of retirement, this time to
go into a business I knew; something I really loved. After
ten years of meditation and writing, I decided to open a
gallery. In May of 1948 I took the space Sam Kootz had
given up on Fifty-seventh Street.

Pablo Picasso

Femme à la Mandoline

1 9 1 1

The list of exhibitions I wanted to do was so long that
even today I'm still working on it. One can do only eight
shows a year, so eighty ideas take a decade. Our opening
exhibition was given over to Léger, a show with important
paintings I had on loan from European collections. Only one
was sold. We followed with one-man shows of Kandinsky,
Mondrian, Schwitters, Albers – all definitive shows. Still
nothing happened. Rather than revert to something more
seductive and more salable, we insisted upon showing more
difficult works. Incidentally, the collection I gave to The
Museum of Modern Art about fourteen years ago consisted
mostly of paintings of this caliber – paintings that couldn't
sell. The harder road we had chosen brought lean results,
and by the end of the second year I was tempted to close
the gallery. At that time the Baroness Rebay came in with
Solomon Guggenheim, and they bought three great Mondrian paintings and one by Léger. That encouraged us to
remain. Slowly others began to see the light, people of my
generation, not only New York residents but collectors from
Baltimore, Chicago, and the West Coast as well.

Women seemed more intuitive than men. I remember
the first time we exhibited some very tough early Dubuffets,
paintings with heavy impasto; men had difficulty but many
women responded favorably. They understood intuitively,
and some convinced their husbands. While men often
respond objectively to works of art, women are more

instinctive and seem receptive to greater cultural penetration and understanding.

We continued with exhibitions of the School of Paris, and by late 1951 began to include one-man exhibitions of important American painters. The Pollock generation was shown side by side with the Picasso generation, the acknowledged masters of Europe. Clement Greenberg later found that such juxtapositions helped the public make the transition, the very long step from Cubism and Surrealism to the New York School.

Jackson Pollock visited our gallery at the time we were hanging our first show and stayed the whole afternoon. He was interested in how we hung it, at the same time sizing up the gallery space. Later on, after he had left Betty Parsons, Lee Krasner asked me if I was interested in handling Pollock. We agreed that I would do an exhibition of his work every November, beginning that year. His first show covered a wide range of his work, including his drip paintings.

De Kooning came over to us late in 1952. I had known him through Gorky from the time he arrived in America as a Dutch stowaway in 1928. He was a struggling artist, very quiet, painting very little and destroying most of what he did. His first show at the gallery, a group of paintings I liked very much, were paintings of the Women.

It hadn't occurred to me that having both Pollock and de Kooning in the gallery was so significant to their peers, but gradually other artists, including Franz Kline, Gorky, Rothko, and Motherwell, joined the gallery. In turn they were given one-man exhibitions.

Jackson Pollock

Autumn Rhythm

1 9 5 0

Willem de Kooning

Woman I

1 9 5 0 – 5 2

Pollock was very jealous of the gallery's position and of the exhibitions we held. He was not happy with out first Matta exhibition, a show of early paintings of works that had strongly influenced Gorky and others. Pollock's conclusion here was "this is not up to your level." I'm not sure he was right, but it does show how meticulous he was about his acceptance of the gallery, artists all of whom impressed me greatly.

We put on consecutive exhibitions of American artists which were real knockouts, but sales were slow. Out of the exhibition of de Kooning's *Women*, only one or two sold, and

Franz Kline

Turbin (Black & White)

1 9 5 8 – 5 9

Mark Rothko

Light Over Grey

1 9 5 6

those for around $1,800. Pollock never enjoyed the sweet smell of success; an eighteen-foot painting called *One* was sold in 1952 for $8,000, which was to stand as the greatest amount we received for a Pollock during his lifetime. Twenty years later I bought it back for $350,000 and gave it to The Museum of Modern Art. We sold *Blue Poles,* a somewhat smaller picture, for $6,000, and eventually it was sold to the Canberra Museum in Australia for a reputed $2 million.

But we struggled along with our artists, and by their second or third exhibition, things began to click. Our third de Kooning show in 1959 sold out on the morning of the opening, quite unprecedented. When Franz Kline joined the gallery he said, "You know, I haven't been selling any pictures. My dealer had them priced at $3,000. What do you think?" I said, "Let's make them $1,500." Quite a few sales resulted. Later we sold them at $3,000, and then $6,000. By the end of Kline's lifetime his price had reached eighteen to twenty thousand, piddling when we consider his prices today. Unfortunately, like Pollock, he died too early to enjoy the fruits of his success. Franz was a wonderful person, the salt of the earth. He could never say no; a beautiful attitude and one that worked often to his disadvantage.

Rothko, on the other hand, was difficult even before he was recognized. We gave him three or four exhibitions which he himself installed exactingly. Eventually he left the gallery, which is a story unto itself. He was the only artist in our experience who decided to handle his own sales. I reminded him that it would take time away from painting and that it was impossible to do both things well. Eventually an offer by another gallery for a great number of his works at a considerable figure was too tempting for him to resist.

We followed with Motherwell shows, and later on Guston joined the gallery, making a total affiliation of ten leading Abstract Expressionists.

Our first Pop exhibition was held in 1961, under the title The New Realists. As a result of this, many younger artists joined the gallery, among them Dine, Oldenburg, Segal, and Wesselmann. This was a step that the older artists, particularly Guston, Motherwell, Gottlieb, and Rothko, strongly opposed. They held a protest meeting and decided not to be associated with what they believed to be Johnnys-come-lately, and withdrew from the gallery as a body. I tried to induce them to stay, explaining that the younger artists

Tom Wesselmann

Great American Nude #73

1 9 6 5

could not be considered competitive, but all in vain. As disturbing as it was, we continued with the Pop generation, which in the meantime has made its own reputation.

Incidentally, Bill de Kooning was one of the artists who attended that fateful meeting. I later heard that he offered no protest. He was the only one who stayed with the gallery. I always felt that Pollock and Kline, both of whom had died, would have remained as well.

Many people find it difficult to step from one generation to the next. The older public, critics included, who had been excited by our Cubist or Fauvist exhibitions rarely came to the shows of the Pollock generation, and the very people who accepted the latter in turn dropped away when we began to show the Pop generation. Today we see an army of new faces every time we show the work of a young artist. Each brings a whole new public. New generations of artists appear so frequently that keeping pace is difficult. Each with new ideas finds a new audience, and this I suppose is as it should be, for each generation, whether artist or viewer, is alike in some basic esthetic. The older collector, however, does not often go along with the changing ideas of each new generation, but when he does, esthetically his life is enriched. The work he acquires of each new artist whether a masterpiece or not offers ample visual pleasure.

Prospective buyers often ask for advice, and the best I can offer is to keep looking; eventually you will see. Try for an open mind and an open eye; thus equipped, new horizons will be in the offing. A dealer should avoid imposing his own findings upon a client, however willing the client may be to listen. Years ago a client and friend of Curt Valentin asked me if I would show him a few Klee paintings, which I was glad to do. Because he seemed interested, as we viewed the work together I touched upon certain interesting pictorial inventions on the part of the artist. When I met Valentin at lunch the next day he asked, "What on earth did you do to our friend? He ran out of your gallery and told me you were trying to educate him!" No longer do I impose esthetic judgments gratuitously.

Making a collection, I feel, is a personal thing and should reflect the collector's own judgment. I might suggest he visit other galleries and also museums in order to gain an overall view of what is happening and continue from there. Alfred Barr once said that museums are right in their choices 10 percent of the time. He was being modest, for The Museum of Modern Art has a very much better record. For me, it seems that 90 percent is a tolerable average, and collectors should try for that.

The Museum of Modern Art has done the most to promote understanding and appreciation of twentieth-century art. At the very start, its backers were well known and respected, and their choice of a young, alert director, Alfred Barr, was both wise and foresighted. The magnificent exhibitions held there which I saw and enjoyed over the years have been a great education for me.

We remain interested in younger artists many of whom are included in frequent group shows. My son Carroll keeps in touch with this situation and visits artists studios and reserves time for them as well when they bring their new work to the gallery.

Each generation has its own direction, its own prejudices, good or bad. Today art is in a state of great pluralism, and I'm far from able to prophesy what the next direction in art will be. But whatever turn it takes, it will come, as it always has, from some unexpected source.

George Segal

The Hustle: The Four-Hand

Pass

1 9 8 0

Tibor
de Nagy

Tibor de Nagy (born 1910, Debrecen, Hungary) was educated as an economist in his native country and came to the United States after World War II. In November 1950 he opened a gallery with the art critic John Bernard Myers. By sponsoring theatrical productions and literary readings, his gallery encouraged collaboration between artists and writers.

My father was an avid collector of modern art, and he began taking me to galleries in Budapest when I was five. Later on he trained my eye with a little game. "I've selected two paintings to buy," he would say after we had seen an exhibition. "But I'm going to take them home, Tibor, only if you can guess which ones they are." At first I failed, but soon I could pick out his selections immediately.

I studied economics in the university and eventually worked at the national bank of Hungary. When I started to build my own art collection, I didn't want to copy my father. So instead of contemporary art, I went back to the old masters, collecting Flemish and seventeenth- and eighteenth-century Italian works. The entire collection was destroyed in World War II by a British airplane that crashed into my villa.

In the years after the War, I was imprisoned three times, first by the Germans and then twice by the Russians. Finally I managed to escape in 1948 and, with a little money from the sale of some jewelry, I joined my wife and daughter in the United States. Landing in New York a disillusioned, spoiled Hungarian romantic, with memories of prison and the loss of people dear to me fresh in my mind, I was desperate to find new values and a new life.

While I was waiting for a post in the World Bank, a young man persuaded me to invest in, of all things, a marionette company, which he felt would become important on television. His name was John Bernard Myers. This was no common marionette company. Jackson Pollock, Willem de Kooning, and Franz Kline were all involved, and Ned Rorem wrote music for us while Kurt Seligman was making hand puppets. In fact, Pollock carved one out of wood, but unfortunately it disappeared. That would be a very important little puppet today.

John Myers was art editor of the famous *View* magazine, which Charles Henri Ford had started. Myers kept up a wide range of interests, and soon the artists we knew began encouraging us to open a gallery. With some promises of financing, I signed a lease on a place off Third Avenue, where the elevated train was still running. It was 1950, not easy times, and when the money did not come through all seemed lost.

Out of nowhere Dwight Ripley appeared, an absolutely brilliant person: poet, artist, botanist, and a great collector of art. Unfortunately, like his friend Dylan Thomas, Ripley was a heavy drinker. But for six years he paid our gallery's rent. Without a patron like Dwight, what gallery could have given Kenneth Noland, Carl Andre, Ron Gorchov, Jane Freilicher, Larry Rivers, and Red Grooms their first one-man shows, as we did?

Our opening show was of sand sculptures by Costantino Nivola, resembling the gravestones in Sardinian cemeteries. Beautiful work, but Tino didn't fully command his material, and the sculptures disintegrated into sand.

Then came Grace Hartigan, calling herself George Hartigan with George Sand in mind, and the thought that a man's name would receive more notice. I was opposed to it, but she insisted. As Grace gained success, we were able to go back to her real name, but meanwhile the first sale we made was a painting by "George Hartigan" for $75.

Larry Rivers still felt the influence of French artists like Bonnard in those days, but with a very American feeling from the outset. He was doing his best paintings at that time, I daresay. His shows were wonderful: Rivers did lots of still lifes and was beginnning to take on ambitious sub-beloved mother-in-law, died, Larry painted cemeteries for a while. When he came back from France he did the marvelous French Money series, and another, the Playing Cards series. His work began selling quite well, and he was the first artist who brought money into the gallery. It was Gloria Vanderbilt who purchased the first Rivers from us. Showing that work was a rewarding experience. He was very much a man of the moment: Larry was committed to bringing figur-

Announcement for exhibition

of paintings and drawings by

"George Hartigan," March

25–April 12, 1952

Red Grooms

Tibor de Nagy Presents

1 9 6 3

Fairfield Porter

Portrait of Tibor de Nagy

1 9 5 8

Larry Rivers

Frank O'Hara Double

Portrait

1 9 5 5

ative painting up to date in an America of jazz and Jack Kerouac.

I have always handled both figurative and nonfigurative artists. It was always satisfying to show the work of Fairfield Porter, a great painter whom I miss dearly. Through the fifties we also had artists like Al Leslie, who was then doing huge, beautiful abstract paintings, and Robert Goodnough.

All these new artists had a completely American feeling to them, just the thing that John Myers and I were after. We began to publish writing by the new American poets, as a gallery activity. Myers was very involved with poets and writers, as were the artists themselves. We were the first to publish Frank O'Hara, and John Ashbery's *Turandot*, Kenward Elmslie, Kenneth Koch, Jimmy Schuyler. Today those pamphlets are quite precious, as is the lithograph series, *Stones*, that Frank O'Hara and Larry Rivers did together.

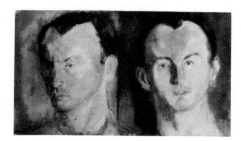

The atmosphere in the arts seemed completely different than it is today. More genuine. We would hold big discussions about the philosophies of abstraction or the writing of Ezra Pound. We were all poor anyway, and you heard much less talk about money. All that changed in the sixties when Castelli came into the picture with Pop Art. Castelli is an excellent public relations man; he has a real talent for it. But public relations in art, such as the media fanfare that publicizes high auction prices, is something I have never liked. I've seen German dealers come to New York and not look around, just ask for those few names they had heard about. Such trends are, after all, only fashion, and I never liked that, no matter how lucrative it was. In that sense, I'm very European. Good art sells itself, and I avoided working with PR and with credit, although both are major components for financial success. My gallery never had the machinery for it like Castelli had with Ivan Karp installed in his gallery. I've always believed that Karp, in terms of public relations, was instrumental to Castelli's success.

Word of mouth is another story, and it helps artists, especially early in their careers. There again it shouldn't look like an advertising campaign building up an Andy Warhol. But what artist doesn't like seeing his name in the magazines? Artists are very egocentric people, after all, and when it comes to their careers they usually couldn't care less what happens to a gallery. It has always been a very bitter pill for me to see artists leave my gallery. When Castelli built up his gallery with Rauschenberg and Johns, he was very lucky to find such loyal artists.

Helen Frankenthaler was the first artist to leave us. She had joined the gallery right out of Bennington. But her husband, Robert Motherwell, didn't get along with John Myers at all. Motherwell himself told me that he talked Helen into leaving us. She went with André Emmerich, where she's been ever since.

Kenneth Noland started with us, too, but when Clement Greenberg took over directorship of the French & Co. gallery, naturally Noland went over to Clem, his best friend. But in this case we had found Noland by way of Greenberg in the first place. Greenberg used to like our gallery because he found it lively; the fact that we once had his blessing is used against us today by the anti-Greenberg contingent. But when Greenberg comes in today, he approves of, at most, only half of our artists.

Changes in art, and in the way it is collected, are bound to occur over the years. My collectors have come to me more out of disinterested appreciation than with an eye toward investment. A collector like Robert Scull hardly ever bought from me; he went to Castelli. Instead, I had collectors like Alexander Bing, the real-estate man, who really became a friend of the artists, donating paintings to museums to help build reputations. He helped Rivers and Hartigan in this way, and in an artist's early days it helps to be listed in one or two museums.

Joseph Hirshhorn came to us often from the mid-fifties on, when he already had quite a developed eye. Like Peggy Guggenheim before him, he felt he had the right to buy inexpensively. Inclusion in collections such as theirs, they believed, gave an artist a very real boost; therefore they took discounts for granted, and it was in the best interests of everyone to cut prices for clients like these. Hirshhorn enjoyed haggling. It was part of his game. He would come into the gallery and say he had fifteen minutes until his

Kenneth Noland

Curious Course

1 9 7 5

Robert Goodnough

Excursion

1 9 6 3 – 6 4

plane took off and he wanted this, this, this, and this. "Give me the price list," he'd say. "You people have become so expensive that I can't deal with you anymore. How much is that? Ten thousand? Alright, I'll give you five or else forget it." He got the paintings. That was Joseph Hirshhorn.

There was a time when Alfred Barr and Dorothy Miller from The Museum of Modern Art would come to the gallery once a month. They were interested in everything new, and when the Rockefellers came and bought it was thanks to the advice of Alfred Barr and Dorothy Miller. The Rockefellers were good customers. Nelson bought a number of Hartigan's paintings. David Rockefeller once wanted a Fairfield Porter to take to the sheik of Kuwait as a gift. He came and bought one painting for the sheik and two for himself. We delivered them to his home on approval, and the next Monday I opened the newspaper: KUWAIT SHEIK DEAD. The deal seemed to be off, but Rockefeller, typically, came around and said he'd keep all three.

Our big collectors today are corporations, which sounds beautiful in principle. But I believe the best large collections of the past were all built by one person's eye. Unfortunately, not all corporate art advisors can use their integrity, and, willingly or unwillingly, act as interior decorators. What will be good on that wall? What will make the vice-president happy? That's a far cry from building a great collection.

My greatest satisfaction as a dealer is in seeing artists grow. As a young man I was a spoiled brat; I loved to own things, to grab, to surround myself with luxury. Life has shown me that my values were wrong, and I have learned that the act of merely possessing art can be heartless and empty when we lose sight of the goals that the artists themselves are working toward. I got rid of the desire to possess: seeing is reward enough for me now.

47

Alexandre
Iolas

Alexandre Iolas (born 1908, Alexandria, Egypt) ran away from the family cotton business to study ballet in Paris. There his interest gradually shifted from the world of dance to Surrealist art, and he opened the Hugo Gallery in 1944 after arriving in New York. In 1955 he founded the Jackson-Iolas Gallery in partnership with another former dancer, Brooks Jackson.

For me a gallery is absolute theater. Arranging the exhibitions, the lighting, the openings – it all goes together, and if it's done well, it's magnificent. I've always thought of myself as a performer. I started out as a dancer, but I've ended up dealing with art because ballet people are really terrible; so ignorant and stupid it's amazing. They may be truly divine on stage, but after the performance they return to earth.

I am pure Greek, but like my mother and father and my grandparents, I was born in Egypt. There was a great Greek community in Cairo, with wonderful schools. Egyptian Greeks are not like Greek Greeks, who are so uncultured. In Egypt we took part in all the cultures – Greek, English, French, Egyptian. Life there was very alive and cosmopolitan.

The first time I saw ballet was when Pavlova came to Cairo. It was amazing: "My God! How do they do that?" I was intrigued. At that time it was well understood that my father wanted me to go into his cotton business, but I wanted to become an *artiste*.

Every summer my father would take me up the Nile to Upper Egypt during that wonderful oriental heat. We would visit the pashas. He was tough on me, very strict, but I really was a bit unbalanced when I was young; at seventy-four I am still completely crazy. But I'm a genuine crazy, nothing cooked up. It comes to me like breathing.

There was only one thing to do, so I escaped from home and went to Paris. I started going to school to become a ballet dancer and proved to be unusually talented. My lessons were given to me free, and every day the professors invited me to keep them company after classes. I don't know why. Perhaps they found my craziness charming.

My first encounter with an art gallery took place one day as I was walking on the rue Matignon. I was about seventeen years old. There was a painting in the window, and for some reason I stopped in front of it. What was this painting doing there in the window? I wondered. The next day I passed the window again. I was drawn to the picture as if by magic, and stood there looking at it. I never thought of going in. I'd never been in a gallery in my life. But by the fourth day, I got up my courage and went in and asked someone, "Excuse me, what is that in the window?" "It's a de Chirico." "What is a de Chirico?" The man in the gallery was

Russian, and very patient. "But who *is* de Chirico?" A young painter of Italian descent, I was told, whose work is full of metaphysical images. "How much does it cost?" "Two thousand dollars." A masterpiece. You could buy masterpieces in those days for even less than that. He gave me a little book on de Chirico as a present.

Every day after school I began going to this gallery. The dealer and I became friends – I forget his name, Raoul Levin, something like that. One day a grandson of Cézanne came into the gallery. I had never heard of Cézanne. I was a peasant from Egypt! Eventually, with the small allowance of money my mother was sneaking to me from Egypt, I bought a little Cézanne drawing.

Man Ray

Untitled

1 9 5 9

I also used to sell my hair to make ends meet. It was 1925, and fake eyelashes had just come onto the market. I have curly hair, and one day Antoine the coiffeur asked me, "Can I buy your hair?" He's crazy, I thought. But I went along with it, and he would cut off the ends of my hair and glue them into false eyelashes. Marlene Dietrich wore them. I was paid for doing this; it was my income. I then bought the painting by de Chirico that had so fascinated me.

My life continued on in this way; it was a double life. Already, ballet was not enough for me. Oh, it was wonderful, the vision of it, but now I also had the art. Little by little, I began to meet the artists. I went to Raoul Dufy, and he made a beautiful drawing of me which I still have. I met Bérard, Picasso, Braque. Then, at the masked ball of Rochas I was introduced to Man Ray. It was to be a memorable occasion for me because that night was also the first time I saw Max Ernst. He was in pajama pants and had eyes painted all over his naked torso, with false eyelashes, of course!

It was very exciting for me to meet those famous artists over the years, all the tra-la-la: Marcel Duchamp, Éluard, Leonor Fini, and the rest. At last, I met de Chirico himself, and we became great friends. He was a man of extraordinary genius. Max Ernst was the person I liked the most, to whom I was most attracted. But it was Victor Brauner who, in spite of being completely unknown, truly advanced painting, the way of thinking about art. I believe that Brauner made a revolution which we do not yet see clearly.

Berlin in the early thirties was an exciting city, very much in vogue. The theater was avant-garde, with Bertolt Brecht and Kurt Weill. The music was extraordinary,

Schoenberg and all that. It was very much alive in the pre-Hitler period, and crazy, absolutely crazy. A bit like New York today but more chic. The Germans are not chic at all; in fact they are very kitsch. But they have a chic by being kitsch. In Berlin in 1933 when Hitler was coming into power, one night I encountered two brown-shirt boys. Because of my dark, curly hair, I was beaten to hell as they shouted, "Dirty Jew! Dirty Jew!" I went straight back to Paris.

The first time I came to New York was in 1935, when George Balanchine engaged me to dance at the Metropolitan Opera. Eventually I became the director of the Marquis de Cuevas Ballet. I became great friends with de Cuevas. I brought Balanchine to him, Menotti, Prokofiev, and then Stravinsky, thinking the Marquis might commission a ballet score. But it didn't click. "The poor marquis," said Stravinsky, "he is very naive. He thinks I am writing in the language of *Coppelia*. He doesn't know that I engrave in granite." *Que je sculpte en granit*. He was talking about *Scheherazade*, about things that were far away from de Cuevas's Corsican mentality.

I also engaged superb dancers like Brooks Jackson for the ballet company, but de Cuevas and I began to fight. He didn't know anything about art, although he was very sensitive. He liked Dali because Dali was Spanish, but he didn't really know what art was all about. He couldn't understand Picasso, what Picasso really meant. I adored Picasso. His paintings were such a shock. But still, I think that the good de Chiricos are much more important than all the masterpieces of Picasso put together. De Chirico: a predestructive painter and a postdestructive painter. If all the world is ruined by bombs, it's going to look like a de Chirico.

I have always hated being established, settled down. When my gallery in Paris started to become completely

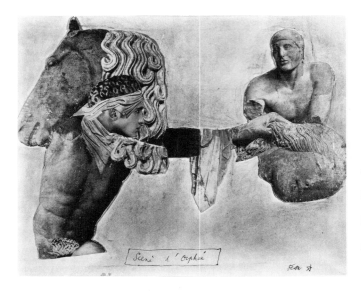

Jean Cocteau

Scene from the

ballet Orpheus

no   date

secure, I moved on to Milan, and when the same thing happened there, to Geneva, then to New York. I concentrated for many years mostly on European artists, but now all my people are dead: Max Ernst, Christian Rohlfs, Fautrier, Gromaire, de Chirico, Cocteau, Magritte. I'm like a widow.

There is enough movement and madness in life that I don't see why anyone needs to look to the past. But I want to be remembered dancing, young, not as an old hag falling to pieces. A dancing pose, a statue, a divine pose, even naked. Very avant-garde, like the Countess de Noailles. Cocteau was never her lover; he was her pimp. Decidedly a better position. I had shows, of course, of Cocteau's work in my gallery in New York, and he often came over.

In the early fifties, Leo Castelli and Sidney Janis used to come into my gallery. Leo had no gallery of his own yet. He and Sidney were clients, fake clients, but so interested. They were nice, and what they had, both of them, was intellectual and artistic interest in what my gallery was showing in the early fifties. I was always pleased to have them come in.

Magritte

Madame Recamier de David

1 9 6 7

I do exactly what I want in my life and work, what I like, what I love, independent of nationalities and things like that. I am antinationalistic in art. I definitely do not believe in cultural boundaries that require a passport to cross. Of course, the French, Italian, and German schools are more advanced in the history of art, because they are a few centuries older than America. But if you look at American art of thirty, forty years ago, it was based on the principles you recognized as coming from European art. A cowboy in place of Millet's peasant. Today American art is the greatest expression of modern art as we know it.

What can be said about art? Analyze? Things like that are none of my business. I hate to talk like a connoisseur of art. I'm not a connoisseur; really I have nothing to do with it. People teach me sometimes and then I read in secret to learn a few things about it like names and dates. But I forget them immediately.

Art has no words. Words have nothing to do with art, absolutely nothing. That's the wonderful thing about it, the magic of it. It's a mistake to be too intelligent: you become professorial, didactic. When you start talking about art in that manner, what a bore! Schapiro and all those critics. It's not possible. Art has nothing to do with anything like that.

Talking about art always seems the best way for me to begin a good quarrel. I went to a young artist's studio not long ago, Julian Schnabel. It was quite a horrible experience – all those cups, all those broken teapots that he uses in his paintings. But I liked very much a few of the things, the things he had really resolved without showing off. The sensibility.

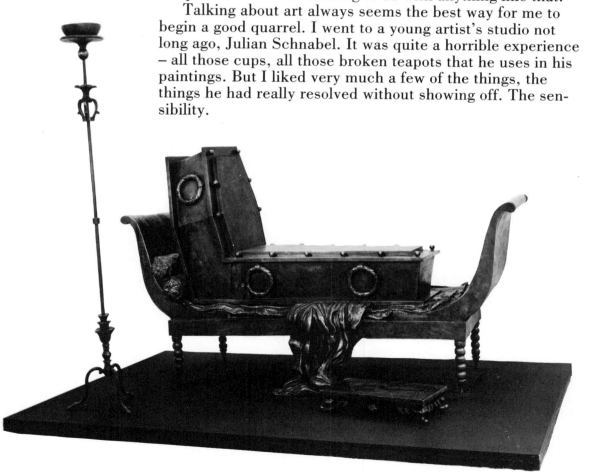

Early on, I did an exhibition of Andy Warhol in my gallery, drawings of shoes and models for shoes, things like that. The boy is a very important artist, Andy, because he helped America. He mixes very much with youth, and with all the chic people – you know, the bums. When you have such a stupid expression as Andy has – when he is being silent, before the smile starts – when you look like that, you can do anything you want in the world. As Christ said to all those priests, "Suffer the little children to come unto me," and Warhol is a horrible child. He has helped America to get rid of its puritanism, either with his half-pornographic, half-esthetic films or else with his portraits of the fake stars he has around him and the real stars he has always liked. He's an amazing person, and probably someday he will be considered a saint.

But my man is Robert Rauschenberg. He is very much influenced by Max Ernst and he'll never know it. Those collages are versions of Max Ernst. But you could see immediately that it was a very wise direction for Rauschenberg to take, for an American artist to take. As with Warhol, when Rauschenberg arrived on the scene it was like the appearance of a divine prophet. It was very important for America, more important for America than for art itself.

On the other hand, Cy Twombly is an artist I cannot stand. No, I can't take his delicate approach, and that all-white background of his. I like him very much as a person, and his wife, and his beautiful house in Rome. He is a very nice man, and very clever, but I think that he has no sensitivity at all. I prefer the work of Rauschenberg because he makes mistakes. He is human; he goes and tries again.

There is another artist I liked more in the beginning of his career, and that is Ed Ruscha. I saw a splendid exhibition of his in Italy – beautiful, detached. Also, it has no pattern, which I like. No patterns that are introduced as knowledge, to be talked about, that you are asked to suffer about. I don't know what he is doing now. I wanted to visit him when I was in Los Angeles, but he wasn't answering his phone.

Joseph Cornell was someone else I liked very much as a human being. I did seven shows of Cornell's work, and every time it was an unforgettable experience. He was such a genuinely poetic person, almost to the extent that he was on the very brink of the ridiculous. He had nothing measured. But he was certainly by no means mad. It was just

Joseph Cornell

Taglioni's Jewel Casket

1 9 4 0

William Copley (CPLY)

The Champ

1 9 7 0

that he allowed himself an exuberance. I had great contact with his work, whatever it was, whether it was a Medici box, or a box full of birds. I liked it because it was a plunge into the past, totally unique. He was in that sense a necrophiliac, pulling you with him back into that past where he found beautiful visions. He was a real artist with visions of beautiful girls.

I used to go to Cornell's home on Utopia Parkway, in Queens, New York. He had an invalid brother who was retarded and had difficulty speaking. He was carried around in a chair. Cornell loved his brother, and the meals he made always consisted of dishes like nuts, fruit Jello of the most incredible colors, things like that. There was never any real food, but it was always colorful. He used to squeeze violets on top of mushroom soup to make it lilac-colored. Cornell didn't eat much himself, but he adored chocolates, cakes, nuts. Above all, Greek pastries were something he could not resist. He was such an emaciated man, so thin, and he spoke with a beautiful voice.

How can one's likes and dislikes be explained? For example, geometrical art bores me to death. I don't move easily in front of one of Frank Stella's paintings. If you give me one as a present, I will return it to you. I have no use for it. Geometry must remain more mysterious. Earlier in this century people tried to make that geometrical art, and what happened? Finally a stupid man came along, named Mondrian, beating his head against the wall, trying so hard. You don't go anyplace like that. Art is a vehicle that transports us, but do you arrive at paradise by a straight line? I think not.

As for paradise, that you decorate the way you want. It has very high ceilings and very high rent. I'll wait to see what they have to sell there; it's a big market. In the inferno, everything is rotten quality. But in paradise they are very well organized, the furniture is nice, and everything has your initials monogrammed on, the color of pigeons. But it's a bore, naturally. The inferno, too, must have its share of tedium, but I'm sure it must be a bit more amusing. Dante was a very shrewd man to have the best of both places, even though he was impotent. But in this art business, even though dealers don't create it themselves, it's all for the love of art. After all, it's better to be a bad lover than to be impotent.

Andre Emmerich.   Los Angeles   3rd April 1982   CH.

Andre
Emmerich

André Emmerich (born 1924) studied at Amsterdam
Lyceum and Oberlin College. After a career as a writer,
he turned to art dealing in October 1954, later becoming the primary dealer for Color Field painters, such as
Kenneth Noland, Morris Louis, and Helen Frankenthaler, while maintaining his passion for pre-Columbian
antiquities.

I'm a third-generation art dealer. There was no escaping it with a family in which my parents were collectors, my aunt a painter, my grandfather a major dealer in Paris before the First World War. An uncle had a gallery in Paris in the late 1930s. But when I was growing up I did not want to become a dealer, partly because I had always been told that I'd be such a good one. I became what seemed much more exciting: a writer, editor, publisher, promotion and advertising man. My faculty advisor at Oberlin said I'd never know English well enough to write, even though I cited Conrad. Well, for ten years I made a living as a writer, everything from advertisements to art criticism. But more and more I felt I wanted to work with things that really gripped me, that I had a gut reaction to. The great publishers and editors – William Randolph Hearst, the Dewitt Wallaces, Henry Luce, Hugh Hefner, Helen Gurley Brown – these are all people who have a gut feeling for what interests people out there. They are in fact a lot like those people. I was not.

With art, however, I found I did have an intense response that very often was shared by others. I have never worried about the salability of art because I assumed that if I like something very much, I was not so unique and there would be others who respond as I do. That feeling in the pit of my stomach is what has always dictated my decisions about art and artists.

Art dealers are often called tastemakers. I think that's a misconception. I am no more a tastemaker than Leo Castelli is. What we are is leaders of the pack. Why? Because we experience early what others seem to experience a little later on. The whole game lies in being able to identify and experience trends in advance, by the seat of your pants, by feeling and enthusiasm. Art dealers are like surfboard riders. You can't make a wave. If there aren't any waves out there, you're dead. But the good surfboard rider can sense which of the waves coming in will be the good ones, the ones that will last. Successful art dealers have a feeling for hitting the right wave.

Many years ago I began collecting pre-Columbian art, and a friend of mine once asked me how I was so clever as to get involved with pre-Columbian art just at the right moment. There's really only one answer. I got interested in it just as I got interested in girls; they had always been there, but at a certain moment it occurs to you how exciting

Gold bird pendant with

double crocodile headdress.

Diquis Delta, Costa Rica

A. D. 8 0 0 –

1 5 0 0

they are. Our responses to things are constantly changing. The same thing happens with art. I had a shock when I saw the Pollock retrospective at The Museum of Modern Art in 1967. I remembered many of those paintings from earlier shows. The interesting thing is that when I'd seen them in the late forties I had been overwhelmed by their seeming violence, brutality, dynamism. When I saw them in the retrospective, they were minuets, almost Mozart-like in their delicacy and subtlety. The paintings hadn't changed; it was my own mindset that had changed.

It is very difficult to explain to someone born after 1950 how *radical* Abstract Expressionism felt, how rough and ready it looked to us at the time. Recently at Christie's a ten-foot Franz Kline was up for auction, a painting done on the barn door of his studio in East Hampton. It is classic Abstract Expressionism. When it was painted it looked as rough and violent as can be imagined. A critic as sophisticated as Harold Rosenberg called painting like that Action Painting; painting that was all action, all raw spontaneity.

The only analogy I can think of is when you are at the beach in summer and there are lots of women in bikinis, you don't notice that they are in bikinis. There is no sense of shock at the bareness of their bodies. If a woman would walk into a gallery or a cocktail party wearing a bikini, we would all be boggle-eyed. Pollock and Kline both appeared like a woman in a bikini at a cocktail party. This is one of the hardest things to do, to convey that sense of shock, the newness.

Remember, too, there is never just one trend going on in art, never just one feeling. In the twentieth century a number of major movements coexisted without much interaction with each other. Mondrian and Matisse lived at the same time, together with Klee and Soutine. Old man Monet painted his water lilies while Cubism was being invented and after it was left behind by its two best exponents, Braque and Picasso. A great many things exist side by side. One obviously goes for what one is most excited by. I once made up an imaginary motto for an art dealer: *Credo ergo exposito.* I believe, therefore I show. Pre-Columbian art excited me. And early on I was very moved by a number of painters whom I showed when I first opened my New York gallery in 1956.

I was never involved with Pop Art. When it came right down to it, I had to make a choice as to what kind of art I

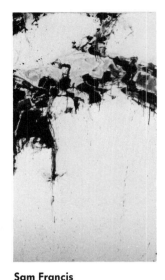

Sam Francis

Muted No. 2

1 9 5 7

wanted to show, and I made as personal and subjective a choice as deciding between a beautiful fresh pear and chocolate ice cream.

One of the tragedies of the art world today is the internecine warfare, the hostility, the oppositional strain. I think it goes back all the way through the history of modernism. Art provokes an enormous amount of hostility. I was on a panel in May 1980 and talked about the art I like, particularly two artists I value highly and have shown for a long time, Helen Frankenthaler and Jules Olitski. Suddenly a passionate advocate of very different kinds of art stood up and said, "So glad you talked about them and showed slides. I'd forgotten how much I hate their work. It is wonderful to relish that hatred again." I felt like throwing up at hearing that said about things I find very beautiful and very tender. It's that kind of hatred that leads to the sort of destruction you had in the French Revolution, Nazi Germany, and the Cultural Revolution in China. These feelings are very, very strong. It's sad. I am far more tolerant in my basic approach than a lot of the partisans all around, and their narrow-mindedness troubles me. I don't think the artists themselves have such feelings of hostility. It's always the hangers-on. They are more Catholic than the Pope.

I have grave questions about government activity in art. We've seen what happened to the universities once the government started to give large grants. Senator Moynihan, whom I like and admire enormously, wrote an article on the damaging effects of excessive government impact on universities. I have seen the same thing happening in art, and I see it as unfortunate. That is not how Velasquez painted the Rokeby Venus nor Cézanne the Mont St. Victoire. They produced that privately.

I have a feeling that there was an extraordinary period in America, which probably began with the fall of Paris in 1940 and led up to the postwar flowering of American art: Abstract Expressionism's first generation, Pollock, Hofmann, de Kooning; the second and third generations; and then Color Field and artists like Stella and Johns. I think, however, there are very few major new artists of the seventies who hadn't already been noted by the end of the sixties.

For some time I've felt we have been in a relatively sterile period in terms of emerging talent, new visual ideas, great painting being done by new people. Today both here and abroad I see an enormous desire to seek out young tal-

Morris Louis

Moving In

1 9 6 1

ent. But I see very little that is of quality. Lots of local interest, but not much of staggering importance. I think the best
painting today is still being done by people who first
emerged in the fifties and sixties. Of course I sometimes
wonder if I believe this because I'm fifty-nine and hung up
on my own generation!

The same thing has happened in other periods. The first
quarter of the nineteenth century for example: A great artist? Goya, David, if you wish, but not much else. Ingres,
Corot, and Courbet were just getting going, really flourishing, in the second quarter. Delacroix, just getting going. It's
all later. Gainsborough, Romney, Hogarth, all dead. It was a
very dull moment, everywhere. The German Casper David
Friedrich and American Luminists come in the second
quarter. So then, as you go down the nineteenth century it
gets richer, and in the last quarter you have the Impressionists, an extraordinary burst of vitality, but still only barely a
dozen.

Critics don't invent talent, and I can only say that galleries don't work with them; you usually work against them.
There are two kinds of critics, those who review shows for
the newspapers and art magazines, and those few writers
who are true critics, such as Clement Greenberg, the late
Harold Rosenberg, William Rubin; these are art thinkers if
you will whose essays you read if you want to gain an under-

Helen Frankenthaler

Tangerine

1 9 6 4

Hans Hofmann

Ora Pro Nobis

1 9 6 4

standing about the work of an artist. Newspaper and monthly magazine art critics have a distinct impact on gallery attendance, but less so on sales. I gather that the critics are crucial for music and movies and theater, wherever it's a question of attendance over a short period of time and a small expenditure of money for a ticket. But a large expenditure of money for a painting or sculpture isn't so easily affected by critics who write for media with a short life expectancy. Yesterday's newspaper is used to wrap fish.

Historically, the *New York Times* has been notoriously wrong. My suggestion to anyone interested in art is to go back to the library and pull down random issues of the *New York Times* or the art magazines of previous decades and see what was reviewed, reproduced, and advertised with enthusiasm, applauded and given importance. What was neglected as minor either verbally or through placement of reproductions, not to mention overlooked entirely?

How was Pollock treated? It's not just how Pollock was treated, or Morris Louis, or Hofmann, or any number of people. What was treated with importance then often is not even remembered now.

Maintaining rather than establishing recognition is another thing altogether. Helen Frankenthaler is a well-known artist, and all you have to do is print the name and people come flocking to see an exhibition. But one still publishes catalogues with color plates to show what the new

Kenneth Noland

Saturday Night

1 9 6 5

work looks like, to document for the longer term an exhibition which hangs but for a month. We still do shows, for the purpose of a show is esthetics, not sales.

Dealers should not rely on critics to get their artists publicized, or talked about, or interpreted. One of the crucial roles of a dealer is helping people to see. Olitski is a painter I think very highly of. I think he's one of the great painters, but he's a painter whose work many cannot *see* on brief first exposure. You have to look at Olitski a little longer, and then you begin to see that there is a world in his paintings. My job with Olitski is to get people to sit down and look at a picture so they can come to see what's in it, and then they may make their decision as they see fit.

It is very important that a dealer not sell too hard. There are, of course, high-pressure salesmen in art just as there are in other fields, but personally I don't like to sell. I let the work of art speak for itself to the possible buyer or curator or critic, and perhaps I can share my enthusiasm for it. Good art dealers don't sell art; they allow people to acquire it.

Art dealers sometimes have a whole psychological problem, and some of us fall victim to it. There is a phrase someone used, "Upper Bohemia." That certainly is my world; art dealers are quintessentially middle class, with rather small means in relation to the people they deal with,

Jules Olitski

Nathalie Type — 3

1 9 7 6

Al Held

Inversion XII

1 9 7 7

David Hockney

Paper Pool #10

"Midnight Pool"

1 9 7 8

who are often very, very rich. We talk quite casually about $100,000 as a modest amount, while of course in terms of groceries and rent and school tuition, it's a staggering sum. There is art money and living money. You cannot and must not confuse the two.

A dealer must be comfortable in dealing with the rich, without losing either his self-respect or his self-confidence. Nor can he allow himself to be bullied. You must know you are with them but not of them. Some colleagues of mine suddenly find it impossible to conceive that they were not born with a silver spoon; it's a problem, really, of inner integrity.

The salvation of an art dealer lies in being able to do anything he likes. It's a highly individualistic business, a business that demands that you take risks both in terms of the art you select and the way you conduct your business. But the one thing you must never do is stoop to marketing strategies, as in the marketing of LeRoy Neiman, whereby the artist's images are endlessly reproduced as prints and decorative graphics aimed at cleaning up on the widest market possible. That's not art; it's merchandise. There's a very fine line that you come to, and beyond it lies pure merchandising. Perhaps like the clergy, who constantly confront matters of the highest moral content, art dealers must guard against cynicism when they view art as an everyday thing or a product to sell. When that happens, you'd better get out of art and into something you can frankly market. You have to love the art, not the selling. My grandfather would say, "What is the difference between the *marchand d'art* and the *marchand amateur?* The *marchand d'art* loves art—the *marchand amateur* likes being a *marchand.*" Patience and integrity, and continued belief in art itself, those are the crucial things.

Joan
Washburn

Joan Washburn (born 1929, New York City) followed her art history studies at Middlebury College with an apprenticeship under the art dealer Antoinette Kraushaar, and since 1971 has devoted her own gallery to American artists from Luminist Martin Johnson Heade to Jack Youngerman.

Why collect art? Why listen to music? Why get up in the morning? Unless it gives you pleasure, there's no point. I cannot imagine living without something that is there only to be looked at, beginning with the first Utrillo reproduction that one puts up as a freshman in college.

Ideas grow and change, which is the thing people should always remember. In my case, I went through my Utrillo period, my Vlaminck period. It's strange how the work of such artists is almost killed by reproduction; every so often you find yourself confronted by an original Van Gogh in a museum, and suddenly that whole first undergraduate experience comes back to you all over again.

It's a mistake for a dealer to run out looking specifically for an artist who works in the latest style. If an art dealer paid attention only to the marketplace he would just be driven mad. Sometimes going against fashion can, in the long run, have its own rewards. At times it can be a question of how to handle a changing marketplace or a once-mainstream artist who is no longer in vogue.

The thing I love most is doing the actual exhibition, the gathering together, the discovering, whether it be a show seeking the most succinct presentation of one artist or a show intended to enlarge a certain aspect of a historical period.

When I graduated I had a hundred dollars left from an art history scholarship, and for eight weeks I madly set out to learn shorthand. The following September I looked for a job, knowing that if I didn't get one quickly I would forget what little shorthand I knew. An employment agency had one job for me but thought I wouldn't like it: it was at an art gallery. They told me there wouldn't be much social life because there was only one person in the gallery. I couldn't have been more fortunate, because that person was Antoinette Kraushaar.

It was 1951, and everything was breaking wide open. The whole art world was right there between Madison and Fifth on Fifty-seventh Street. One could see every exhibition of importance at Sidney Janis, Betty Parsons, and Charlie Egan. We were in the same building as Curt Valentin and Marian Willard. Knoedler's was on Fifty-seventh. It proved an excellent opportunity to learn about the first fifty years of American painting.

Miss Kraushaar concentrated on painters like John Sloan

and Maurice Prendergast, estates containing a large body of material. There were also contemporaries. She is a wonderful person and introduced me to the way a gallery should be run.

In those days universities didn't even offer graduate-school programs in American art history; all I knew about contemporary American art ended at the Ash-Can School. Few books on contemporary art existed, nobody had written about the thirties and forties, and only the Stieglitz group was well documented by library material.

It was all going on: painters came in and out of the gallery talking about the new art, and everybody raced to see new exhibitions of artists like Pollock and de Kooning. It was coming right out of the studios at that point.

After two years, however, I wanted to see something of Europe. After five months there, I returned to New York and decided to marry. I state it that way because my husband lived in Hartford; I did not want to live in Hartford. Nevertheless I was there two years until I finally couldn't take it anymore. I did, however, have a wonderful learning experience working at the Wadsworth Atheneum, where I was director of public relations. Hartford was such a letdown after Fifty-seventh Street. I finally told my husband, "I love you truly, but I can't bear this town." We moved to Manhattan.

There I was, at a loss again. I didn't want to continue in museum work and couldn't afford to go back to school; besides, I could not afford the low pay offered by institutions. I worked at The Museum of Modern Art for two weeks before my next position presented itself at the Graham Gallery.

The third floor there was devoted entirely to contemporary painters, and that took up the next twelve years of my life. When Bob Graham's sons graduated from college and entered the business I told the family that I was going to step out, which seemed the brightest thing for me to do. I then worked at the Cordier-Ekstrom Gallery for two years.

In 1971 I learned from the artist Alan Gussow that the art dealer Lou Pollack had died and that the artists in his gallery were very much concerned about their future. Gussow asked me if there was any way I could buy the Peridot Gallery as Pollack had left it. I took the plunge by borrowing money, holding my breath, and going through absolute terror. It required a great deal of patience on the part of my

Ilya Bolotowsky

Blue Rhomb

1 9 8 1

husband. We had two children, and the least sensible thing was to leave my job and paycheck to be totally dependent on my husband's income and the earnings of my own gallery.

I continued the schedule for that season because Lou Pollack had set it up before he died. The next exhibition year I started more historical exhibitions, with important nineteenth-century shows as well as one-man shows. The first historical show we held and one that particularly pleased me was an exhibition of portraits by Joshua Johnson, reputedly the first known black artist in America, who worked in Baltimore from 1800 to 1830. I also was interested in American abstract artists of the thirties, the WPA, and the Stieglitz group.

I acquired a taste for doing historical exhibitions when I worked at the Graham Gallery. I like to reconstruct exhibitions such as 291, WPA murals or *Vanity Fair* photographs because many of us learn art history through somebody else's written interpretations rather than from the work itself. Dealers can cooperate by lending work for such exhibitions, particularly if the idea interests them. James Goodman told me where to find an early Calder, and I helped him authenticate four Légers done under the WPA.

Two years after we opened the gallery, Parke-Bernet approached me to take over their American painting department. A serious recession was going on, so I gave it a lot of thought and concluded that I would do it, provided I could continue my own gallery. I never thought Parke-Bernet would accept terms like that, but they did, probably because my gallery was so small that they saw no conflict.

There I was with two children and two jobs. I told my new employers that I would try it for two years, by which time I would know how things were going. Auctions and galleries were suffering at that time, and it was a lot of hard work. I couldn't do it today, but it was a wonderful experience, totally different.

Auction houses cannot conceivably build up an artist's career, which is why galleries are essential for the growth and development of an artist. Once the artist has that reputation, then auctions can be a means of confirming it. They can also destroy it. But it is the galleries that do the day-to-day work, year after year.

Auctions do give people confidence when they see the prices that works of art can achieve. Auction houses also have elaborate public-relations systems concerned with the whole question of prices. Sometimes the public is fearful of the mysteries of an art gallery; they don't know whom to trust.

Those record auction prices quoted by newspapers can be misleading. When you read about the highest price ever paid for the work of a certain artist, a dealer can know that he himself has sold a work by the same artist for a higher sum, but dealers don't phone the *New York Times* announcing their latest triumphs. You'd lose the client, offend the critics, and infuriate the seller.

In contrast to auction houses, a gallery offers a program of ideas. One should specialize, but I just can't. The same is true of many dealers, which people don't realize. Look at Sidney Janis and his long involvement with folk art, or André Emmerich and his love for ancient art.

You sometimes have to play it by ear with people in this business. My first lesson took place soon after I began working for Antoinette. There was an artist named Vaughan Flannery who painted horses and farmhouses, spending weeks with families in the country just as English painters had done. I was alone one day in the gallery with an exhibition of Flannery's work, and a rather attractive gentleman came in and evinced interest. Not knowing anything about the subject, I launched into a long monologue. Antoinette came in and found me talking on and on about horses and polo matches. It was only afterward that she told me I had been lecturing Alfred G. Vanderbilt.

Prices rise astronomically in many cases, and since I have dealt with American art, we need only look at the prices for Prendergast watercolors when I started out. A fine example could be had for $500. But it must be recalled that until the fifties, when the art schools started churning out so many artists, there had been very few visual artists in America. Therefore, we have a vast number of collectors today for a dwindling supply of American paintings. This ratio changed after the fifties, when art became a bit more respectable and the GI Bill launched so many artists' careers.

The attention paid to art is marvelous now, but it's too bad that there aren't more newspapers that give coverage to the visual arts. When I began in 1951 the *Herald Tribune* and the *World-Telegram* were both published. In view of the number of exhibitions each month, a terrible burden is placed on the *New York Times* today.

An art dealer has to relate to critics on a one-to-one basis, as people; some are interested in one special area, some in many. One positive aspect of presenting as varied an exhibition season as our gallery does arises when critics unexpectedly discover one artist when they have come to see another.

When Sidney Janis held those first exhibitions of Pollock or de Kooning, there was always a Brancusi or a Mondrian in the back room. It gave a great sense of continuity, one thing leading to the next, encouraging historical understanding of the new art. That would be a very difficult task today. Of course, galleries handling a full stable of contemporary artists are very important. Betty Parsons and Eleanor Ward were, in their day, examples of such galleries. I shall never forget the Joseph Cornell exhibition at Eleanor Ward's Stable Gallery. The show gave you the feeling that you were discovering Cornell and that no one else knew about him.

I saw the first Andy Warhol show, the Brillo boxes, at the Stable Gallery. I went to the opening with James Harvey, a painter supporting himself as a freelance package designer. It was he who had designed the actual Brillo box, and strangely enough, he was also a friend of Andy's. Jim nearly collapsed when we went in and saw people actually

Leon Polk Smith

Form Space—Black Red

1 9 8 1

buying Warhol's identical version. All Jim could do was to write it off as part of the madness of life.

I work more with museums than with private collectors; a curator will come to me for information about an obscure artist, and because of their specialized understanding museums will sometimes be very adventurous in their buying. In 1980 we sold a painting to the Metropolitan Museum by the little-known painter Leon Kelly, because the curator recognized Kelly's importance in relation to Arshile Gorky. Such an acquisition is possible only when a museum understands the significance of a particular artist in a specific period. Collectors tend to invest in names. Museums, on the other hand, relish those obscure links in art history that fascinate me, too.

Many dealers don't necessarily want to sell work to museums because that painting will rarely be seen on the market again. This is very important, and it brings me to a difficult subject in the art market: the role of private dealers.

Private dealers make it harder for galleries in some ways than auctions do. The great French galleries, like great galleries everywhere, were built through selling paintings which were returned to them to be resold years later. In this way, a painting's provenance is recorded and the gallery is

Jack Youngerman

Huracan

1 9 8 1

Marsden Hartley

Berlin Abstraction

1 9 1 4 – 1 5

supported by recurrent sales. Today, there are many, many private dealers who syphon paintings away from galleries. These private dealers put absolutely nothing back into the art world. They sell art like real estate.

Galleries should be nourished, protected, and in some cases even revered. We do a tremendous amount of work, with the cost of doing exhibitions often going unrecovered. Certain exhibitions are done at an absolute loss, yet these shows are free to the public. Most museums aren't free. Private dealers have none of the overhead. If a major work can be pried out of a collection, the private dealer will sell it with no exposure to the public or benefit to the artist; the gallery that first pioneered the career of this artist suffers a loss, and the painting's history is unrecorded.

In 1977, we moved the gallery to 42 East Fifty-seventh Street, where the legendary art dealer Julien Levy once had his gallery. In 1980, we opened another gallery in Soho. The last thing I needed was a second gallery, but when I saw the space on Greene Street I fell in love with it. I had just sold a very important painting by Marsden Hartley, so I did it. The only dealer who thought I should open the second gallery was Castelli, who told me, "If the space speaks to you, do it." With his four galleries, he's about as practical as I am.

Soho galleries attract a different collector, a more general public, with greater attendance than uptown. Museum curators visit Soho, and private collectors certainly make the rounds every couple of months. Our clients on Fifty-seventh Street consist of people who already know what we offer and seek us out for specific reasons.

With our large space in Soho I have been able to install exhibitions that had been only frustrated ideas in the past. We opened in 1980 with an exhibition for which Ilya Bolotowsky reconstructed his WPA murals of the thirties. The next show, "From Matisse to American Abstract Painting," included work by artists like Jack Youngerman and Ellsworth Kelly. The Kelly was a small oil on loan from Irving Blum, the first he acquired.

When a season finishes and we close for the summer, it is the anticipation of doing such shows in the year ahead that makes me happy to open the first fall exhibition and face the season again. This year we opened another floor on Fifty-seventh Street, and the season began with paintings by David Smith from the 30s and 40s that had never been exhibited in New York. It's hard but wonderful work.

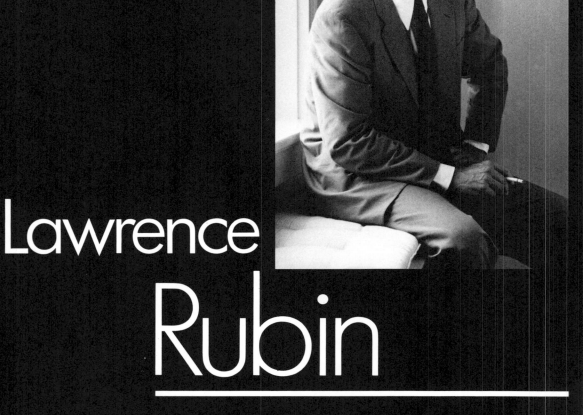

Lawrence
Rubin

Lawrence Rubin (born 1933, New York City) graduated from Brown University in 1955 and continued his studies in art at the University of Paris. His first gallery, Galerie Neufville, opened in Paris in the summer of 1959 and offered the European public a look at the best contemporary American painting. After operating the Lawrence Rubin Gallery in New York from 1969–1973, Rubin joined Armand Hammer's Knoedler & Co., becoming its president and director in 1977.

he first art dealer who inspired me was Sidney Janis. I was still a student at college when I started going to Fifty-seventh Street, and I found the exhibitions at his gallery especially stirring and beautiful. Even when the artist didn't particularly interest me, there was always something spectacular in the way Janis selected and mounted the work. Later, certain shows at Castelli were also inspirational, but I knew from the start that my way of looking at art was very different from his: I am much less interested in the knockout blow in the first round and tend to be suspicious if something hits too hard, too soon.

My real interest has always centered on painting, and I use that word very specifically, rather than the general term *art*. Perhaps more than other dealers I have kept a straighter course in a time that has witnessed so many spinoffs related to photography and theater. Dealers less restricted in their views, more catholic in their tastes, allow themselves an interest in those aspects of art, but from the outset I have stayed close to painting.

I became an art dealer in 1956 when I graduated from college and took a job with a gallery in Rome. A year later I moved to Paris and became a partner in the Galerie du Dragon, which was already involved with Surrealist painters like Max Ernst, Matta, and Wifredo Lam.

Twice a year I would come to New York and spend a month catching up on American art. It wasn't as if I had to guess; by the late fifties you didn't have to be a genius to recognize Rothko, Newman, and Kline. I saw their importance, but meeting Clement Greenberg in 1959 accelerated the process. I learned a great deal from the way he sized up a picture, analyzing its elements more dramatically than anyone else I knew. I don't see anyone on the scene today who matches him.

I opened my own Paris gallery in 1959 under the name Galerie Neufville, with a show of American painters. It was not easy to put the large canvases of Motherwell, Rothko, Kline, Newman, and Gottlieb into the small gallery space I had. That fall I began showing the work of younger American painters who had come to my attention through Greenberg: Stella, Morris Louis, Noland, Ellsworth Kelly.

The Parisian public greeted these American painters with total indifference. Anybody who claims there was real interest in American art in France at that time is fibbing: it was all uphill, and there was no exchange. Rauschenberg and Johns already had arrangements with the Larcade Gallery in Paris, but both remained truly American painters. Ellsworth Kelly lived in Paris, but his work is much more typical of American art of the time. He may feel otherwise, of course.

Fortunately, there were always a few receptive Europeans. From 1960 to 1963, dealers like the late Alfred Schmela in Dusseldorf and Beatrice Monti in Milan showed American painters through me, making a few sales from each exhibition. Collectors, a handful of Belgian industrialists and a couple of Germans and Northern Italians, were beginning to buy Americans. One man in particular, Phillipe d'Autremont, kept my gallery alive. A Belgian, he had probably the largest collection of twentieth-century art in the world. I was able to convince him there was something important in current American painting, and by 1960 he was simply asking me to buy the biggest and best pictures I could find for him, whatever the price. I sold him between thirty and forty pictures over the years: Rauschenberg, de Kooning, Still, Louis, Noland, Stella and others.

In 1965 I moved to London, where a close friend and partner was running the Kasmin Gallery. Kasmin had been showing all the painters I represented. After a year I concluded that "Swinging London" had less to do with painting than with fashion and pop music. No matter what, New York was the most active city for art. I had to come back and face the music.

I bought a house on Ninety-first Street and set up as a private dealer in January 1967, handling all the artists I had dealt with in Paris. In 1969 I opened the Lawrence Rubin Gallery on Fifty-seventh Street, adding painters like Jules Olitski and Friedel Dzubas.

Jules Olitski

Thales Enthralled 1

1 9 7 8

Friedel Dzubas

Agmont

1 9 8 1

Judgment is the important thing for a dealer. I feel a close tie with my collectors, in the sense that some of them, if they don't *depend* on me, certainly look to me for direction. I always look for new painters, but I am not driven by the overriding need to find somebody new. The last thing I would do is to bring in a succession of young artists whose work I liked and then find out a year later that they were not stickers, that I didn't really like the work at all. I probably feel that way more than any other dealer in New York. I am tougher and slower because I intend to stay with my artists for years, with a commitment to the collector for the long term as well.

When you see a talented young artist, the first question is one of staying power. Will he go on, will he develop? All too often, the answer is no. I would rather sit back and follow the artist's work for a couple of years. Instead of asking half a dozen artists to join the gallery, I stick to the one I want for as long as it takes.

The first show of Richard Diebenkorn I saw was at the Poindexter Gallery in 1962. Five years later, on my first trip to California, I met Diebenkorn and asked him to join my gallery. He was noncommittal and a few months later joined the Marlborough Gallery. Five years ago Diebenkorn became free. I asked again, and I've been showing his work ever since.

Rarely does a gallery handle as small a stable as I do. But for me, personal contact with the artist is of total importance. I work with ten living artists: Diebenkorn, Darby Barnard, Nancy Graves, Friedel Dzubas, Herbert Ferber, Howard Hodgkin, Robert Motherwell, Jules Olitski, John Walker, and Frank Stella. I feel very close to all my artists

Richard Diebenkorn

Ocean Park #117

1 9 7 9

and like to think that they are all my friends, despite the problems that arise between all dealers and their artists. But when it comes to art itself, I never go on personalities, only on what I see in the pictures.

When I met Dr. Armand Hammer, Knoedler's owner, I was bowled over in many ways, but not so much that I didn't know simply to continue what I had already been doing. The notion of working with Knoedler intrigued me, I liked Dr. Hammer, and I felt I would lose none of my freedom by getting involved. Also, a lot of money would be available to do things that I had not been able to do on my own, such as dealing with the work of earlier twentieth-century painters like Léger, Miró, Picasso. I wanted to show those artists simultaneously with American post–World War II painting. In 1973, we formed a joint venture, a fifty-fifty partnership called Knoedler Contemporary Art, which went on for a few years. The older business of Knoedler & Company had not been going too well, so Dr. Hammer asked if I would take over the whole thing and give it a new direction. After dealing in American art for fifteen years I had come to

John Walker

In Truth I

1 9 8 1 – 8 2

feel a little stale; Knoedler came as an opportunity to get a much broader mix.

Every single collector from the old days followed me to Knoedler. I've had very few dropouts, which is like my relation with artists. One of those collectors had given me the $3,000 I needed to go into business at the beginning. I know every picture in each of their collections and I know what they should have.

The toughest question to answer when talking about art collecting is why collect at all. Obviously, the answer is multiple. Some collectors are motivated by a very poetic notion of the way they would like to live, what they would like to think about when not thinking about their daily business. For others, it starts with greed, not just the money aspect, but also the drive to have, to accumulate, to keep. Those are the two poles, and every shade of gray between the two can be found.

Many collectors are my friends, and it's easy to be open and express doubt about a certain picture or my faith in another. I tell them what I paid for it, and sometimes I am making a staggering profit. If the collector knows this, nothing can happen to damage his belief. A collector who is a businessman understands the need to make money and would rather hear what I make than have me trick him into thinking my profit is a small one. If I am making a lot on a picture, then my belief must be all the stronger to justify the collector purchasing it.

At one time or another, all my collectors have grown tired of certain pictures and sold them back. There is a continual coming and going. Sometimes the picture that was available when they bought it is not as good as a work by the same artist that later comes onto the market. I would not want the collector to think that the painting they have is the one they must keep forever; I am just as involved in improving a collection as I am in placing works in it at the outset.

The beginning collector should start by looking, getting to know every picture in the museums, then going around to the galleries to see all the paintings he possibly can before ever buying one. I don't believe a collector needs to start with prints if he eventually wants to collect paintings. Above all, I think a collector should wait at least a year before buying anything; frankly, I think people really should wait three years. Sometimes, unfortunately, there is the feeling of rushing against time right now in art, and they get nervous and don't want to wait.

I must stress the importance museums have in forming our eye. Only by going to museums can any student or collector learn what good painting is, and in New York we are very lucky to have the world's most important teaching instrument for modern art, The Museum of Modern Art.

Museums should not buy everything new under the sun as soon as it appears on the scene. They don't have to. If I were running a museum, I would want to wait not only to identify the artist who will carry the day or the decade or the century, but also to be able to choose from that painter's work rather than simply snapping up the first thing at his first exhibition.

Then there are the auction houses. Art dealers' business has been affected by auctions, but auction houses are incapable of dealing with current art so they are no threat in terms of living painters. Still, they have been very competitive in cutting into what was once the dealer's domain. Resale used to be a substantial part of a dealer's business, and it has lessened because auction houses are getting the business instead. When I started my career, I survived by dealing in older works of art. If people's attention had been turned toward auctions as it is today, I probably could not have gotten those works. A collector must be more sure of his eye at the auction, since there are just a couple of days to look at the paintings before the auction and five minutes to buy it during the sale. When he takes it home, it's his. Most dealers will let a collector try something out, and that way the collector can have better knowledge of what he is buying. Beginning collectors would be foolhardy to buy at auction.

It is a totally different experience for a dealer to represent the estate of an artist rather than a living artist. When dealing with an artist's estate, you are dealing usually with works that have been recognized, that have been around for a certain time and have received a certain value in the market place, and you are dealing with relatives of the artist rather than the artist himself. It's a different cup of tea. Dealing with a living artist is a much more exciting thing, a more human one. A young artist on his first or second show, who is probably not selling too well, depends on you to get him enough money to paint, to live a little less shabbily than he might otherwise need do. Obviously, it is important whether an estate is worth $5 million or $10 million, but

Robert Motherwell

Portal

1 9 8 2

Frank Stella

Talladega

1 9 8 1

Nancy Graves

Fanne Figura

1 9 8 2

somehow you cannot bring yourself to worry as much about something like that as you can worry whether a living artist is going to have another meal on the table.

Of course, in either case, the work itself, no matter what the price or age, does not change. It's the way that it is treated that changes. In 1959 when I showed Frank Stella for the first time, the paintings were $350 retail. I recently sold one of those paintings for $350,000. The work had not changed one iota. Clearly, something had changed dramatically in the public's view of that painting.

In a historic sense, I always dreamed of being like the early French dealers Vollard and Kahnweiler, who set out to discover and then support the greatest artists of their day – Picasso, Braque, Léger. But my personal image as an art dealer has no bearing on my work. It seems very clear that there are certain dealers for whom a lot of the fun lies in being identified with that image. I have been totally uninterested in that from the very beginning; it's no accident that only once in my career have I operated in my own name.

It's always been my feeling that, in the end, it is the artists and not the dealers who are important. Rather than beat my head against the wall to compete with the artists in reputation, I prefer to submerge myself in the gallery. I'm interested only in the long term; I care less about what people think of the Knoedler Gallery today than what they will think in twenty years. Looking back, people can say that *this* gallery was the best, or one of the best, for having maintained a certain quality in a world in which the handmade has been shrinking almost to nonexistence. That would be meaningful.

Leo *Castelli*

Leo Castelli (born 1907, Trieste, Italy) took a degree in law from the University of Milan and put aside careers in insurance and banking to open a gallery in Paris in 1939. Escaping the occupation, he arrived in New York in 1941. His continuing interest in art culminated with the opening of his gallery in 1957. His promotion of artists, including Jasper Johns, Robert Rauschenberg, Andy Warhol, Roy Lichtenstein, Dan Flavin, and Donald Judd, transformed the art world as we know it today.

The fact that I was born in Trieste, and that I lived the early years of my life there, has a certain relevance even though it is so far in the past. As the seaport of the great Austro-Hungarian empire, Trieste was a strange city; although Italian, it was deeply influenced by the culture that came from Vienna.

Literature was the first passion in my life, and it was, as I suppose it is for many of us, a way of finding out about myself. My father was a bank executive, and during World War I my family went to Vienna. By the time we moved back to Trieste three years later, I had learned to speak and read German. Soon I also became fluent in French and English, and discovered the world of the great contemporary writers: Thomas Mann, Proust, Joyce, Eliot, Dostoyevsky, and Freud. I was exploring it on my own, without any assistance.

My father felt I should have a career in business, so after I finished law school he managed to have me placed in an insurance company. Life was pleasant and gay in Trieste and the people I worked for didn't ask much of me. I tried it for a year, but finally told my father that I wanted to quit and study comparative literature and become a teacher. My father was a wonderful man, a businessman, yes, but also very understanding. He made a bargain with me: if after working in a branch office of the insurance company in Rumania for a year I still wanted a career in literature, he would be happy to support my studies.

So in the spring of 1932 I went to Bucharest. I was as bored as ever with the insurance business, but my social life had surprises in store. After a few months I met Ileana Schapira, the daughter of a Rumanian industrialist, and we married the following autumn. Ileana shared my love of literature, and we also seemed to bring out in each other an interest in collecting, mainly antiques at that time. Soon we were roaming the Rumanian countryside looking for art objects, rustic versions of more refined work done in Austria or Hungary. Hunting for those things was to be the beginning of our careers in art.

My father-in-law was very wealthy, so we could afford practically anything: travel, a beautiful apartment, antiques, whatever. I stayed with the insurance company for a while and then turned to banking. Ileana's father had great pull so after a year or so I got a position with the Paris branch of the Banca d'Italia. I did not like banking any more than insurance, but Paris was more entertaining in every respect than hanging on in Bucharest. We made a lot of friends there, among them René Drouin, a young architect and interior designer with whom I loved to talk about art and architecture. Since I was very dissatisfied with my job, and since he was an aspiring designer with talent but no money, Drouin suggested we open a gallery displaying paintings, contemporary furniture, and objets d'art, much of it which he would design himself in the current Art Deco style.

Not long after, while walking through the Place Vendome, we saw a "For Rent" sign between the Hotel Ritz and Schiaparelli's. Bravely, we went in and had a look at the space. It was sensational. There was a fantastic suite of rooms that gave on to the Ritz gardens. Just beautiful. Ileana's father approved our project and put up the capital for our new enterprise. I quit the bank and plunged into the gallery full time.

I knew almost nothing about contemporary art at the time, much less than Ileana, who had spent many hours wandering around museums in her childhood. My earliest knowledge came from Trieste – and literature. It was during the Fascist era, but somehow the proprietor of this extraordinary bookshop I frequented managed to procure everything that was important in art and other domains. I went in one day and bought a book called *Since Cézanne* by Clive Bell. Everything I know about art starts with that book.

But it was Leonor Fini who set the stage for our gallery at the beginning. I had known her in Trieste as a child, and she was now a well-known painter and member of the Paris Surrealist group. When I told her about our venture, she said, "We will accomplish great things there! I will introduce you to all the important painters: Max Ernst, Dali, Tchelitchew." Well, Leonor and those artists took over the artistic direction of the gallery, much to Drouin's distress. His Art Deco furniture was overshadowed by the fantastic creations of our Surrealist friends: Leonor designed an armoire with doors in the shape of swan-women, and Eugene Berman one that represented romantic ruins. Meret Oppenheim sculpted a hand mirror surrounded by flowing hair. Because of technical problems, Dali didn't come through with the breathing chair he had promised. The first show was of a single work: Pavel Tchelitchew's "Phenomena." *Le tout Paris* showed up for the opening, and we really seemed to be on our way. That was the spring of 1939.

We probably would have been very successful, but the war interrupted all that. Drouin joined the army, and Ileana and I went to her father's villa in Cannes. Fortunately, the south of France remained free when the German invasion came in June 1940, and we had ample time to get out, although by very complicated routes through Algeria, Morocco, and Spain.

When we arrived in New York in 1941, I was surprised to learn that people in the Surrealist art world knew about our short-lived Paris gallery. The dealer Julien Levy and Peggy Guggenheim had received interesting reports about our activity. A year or so after our arrival we moved to the fourth floor of a town house at 4 East Seventy-seventh Street, which Ileana's father had bought and remodeled into apartments for himself and his family. I joined the United States Army in 1943 and eventually was sent back to Rumania as an interpreter for the Allied Control Commission.

I was discharged from the army in 1946, but the previous year I managed to go to Paris on furlough. To my surprise, the gallery was back in operation, but the Surrealists had vanished, and had been replaced by a most interesting group of artists: Kandinsky, Dubuffet, de Stael, Pevsner.

I decided then and there that I wanted to remain involved with the gallery, but as its representative in New York. To save money, Drouin would take paintings off their stretchers and fly them to New York with a pilot friend, and I'd go out to the airport and get them. It was all done in a rather homespun manner.

One of my clients was the Baroness Hilla Rebay, whose passion for Kandinsky was all consuming. She bought quite a number of his paintings for the collection of her friend Solomon Guggenheim, which was located at the Plaza Hotel at that time. Being an inveterate collector myself, I also bought a few paintings: two oils by Klee and a Mondrian. Their prices were, by today's standards, incredibly low, so that even with my modest means I could afford them. I had paid $2,000 each for those three paintings and was reluctantly obliged to sell them a few years later at what seemed a decent profit. Eleven thousand for the three. Today they would be worth at least $2 million.

While I indulged in these activities, I was supposed to

be working for one of my father-in-law's subsidiary companies, a sweater factory. Although I tried to do my best, my
heart and mind were elsewhere, either on East Tenth Street
with the artists, or at The Museum of Modern Art. It's
incredible collection was educating my eye more than anything else. There was nothing comparable in Europe. Alfred
Barr, the museum's director, was my great teacher in the
way he chose, analyzed, and presented the art of our century.

By this time there was no doubt in my mind that I
wanted to stay in America. As I could no longer help
Drouin, I decided to pull out of the Paris connection. That
was in 1949. Even though things were going pretty badly,
Drouin let me have a few good paintings by Dubuffet, Kandinsky, and Léger.

I was now in the thick of it in New York. Pollock, Kline,
Rothko, de Kooning, and Still were in the process of creating a new revolutionary school of painting, assisted in their
efforts by two enormously influential critical writers, Harold
Rosenberg and Clement Greenberg.

I have always been guilty of hero worship. For me, great
artists and great writers are in the same class as great war-
riors and great statesmen. And if I had admired Max Ernst
or Dali in Europe, other heroes appeared now in New York.
The two greatest were Pollock and de Kooning.

I knew Pollock well, and can say that despite his rough
edges, he was a highly sensitive and lovable man. In the
early fifties Ileana and I had a house in East Hampton, and
as de Kooning was our good friend we were delighted to
provide him with space where he could work during the
summer. He constructed a studio for himself where he
could be alone, and he struggled and struggled but at the
end of four long months, he destroyed everything that he
had done. Somehow though, I think that they were very productive years for him. Both he and his wife, Elaine, were
wonderful company, and when they were around a lot of
artists would gather at our house: Ludwig Sander, a marvelous man who also did a Mondrianesque sort of abstract
paintings; Franz Kline, a very poor driver who bought a Fer-
rari because he wanted one; and of course, Pollock, who
lived in the neighborhood. Pollock would come over in his
model T Ford (immortalized in a marvelous photograph by
Hans Namuth), jump out of the car without turning off the
motor and storm into the house, perhaps to find de Kooning

or just to make a nuisance of himself. I remember Ileana being terrorized by his behavior, and both of us would wonder what he would do next. If de Kooning was indeed around, there was sure to be a fight. The truth is that they were actually good friends, but they would tease each other relentlessly, and sometimes the teasing would get out of hand. As painters, they were of equal quality, but very different. Perhaps Pollock started from a more original concept, but de Kooning was so good at that time. His paintings were extraordinary.

In those days some artists urged me repeatedly to open a gallery, but I felt it wasn't yet the right time. I considered myself unprepared and too much of a gentleman, in the old European sense, to indulge in commerce. Sam Kootz offered me his space on Fifty-seventh Street when he decided to give it up, but I declined. Instead, Sidney Janis took it over.

I came to know Sidney Janis in the late forties, and we saw quite a lot of each other. In 1950 we did a show together that paired postwar French and American painters who seemed to have something in common: de Kooning and Dubuffet (their figures of women), Gorky and Matta, Kline and Soulages, Pollock and Lanskoy, Rothko and de Stael, and some others. The show was a bit silly, and purists like Charlie Egan, the dealer who handled de Kooning, took a very critical view. It proved one thing, however, that there really was no connection, except on a very superficial level, between European and American painting.

Janis was very alert and well informed. He found out that Matisse's son-in-law, a Frenchman named Duthuit, was writing a book on the Fauve Movement, and we set to work gathering as many of those artists as we could – Derain, Vlaminck, Matisse, Braque, Dufy, and others – for a show that would coincide with the publication of the book. Prices were ridiculously low. I remember buying a Braque nude from Knoedler's for $2,000.

The show was a great success. We sold everything rapidly and made a good profit. Paintings bought at $2,000 went for around $8,000 – a lot of money in those days. The only piece left was the Braque nude, a beautiful work valued at something like $300,000 or more today. The nude was not in great favor then. Just imagine: people preferred landscapes or still lifes.

Around 1951 many of the painters with whom I was

involved, Pollock and de Kooning to mention only two, began getting restless in their galleries. As Janis was showing the most important European artists, it seemed appropriate for these painters to be in a gallery of that caliber. So I said to de Kooning, "Why don't we try to get you into the Janis Gallery? You would be in great company there." I then proposed it to Janis. Janis had been very much aware of the new Americans from the start, and since it was becoming increasingly difficult for him to procure good work from Europe, he had to diversify. Here was the occasion. So de Kooning joined the gallery. Then Pollock came to me and said, "Now that de Kooning is at Janis, I'd like to get in there too." This time Janis hesitated; as much as he admired Pollock, he felt that in view of his difficult character he might run into a lot of trouble. But in the end the temptation was too great, and Janis took him on. As it turned out, Pollock was easier to handle than de Kooning.

Soon Janis got all the important Abstract Expressionists: Kline, Rothko, Still, Motherwell – an incredible group of major artists. Many people who up to then had been interested in collecting only European art became involved in the American painters because they had great confidence in Janis's taste. His decision to take them on and promote them with all the dedication he had given to the Europeans has been of immeasurable importance to American art.

Robert Rauschenberg first appeared in my life when I saw his now famous white paintings at the Betty Parsons Gallery in 1951. The show consisted of a number of differently shaped canvases painted white. I asked him what they meant, and he explained that the shadows people cast across them formed the subject. That was an idea I was familiar with: the spirit of Dada, and the spirit of Duchamp. I was delighted. In a curious way those white paintings are among the first performance works by an American artist.

That same year I helped organize a show that came to be known as the Ninth Street Show, a celebration of Abstract Expressionism that centered around the work of de Kooning and Franz Kline. I decided to include Rauschenberg in that show, even though at the time the work seemed to have little to do with the Abstract Expressionist dogma. Perhaps it was an advance sign that I already saw beyond the Abstract Expressionists. For whatever reason, from then on I followed his career closely, and remember being overwhelmed by his show of "red paintings" at Charlie Egan's

Gallery the Christmas of 1954.

By 1955, I felt that I couldn't go on doing petty deals with Janis. The sweater business had gone out of existence, and I was at loose ends. The time had come for me to open my own gallery, which I finally did February 1, 1957.

I decided to do it very modestly, in the apartment that Ileana and I had at 4 East Seventy-seventh Street, turning the L-shaped living and dining room into the gallery. My overhead was minimal since Ileana's father owned the house. I had one assistant whose salary was not large, and got simple announcements printed for a few hundred dollars. Running the gallery in the first few years probably cost me less than $1,000 a month. There wasn't even a sign out front. I expected that the quality of my shows would be such that everybody would find out about them.

My first show was a declaration of intention: I wanted to indicate that the American artists were just as important as the European artists, perhaps more so. I placed three of them – de Kooning, Pollock, and David Smith – next to a number of recognized Europeans including Dubuffet, Lèger, Picabia, and Mondrian. The Mondrian came from Harry Holtzman, a friend of the artist who inherited everything Mondrian had when he died. Holtzman wanted $30,000 for it. Pollock was, at that time, selling for maybe $5,000 or $6,000. So $30,000, I told Holtzman, was an outrageous price, and I'd never be able to sell it. He said never mind, it doesn't matter, but that's what the price is. To buy a Mondrian of that caliber today would cost over $1 million, maybe even $2 million, but of course I didn't sell it, and it went back to Holtzman.

My hope was that later shows would include younger European and American artists. But you have your schemes – and then life takes over. It soon became apparent that all the interesting new art was being done in America, and that for the time being at any rate, Europe had had its day. I had no intention, however, of taking my old friends away from Sidney Janis, even though when they had urged me to open my own gallery they presumably wanted to go with me. I knew I had to find new heroes.

The tremendous upsurge of Abstract Expressionism in America transformed the way people looked at art, but by the late fifties, I came to feel that it had lost its fire. Although there were some good painters among the second generation Abstract Expressionists, they were not inventing something new as the great artists of the first generation had done. There were no surprises there.

There are certain moments in the evolution of art when it seems that it is not enough to create in the spirit of the previous generation. There is a feeling that new ideas must appear, and perhaps great contradictions. A dealer must be able to pinpoint these moments when they occur, and to identify which artists embody these new ideas. When I opened my gallery I felt it was one of those moments, and when I came upon them, I felt that Jasper Johns, Bob Rauschenberg, and Cy Twombly, each in his own way represented the quantum leap to something new.

In March, 1957 Meyer Schapiro assembled a show of the younger generation Abstract Expressionists. It was held at the Jewish Museum and included Rauschenberg, whose "red" show at the Egan Gallery two years before I had greatly admired. It had convinced me that he was the most original young artist I had come across in a long time. Joan Mitchell, Larry Rivers, and many others who mostly followed in the footsteps of their elders, were also present. But there was one painting in the show that puzzled me. It was a green painting done in an unfamiliar medium: wax. I couldn't quite make out what it meant, nor had I heard of the name that appeared next to it: Jasper Johns. I thought about that painting long after I went home. I just couldn't get it out of my mind.

Two or three days after seeing the show at the Jewish Museum, I went down to Rauschenberg's studio to select paintings for a show that I was planning to do. Somehow, the name Jasper Johns came up, and I told Bob about the green painting I'd seen. "Jasper Johns? His studio is just below mine." Jasper later came in to bring ice for the drinks, and I suggested going down to see what he was doing. It was uncharacteristic of me to interrupt my visit, and probably Bob was not too happy about it, but he was eager for me to see the work of the friend he admired so much, so we all went down. It was an extraordinary experience: incredibly mature paintings by a young man of twenty-seven, many of them done since 1955. They were masterpieces, an amazing array of images – alphabets, numerals, flags, targets – a treasure trove. To say that I was tremendously impressed is understating it. I was bowled over.

Then and there I asked him to join the gallery. Jasper

Jasper Johns

Small Numbers in Color

1 9 5 9

Jasper Johns

Target with Plaster Casts

1 9 5 5

was very spare with his words. Betty Parsons had been in touch with him several months before, but she hadn't come to his studio. She later said that was the biggest mistake of her life. Jasper told me he would be free to accept my offer.

My closing show of the season, in May, was a group show with the very unspecific title "New Work." I included a flag painting by Jasper Johns, and a Rauschenberg combine painting called "Gloria." The other artists were Norman Bluhm, Morris Louis, Friedel Dzubas, David Budd, Savelli, Marisol, Ortman, and Leslie. Of that group, only Johns and Rauschenberg are still with me.

In January, 1958 I had my first Jasper Johns show. It was probably *the* crucial event in my career as an art dealer, and, I think, an even more crucial one for art history.

The choice of Jasper Johns, about which I felt immensely secure, had to do with my varied background and all its faults. The fact that I had a vaguely amateur approach to art permitted me to make judgments that others would have rejected because they had fixed ideas of what art should be about, of what art should produce at a given time. When I began, I had absorbed a great deal of knowledge that was not structured or prejudiced. I was relatively free. When I first saw Jasper Johns, I of course recognized the influence of Dada – especially Marcel Duchamp, the

great master of them all. But Johns's work was also so fresh
and new because he was, after all, a part of what was happening here in America. John Cage, for example, was a
great influence with his extraordinary ideas on what art was
about. His field was music, but his vision extended to everything that he perceived around him: art, music, literature –
everything.

Tom Hess, the editor of *Art News* and a wonderfully per-
ceptive critic, had heard about Johns from Rauschenberg,
and stopped in to look at the paintings that were lined up
along the walls in preparation for my show. He was visibly
impressed. "Can I take this one with me?" He pointed to a
painting, a yellow, red, and blue target with plaster casts
along the top of four identical faces. He said he'd bring it
back the next day. You cannot imagine the way things were
handled in those days. Without thinking to ask what he
wanted to do with it, I said I guessed the painting was small
enough to fit into a taxi. Not long after that, it appeared in
color on the cover of *Art News* the month of the opening,
January 1958.

When Alfred Barr came to see the show he could hardly
contain his excitement. He felt, quite simply, that it was a
major event in the history of art. He wanted to buy several
paintings and he spent hours picking out this one and that
one, talking out loud to himself about who could be found to
provide the funds. A problem came up about the flag image.
Would it offend the Daughters of the American Revolution?
What could be done?

Barr called Philip Johnson. Would he, as a favor, buy
the painting and hang onto it for the Museum until this issue
of flag desecration was solved? Philip didn't care much for
the painting, but he gave in and bought it for $900. When
the flag image did not turn out to be the problem we thought
it would be, Barr went back to Philip Johnson and said,
"You can give me my flag now." He said, "Your flag? It's
my flag. I've grown to like it very much and want to keep
it." Eventually, he donated the painting to the Museum of
Modern Art as a homage to Alfred Barr.

One painting in Jasper's show contained plaster casts in
little boxes across the top which included, among other
parts of the human body, a green penis in one of the com-
partments. We lived in a more prudish era then, the late
fifties. Barr wanted the piece for the Museum, but asked if
he could keep the lid on that one box covered. He talked it

Robert Rauschenberg

Bed

1 9 5 5

over with Jasper, who said he could, but not all the time. Johns was, at the time, a very shy young man, although very sure of himself when it came to his art. Barr felt he couldn't promise that, and reluctantly decided not to buy the painting. I still have it. At the end of the show, I bought the problematic "Target with Plaster Casts," for $1,200.

I had planned on showing Rauschenberg when I first opened the gallery, but was disturbed by some of the work he did after the "red" show and had put off making a definite commitment. I finally overcame my hesitations, and Bob got his first show one month after Jasper's. We now know, with the benefit of hindsight, that its importance was equal to Jasper's. It contained many of the now famous combine paintings to which all kinds of found objects are attached: a rooster, ties, shoes – anything. I bought "Bed" for my collection: a real pillow and quilt heavily splattered with paint, in which some horrible act – a rape or murder – seemed to have occurred. Or so we thought at the time. Now it seems very mild, very beautiful. The only other sale, a small "Collage with Red," was returned by the lady who bought it saying that she had been forced to relegate it to a closet because the tradesmen and delivery boys broke up laughing whenever they saw it.

Rauschenberg's show, compared to Jasper's lightning success, barely got off the ground, unless one counted the level on which it succeeded in annoying so many viewers. Very few people understood Rauschenberg this early on, although interestingly enough, his work had been shown before, whereas Jasper's work came out of the blue. It was not only the general public who had trouble with Rauschenberg. Alfred Barr did not respond positively to the work at all, and, to his own acute distress, was never able to relate to it. He accepted its importance, however, and later on gratefully accepted Philip Johnson's gift of an important combine painting, "First Landing Jump," for the Modern.

Someone who did understand and appreciate Rauschenberg's work was Alan Solomon, then director of the Andrew Dickson White Museum at Cornell, now the Herbert F. Johnson Museum of Art. The painting he purchased for the museum in 1958 was the first Rauschenberg to enter a public collection. Six years later, Solomon was to play an even more important role in Rauschenberg's career at the Venice Bienale of 1964, when, to everyone's amazement, he won the first prize – a first for an American artist.

One could argue that with Bob and Jasper their early work was their great period of invention. In my view, what Bob did in his combine paintings, and what Johns did in creating his flags, numbers, and targets was just sheer genius. Cy Twombly's work was equally original, but had a quieter approach, going back to some source of inspiration that lies in childhood. His paintings reminded me of a child's random scribbling; there was nothing comparable to it. Although successful in Europe, for many years few understood or accepted his work over here, but I went on showing Cy's paintings from 1959 on, never once doubting their extraordinary quality. Today he is considered the equal of Jasper Johns and Bob Rauschenberg.

Frank Stella was perhaps the most controversial of my artists by the time he had the first show of shaped aluminum paintings at my gallery in 1960. Confronted with his black paintings the year before at his studio, I was reminded of Jasper Johns. But Stella's idea was to reduce painting to its rock bottom essentials so that "what you see is what it is." There lies the whole idea, without confusion. Or so he said at least. I was one of the few who believed him.

This was in 1959, and Dorothy Miller was still shopping for her show of young Americans for The Museum of Modern Art when I took her down to Stella's studio on West

Cy Twombly

Untitled

1 9 6 8

Frank Stella

Gezira

1 9 6 0

Broadway to see his work. Her reaction was immediate: "I *must* have him in my show." I said, "Don't be ridiculous, Dorothy. He's twenty-three years old and hasn't shown anywhere yet. To begin with, it could ruin him to be included in an important show like this one. Besides, I plan to show him in November." Dorothy insisted, "Out of the question. If he's not strong enough to withstand success, then too bad for him. Forget about your show. I *insist* on putting him in mine." Well, she did. And not surprisingly, the group of Stellas shown in her "Sixteen Americans" show was a bombshell. Outrage came as no surprise from the expected quarters: critics like Emily Genauer, who dubbed him the "pinstripe boy," and artists, particularly the Abstract Expressionists, who saw in his black bands and geometric precision an uncompromising, almost ruthless negation of painting as a personal experience.

Undeterred, Alfred Barr wanted to buy the largest painting in the show, a particularly difficult piece, black, of course, called "The Marriage of Squalor and Reason." The price was $1,200 which at the time seemed adequate for a large painting by an artist I considered very good. The trustees refused their consent saying that they didn't care for it, and that it would take up a lot of space in the storage racks where it was destined to remain forever. But Barr was determined. As he was free to acquire works for under $700 without the board's approval, he approached me saying that he would buy it for the museum out of his own purse. I told him okay, that he could have it for $700. Needless to say, since then, it has seen the light upstairs.

That same year I discovered a young artist named Lee Bontecou. I was immediately struck by the incongruity of this very pretty girl and the ferocious, menacing images she used in her sculptures. When it came to her first show, the work had to be taken out of her window with a crane, and when we got to the gallery a whole new door had to be cut to get them in.

Lee's career at my gallery was meteoric. After several successful shows, she stopped working, and for many years now all she has done are drawings and prints. Her work was so powerful and incredibly strong – but it didn't sustain itself. Let's hope she'll come back.

When Roy Lichtenstein came to the gallery in 1961, Ivan Karp, whom I had asked to join the gallery in 1959 as manager, got very excited. So did I. The paintings were blowups

Lee Bontecou

Untitled

1 9 6 2

from comic strips and commercial advertisements that at first seemed to be exact replicas of their models.

Some people said, "So what, he makes comic strips bigger, or he takes images out of art history books or advertisements from phone directories and blows them up – is that to be considered art?" But the fact is that Roy does a very subtle thing to all those images. If you compare the original comic to the result when Lichtenstein paints it, you see that it has gone through, with the fewest possible strokes, a tremendous transformation: from something totally commercial that's just meant to catch your eye or advertise a product, into serious art.

In 1961 I showed Roy in a group show – a wonderful painting of a girl with a beachball. Rauschenberg came by and stood there in amazement, not knowing what to make of it. The next day he came around and said he'd given it some thought and decided he liked this guy Lichtenstein very much.

It took Jasper longer. He didn't feel good about Roy at all, until finally there was a drawing show that included works by Lichtenstein. Without saying, "I like them," Jasper only said that he wanted to have one.

Soon after Roy joined the gallery I became aware of other artists who were drawing on the same subject matter: the mass media and the consumer product. I went to look at

Roy Lichtenstein

Girl with Ball

1 9 6 1

the work of an artist named James Rosenquist, a billboard painter who used fragmented images in his canvases. At the same time a highly successful commercial artist named Andy Warhol was using Campbell soup cans and Coke bottles as a subject matter. I have a precise recollection of Andy coming to see a show of Jasper Johns's drawings. He bought a drawing of a light bulb. That was before he became the real Andy Warhol, although as we know now, what he was doing then was the real Andy Warhol, too.

Warhol very badly wanted to join my gallery, to be with artists he admired, like Johns. I turned him down at first because I felt his work was too similar to Lichtenstein's. Warhol told me I was very much mistaken. Was there another gallery interested? Yes, I was told. If I didn't take him, Andy said, then he had no choice but to go to Eleanor Ward's Stable Gallery. And he did. His show there a year later was fantastic: the Brillo boxes, the Marilyns, and the Elvis paintings. I realized I had made a big mistake.

With Jim Rosenquist, it was the seemingly academic approach that disturbed me. In addition, it seemed too close to Surrealism. But billboards are painted that way. If only I had remembered Magritte! In both artists' work, subject is all, the medium irrelevant. In fact, it is the *absence* of traditional craft that is important to Rosenquist.

Jim joined Richard Bellamy's Green Gallery, and his first

Andy Warhol

Coca Cola Bottles

1 9 6 2

James Rosenquist

F–111

1 9 6 5

show there came after Roy's in the spring of 1962. Both were preceeded by Claes Oldenburg, who had opened his famous "Store" two months earlier – a storefront with replicas of plaster items found in real stores. Pop Art had arrived without anyone knowing it existed, not even the artists making it. Suddenly, people realized that there were two, three, four, five artists who were working with the same ideas and feelings in mind. At this point, the originality of the solitary artist counts for very little; he belongs to what is called the *Zeitgeist*, the spirit, of the moment.

Phenomena of this sort acquire a name, and for want of a better term we go on using it. Pop Art became the common denominator for Warhol, Oldenburg, Lichtenstein, Rosenquist, and others because of the subject matter they all shared: the consumer product.

Pop Art was no more a clear cut movement than Abstract Expressionism, except in the eyes of the media who rose to it like a trout to a fly. In time, the common concern these artists shared turned out not to be that essential – Roy's work is as totally different from Jim's and Claes's and Andy's as theirs is from his. As the individuals transcend its limits, the movement loses meaning. At the time, however, it was considered as a movement, and I worked hard to get thè most important of the Pop artists in my gallery.

Claes Oldenburg

Three-Way Plug—Scale A,

Soft, Brown

1 9 7 0

In 1964 both Rosenquist and Warhol came over to me. Bellamy was closing the Green Gallery and had urged Jim to go with me if he would. In Warhol's case, however, I worried about Eleanor Ward, who was a friend. How could I take Andy away from her? When Warhol convinced me he was going to leave anyway, I finally gave in. I needed Oldenburg to complete my roster of Pop, but by that time he had joined the Janis Gallery, and there he would stay until 1974. Like Julius Caesar, Oldenburg preferred being in

Ellsworth Kelly

View of exhibition

March 8–April 5, 1975

charge of a garrison town rather than second in command at Rome. But I made sure he was always aware that I would like to have him in my gallery, and eventually he felt strong enough to hold his own in my ranks. I had to wait ten years, but eventually I got him.

Ellsworth Kelly had come to me the year before, also from Janis. Other than Stella, I had no artists working in an abstract medium who could match Kelly's incredible subtlety and imagination. He knew that if he ever became dissatisfied with conditions at Janis, rightly or wrongly, that I would be more than pleased to take him on.

When an artist leaves another gallery and joins mine there are often bitter feelings, but in the end I have kept a good relationship with dealers from whom I got important artists. I make it obvious to the artist in question that I like his or her work, and that I think he or she belongs in my gallery rather than another. In this way I am guilty of helping the artist make a decision even though I would never take the initiative. The process is fine-spun, and one of the things, like so many others in a career or in personal life, that is difficult to handle as elegantly as one would want.

At the same time, it is notoriously tricky keeping one's artists, and I think I've been doing a creditable job there. Janis lost his artists little by little, perhaps partly because they were older with idiosyncracies and bad habits acquired in other galleries. Most of my artists were young with no prior gallery experience to speak of before joining mine. We grew up together. I place great importance on that connection, and think it has made a bond between us. Also, I've always identified with my artists' needs and problems, financial or otherwise. I never demanded things from them, and while there wasn't that much of it around, I tried to advance them all the money I could. Above all, I've never told my artists what to do, especially when it comes to their art. Although sometimes I may be unsure of the new work myself, I encourage them to proceed with it – because I know that there has been a tremendous effort on their parts to do something new, not routine, and that they have struggled to get there. But it is not for me to speak *pro domo mea*. For whatever reason, most of my artists have remained loyal to me and the gallery throughout the years.

An important consideration for an artist should be how well his dealer distributes the work, making sure it is shown in other parts of the country as well as Europe. In the early sixties I formed collaborative relationships with dealers outside New York despite the drastic cut in my commission. I want to be candid about my reasons for doing this. One of them certainly was because I was not confident that I could sell my artists' work in New York. Being European, I was comfortable dealing abroad, and naturally looked in that direction. I also knew that little was happening among the young European artists except a longing to get close to their American contemporaries.

John Chamberlain

Mr. Press

1 9 6 1

For a long time no gallery in Europe had bothered with American art, so when my former wife, Ileana Sonnabend, opened her Paris gallery in 1962, we knew that there was an important job to be done. Through Ileana, Rauschenberg, Johns, and many others were seen not only in France, but throughout all of Europe as well. The Sonnabend Gallery soon became a reference point for European collectors, curators, and dealers interested in the new American art. As a result, by 1964 my young artists were much better known abroad than any of the older generation Abstract Expressionists. One explanation for this is that Sidney Janis, because of his established clientele, knew he could sell his artist's work right here in New York, and figured there was no reason to bother with the European market. This, in the end, was a mistake that he made – a mistake made out of strength, whereas I acted out of weakness. But this weakness was to prove useful to me, and to the artists as well. The European market soon became terribly important.

In 1964 Bob Rauschenberg won the Venice Bienale, and for the first time official recognition was given to an American artist by an international forum – an unprecedented event about which quite a bit of ink has been spilled. I was accused of having influenced the jury, which was absurd. It would have been impossible to do. It was just that so much had happened – so much work had been done in Europe by Ileana and myself to make the public understand that Rauschenberg was a major painter that it finally was recognized on this particular occasion.

To the young European artists, Rauschenberg was a hero. *Arte Povera*, an Italian movement whose members identified with the American sensibility of making art out of simple rough elements, came directly out of his combines. And so what seemed to be something that was rigged or influenced by all sorts of maneuvers was partly a natural phenomenon, a groundswell in Rauschenberg's favor, and partly a reflection of the influence his work and ideas had already made on European art.

Around the time I started sharing my artists abroad, I began to do the same thing here with three California dealers: Virginia Dwan, Everett Ellin, and Irving Blum, who

Robert Rauschenberg

Rebus

1 9 5 5

was then at the Ferus Gallery in Los Angeles. I was aware that West Coast collectors would come to New York and complain that by the time they got here, the best works of the artists they wanted were no longer available. My first resolve was to send out only very good material, not just remnants. Slowly, I convinced the collectors that they could find work at local dealers that was of equal quality to what was in New York. This network of galleries in "the provinces" has served me well, and has established an important art market in other parts of the country. Today I have connections with the Margo Leavin Gallery, the James Corcoran Galleries, and the Ace Gallery in Los Angeles; with John Berggruen in San Francisco; with Ronald C. Greenberg in St. Louis; with Janie C. Lee in Houston; with Young-Hoffman in Chicago; and with the Sable-Castelli Gallery in Toronto. Serious collectors no longer feel they have to come to New York to get the best things.

There are many different arrangements when sharing artists, some more complex than others. One gets involved in sharing in a roundabout way, sometimes for personal reasons, sometimes for purely practical ones. But mainly, I collaborate with other dealers because I have more sense than to think I can be on top of everything all of the time.

It was becoming clear to me that on the other side of Pop Art another movement was taking shape in the mid-sixties which was an attempt to reduce and eliminate all that the Pop artists had let into their work. The origins of Minimal Art were de Stijl, Bauhaus, Mondrian, and most importantly, Frank Stella. Without his example, artists that I've shown consistently for the last twenty years – like Judd, Flavin, and Morris (in his more Minimal manifestations) – would not have been able to come into existence.

The Minimalist movement was not something that I initiated. The important artists were obviously Judd, Flavin, and Morris, and I got them all in my gallery through Dick Bellamy. These artists, who had all appeared for the first time in Kynaston McShine's "Primary Structures" show at the Jewish museum in the spring of 1966, had been with Dick Bellamy, but it was not very clear what they were about. They were isolated phenomena, and perhaps the fact that they emerged as part of an important new movement was more my responsibility than the initial discovery of them by Dick. I say this with the benefit of hindsight, but I think perhaps I understood them better than he did. I overlooked

Robert Morris

Untitled

1 9 6 1

Robert Ryman, Sol LeWitt, and Carl Andre which I very much regret – but I forgive myself *some* blind spots.

Again with the help of Richard Bellamy, I found three other artists in the late sixties, right after the Minimalists: Richard Serra, Bruce Nauman, and Keith Sonnier. Soon the work of other Conceptual artists came to my attention by way of the art dealer Gian Enzo Sperone and the collector Panza. These artists were almost completely neglected in the United States until they were brought together for the first time, again by Kynaston McShine in his "Information" show at The Museum of Modern Art in 1970. They were, to name the best, Joseph Kosuth, Robert Barry, Douglas Huebler, and Larry Weiner. To these Americans, I added three Europeans, Hanne Darboven, Laura Grisi, and Jan Dibbets.

People think that with the reputation I have now, I can impose any artist that comes my way. It's not true at all. There has to be some kind of mysterious consensus, without which nothing can be done. There are a number of artists in my gallery that have not been successful. Some never have been, and others were not for years on end before gradually becoming so. Why did I choose them in the first place, and do I now consider that choice a mistake; or do I feel that I was right, and the public or critics or whoever decides these things were wrong? It's very difficult to say, but I feel that if an artist is not successful, the fault may be my own for having chosen him and taken him on when in many cases he would have been much better off in another gallery where the competition from the major artists is less. You see, every artist in my gallery has to compete with Jasper Johns, Rauschenberg, Lichtenstein, and Warhol. The buying public, clients, museums, and others who come to see and buy, are often only interested in those stars, and not in others whom they consider, correctly or incorrectly, second rate; whereas in a smaller gallery with less competition, they might be the main artists. I have not lost many artists, but some of them have felt, quite rightly, that they would be better off in another gallery, like my old friend Friedel Dzubas, who felt he no longer belonged in the gallery after I took on Jasper Johns and Bob Rauschenberg.

Because of the nature of their work, the Minimalists and the Conceptualists have been neither a popular or a com-

Richard Serra

St. John's Rotary Arc

1 9 8 0

mercial success. Actually, Donald Judd is an exception, and a fairly recent one dating from the late seventies. One show after another, I kept on advancing money to these artists, and in the case of Judd, there was also the expense of building the pieces themselves, a great investment that is only now beginning to pay off.

My financial arrangements vary from artist to artist. With some, we split 50-50, but with most, the arrangement is 60 percent for the artist, 40 percent for the gallery. In some cases, the gallery gets even less, one-third or as low as one-quarter of a sale, especially when it comes to commission. Naturally, what has to be considered is the tremendous expense the gallery goes to in providing the space, and in many cases, very expensive announcements, color publications, and all the publicity that goes into magazines. I would say that in general you end up, when everything is said and done, with less than 20 percent. One can see how a group of artists that consistently fails to sell, despite costly shows, becomes a terrific burden on the gallery as a whole – particularly the other artists who must make enough sales to support the ones who don't. Nevertheless, I go on showing the Minimalists and Conceptualists because their work is of great historical importance. It cannot be dismissed or forgotten.

I consider it the gallery's obligation to function as a sort

Joseph Kosuth

One and Three Brooms

(English)

1 9 6 5

Bruce Nauman

Henry Moore Bound to Fail

(Back View)

1 9 6 7

of museum, to show the most important works of art while at the same time providing a reliable base where artists can count on support and exposure. Sales will hopefully come as a consequence. In spite of my ambition, and feeling so sure of myself and my artists. I have never been pushy about making sales. And yet I am a dealer. I have to sell art, and I enjoy the fact that when I have been right, the work has gone up in value. Why be shy about it?

Although the focus of my gallery has never been a money-making one, the commercial part of running a gallery is essential. Unlike museums, galleries are not funded, and must rely on their own resources. More than museums with their ponderous committee choices, it is the daring collector who is central to a gallery's survival. The main reason I never worried or thought about whether or not the artists I "discovered" were going to sell or be understood by the general public was that from the beginning I counted on a handful of sophisticated collectors to feel exactly as I did when someone like Jasper Johns came around.

Who are these collectors? In the early days, there were Ethel and Robert Scull, and at the same time another great team, Burton and Emily Tremaine. Scull, who owned a fleet of taxi cabs called the Scull's Angels, was better known than the Tremaines, although they recently made headlines in connection with the sale of a Jasper Johns painting purchased from me for $900 and sold to the Whitney Museum, alas not through me, for $1 million.

The Sculls and the Tremaines were always in competition with each other over Jasper Johns. Before Jasper's second show in 1960, both went to his studio to make their advance choices. Scull made it there first. He reserved two paintings, and the Tremaines came right after him and picked one called "Device Circle." The next day Scull came back and wanted the same painting. He caused a terrible fuss over the fact that the Tremaines had already bought it.

The Sculls were the type of collectors who wanted to have more than one painting from each important artist. They amassed a large collection at relatively modest cost — $1,000 to $2,000 on an average for Rauschenberg and Johns. The maximum Scull spent was $45,000 for Rosenquist's "F-111." One painter missing from their collection, already difficult to find and expensive, was Jackson Pollock. At one point I found a great Pollock for them, but at $100,000 it was way above their budget.

In 1973 the Sculls' marriage was on the rocks, and they put most of their collection up for auction. For the first time prices were officially established for artists like Johns, who went for over $100,000, and Rauschenbergs and Lichtensteins close to that. The Scull auction was of major importance for the pricing of recent American art.

Many early collectors stopped buying when prices skyrocketed into another orbit, leaving the market open for younger collectors. Si Newhouse is one who has put together a perfect choice of artists, starting with Pollock and de Kooning – as good a collection of contemporary art as can be imagined. Victor Ganz, Agnes Saalfield, Eli Broad, Douglas Cramer, Robert and Jane Meyerhoff, Sydney and Frances Lewis, Charles Saatchi, Peter Palumbo, Don Marron, and Marty Margulies are others who have developed independent and thoughtful collections over the past ten years.

Beyond any doubt the most fervent and extraordinary collector I have ever come across is Count Panza of Milan. When he gets involved with an artist, he buys *en masse*. In the fifties, when nobody else wanted it, he bought Rauschenberg's work – six or more at one stroke. Later on, he was one of the few to buy the Minimalists and the Conceptualists.

The only counterpart to Giuseppe Panza is the German

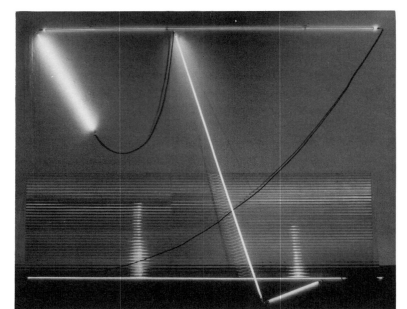

Keith Sonnier

BA-O-BA III

1 9 6 9

Jan Dibbets

Dutch Mountain—Big Sea A

1 9 7 1

collector Dr. Peter Ludwig. Only Jasper Johns has more Jasper Johns paintings than Ludwig, and the sames goes for Rauschenberg. A Lichtenstein painting once caught Dr. Ludwig's eye. Was it available? Unfortunately, I had to tell him it was not. The artist was keeping that particular painting. Later that year we went out to Lichtenstein's studio. Again the subject of this painting was raised, this time to Roy. Indeed, it was not for sale. Dr. Ludwig turned to me and asked how much it would cost if it were available. I told him that normally such a painting would go for $20,000. Immediately he offered $40,000. Roy was very embarrassed. It was not a question of money; he simply did not want to part with the work. But what could he do? One got the feeling that Ludwig would just continue escalating his offer, and by the time we left, Dr. Ludwig owned the painting.

The dedicated collector supports the gallery and the artists with unparalleled commitment in scale and daring. He makes choices way before any general consensus of approval. In this respect, he is as much a champion of uncharted territory as a dealer. None of us could survive without him.

In 1971 I moved part of the gallery operation to 420 West Broadway in Soho. But until the end of 1976, 4 East Seventy-seventh Street remained my headquarters, and I continued to have important shows there too.

At this point I must mention the fact that since the early sixties my major artists had started doing prints in a very serious and consistent way. Universal Limited Art Editions, founded by Tatyana Grosman, Gemini G.E.L. in Los Angeles, Petersburg Press in London, and Ken Tyler were the organizations where prints of an extraordinary quality were produced. They soon became immensely popular with a great number of collectors who could not afford to buy the paintings of Johns, Rauschenberg, or Lichtenstein. My wife, Toiny, feeling that this was an entirely different area which

I could not handle adequately, decided to open a gallery devoted entirely to the exhibition and sale of prints. So in 1969 Castelli Graphics was set up on the ground floor of 4 East Seventy-seventh Street. Its activity expanded rapidly, and soon photographers were added to its roster of artists. When, in 1976, I moved definitely of Soho, Castelli Graphics went up to the floor which I had occupied for so many years.

In 1980 I acquired another gallery at 142 Greene Street. At first I thought it would be a good place to show sculptures and things after I had them at 420 West Broadway, so they would not disappear right away and be forgotten. I thought it would be inexpensive because it was already there, even though it was a bit tacky, and not in very good shape, with a terrible basement where water was dripping down the walls. But upstairs the space was so beautiful aesthetically, with its slim columns and high ceilings, that I began spending more and more money on it. I remade the floor, remade everything. Finally I realized that I couldn't use it for minor purposes, and began showing things that could only be seen in this context: a 50-foot Stella painting called "Racetrack"; a fantastic Judd piece that was 80 feet long and took two months to install; the Richard Serra arc, 120 feet long; Jim Rosenquist's controversial "Star Thief," and other works of similar dimensions.

With this expansion, I rely more and more heavily on my staff to keep things running smoothly. My choices are based more on experience than on theoretical knowledge or a degree in art history, which is not that important. What is really required is practical knowledge – secretarial work, archival work, the pure mechanics of receiving and sending paintings. When you have two or three employees and need more, the people in the gallery itself will find the additional personnel. It is very important that they should be happy and work with others who are congenial. If, which has happened occasionally, I make a choice and my staff is not entirely pleased with it, well, then I give up. I go by what my people decide, not by my own preferences.

But although I have very good employees – and I especially want to mention Susan Brundage, Patty Brundage, Michelle Dreyfuss, John Good, Mame Kennedy, Tom Pehlam, and Terry Wilson as well as so many others before them – although I have this fantastic assistance, still, my personal presence is required at all times. I no longer have time to go to studios to look at work, but I do look at slides, and I see an incredible number of artists a week. And yet, for ten years, I did not take on any new artists whose work I was not unfamiliar with until Julian Schnabel joined the gallery in 1981.

In the late seventies, a new group of artists surfaced under the meaningless label "New Image." I got into the fray after seeing Julian Schnabel's work. At that time, his paintings consisted of an accumulation of broken plates with images emerging from the surface in a very interesting way. They were violent and strong, and I expressed my admiration to Schnabel's dealer, Mary Boone, who had taken a small space on the ground floor of 420 West Broadway. Schnabel is a very ambitious young man, and he felt too confined in that small gallery. One day Mary asked if we could have a combined show of Julian in her and my galleries. I told her I couldn't possibly do that as a one-shot affair, but, if she wanted to, we could come to some sort of agreement about Julian Schnabel. She said fine, and we've been sharing him since then. Very harmoniously. There's never been a problem between Mary and me, ever. We now share another artist, David Salle, and our collaboration continues to be as smooth as it can be. It's something new: someone who has been around as long as I have, working with a very young person like Mary Boone.

I was enormously excited by these events. Schnabel's work made me feel, for the first time in many years, what I had felt about Jasper, Bob, Frank, and Roy when I first saw their work. It was a great experience to be able to recapture that feeling and know that I was still capable of this enthusiasm. Because of his rapid success, his fast climb to the top, there have been many crabby articles written about Schnabel, but, as with the others throughout my history as a dealer, I have no doubts about him or the quality of his work. There are always great enthusiasms and great hostility when you are confronted with originality.

But this is not all. For the first time in many years European artists have been assuming a great importance in the scheme of things. Recently, there have been, at least in Soho, more exhibitions of Italian, German, and, even French artists, than Americans. Some of them – Chia, Cucchi, Clemente, Baselitz, Penck, Immendorf, Kiefer – have become household words. How could I not participate in this new development? In cooperation with the Sperone

Julian Schnabel

Portrait of a Girl

1 9 8 0

Westwater Gallery I have had during the past season very successful exhibitions of Chia and the Frenchman Garouste.

Where do we go from here? It is impossible to say. I was never satisfied with saying to myself, I've done my job, I can't have much more, so why bother. There is still that spirit, let's call it the vanguard spirit, which moves me. And I've always liked breaking away from the familiar and starting over with those artists who redefine what is and what is not art. I see the same inventiveness and originality in my artists' latest works, in their last shows, as I did when they represented the avant garde. And I still get the same tremendous amount of energy from them. So much a part of what they are doing is my life. I am waiting with bated breath to see what new paintings Jasper or Roy or Andy will produce, so when I go to their studios and see their new work, it gives me a tremendous boost. There it is, the material I work with. For instance, quite recently Jasper Johns produced some very great new paintings, one especially. It was a monumental piece using the crosshatch motif with which he started working six years ago. As soon as I saw it, I knew it was a major painting. My feeling about it was communicated to other people who went to see it, like David Whitney and Philip Johnson, and then, through the collector Agnes Saalfield, Philip Johnson saw to it that the painting got into The Museum of Modern Art. An event like that is incredibly life-giving.

My artists have been accused of iconoclasm, of making peculiar paintings just to cause a sensation. All I can say is that in each case I have been convinced of the importance of the work, sure of its substance, in an intuitive way. But what is intiution but the sum of all the knowledge and emotional reactions you have accumulated over the years?

The art scene today is a supermarket compared to the grocery type of operation it was when I first opened my gallery over twenty-five years ago. You can no longer keep your artists today by saying, imperiously, that you will help them survive from month to month on a modest stipend while they finish the work. The artist of the eighties has grand ambitions and the dealer who fails to realize it will soon lose his artists to the enormous competition around him.

For the first time in twenty-five years, European artists are assuming importance in the scheme of things. There is a simultaneous development in Europe and America, a return to figuration but with an expressionistic approach. We can

Roy Lichtenstein

Two Paintings: Craig . . .

1 9 8 3

no longer say it's "all ours."

I have no idea where all of this will lead us. You can't possibly foresee what's going to happen, what techniques will be used, which artists will catch the public's fancy, or what ideas will unfold at just the right moment. The future will always surprise us, thank God.

It has always been part of my ambition to have every major artist and every important movement represented by my gallery. Over the last twenty-five years the only ones to escape me were the color field painters who emerged in the mid-sixties under the sway of the critic, Clement Greenberg: artists like Kenneth, Noland, Morris Louis, Helen Frankenthaler, Larry Poons, and so forth. But perhaps it was all to the good. Otherwise, it would have been a total dictatorship.

The real question for me has always been one of historical importance. After all, a museum has to pick all the good paintings of a period. I felt I should do the same. Obviously, it was not possible, so I forgive myself for overlooking a few.

It's difficult to give one single motivation that has compelled me to do what I have done. The reasons are complex, and in the course of developing this enterprise, many things have changed. Things that seemed easy turned out to be much more difficult; things that seemed difficult turned out to be easier than I ever expected.

My main motivation was to do something that would remain, something of lasting value, and especially something that would help the artists to go on with their work. Thousands of people have seen shows in my gallery, and I like to think that these shows have had their impact on the development of art.

No doubt at first I was particularly receptive to the audacious new attitude toward art because of my personal ambition to make an impression myself. But I hope this desire to be the equal of my heroes, to be a star if you will, has served not only my own ambitions but those of my artists as well.

What has been my greatest satisfaction as an art dealer? Whether or not it's true, I feel, perhaps arrogantly, that any artist would come to me if I asked him. It is very important to feel that you can have something you don't already have; to know that you have a choice, even if you don't exercise that choice. As long as you feel the whole world is at your disposal you're satisfied.

Ileana
Sonnabend

Ileana Sonnabend (born 1914, Bucharest, Rumania) emigrated to the United States during World War II and received a degree in psychology from Columbia University. She worked with her former husband, Leo Castelli, in New York until 1960. Returning to Paris, she opened her first gallery in 1962, showing the best of the new American art. In New York, she opened an Art Deco gallery in 1969 and her present space at 420 West Broadway in 1971 to present new American artists and many major Europeans to the American public.

I've always deplored the fact that the Abstract Expressionists were not properly seen in Europe during the time they were producing their greatest work. The War and its aftermath stood in the way. A decade later, I didn't want that to happen to the rising generation of young American painters. I knew that these were the artists I wanted to show in Europe.

The time was right when I started my gallery in Paris in 1962. Everyone in Europe was looking forward to something new, to recover from the general feeling of boredom with the last waves of the École de Paris. No one knew what direction to go in; for a long time I'd been trying to arrange shows in other galleries, but European dealers wouldn't make the financial commitment to show the new work from America. Finally my husband, Michael, suggested that I try to find a space and show the work myself for a few months. As Michael always says, *Il n'y a que le passager qui dure.*

The first artist who showed in my gallery was Jasper Johns, who had already been seen and well received in Paris at Jean Larcade's Galerie Rive Gauche in the summer of 1958. But I wanted to offer a more controversial side of his work, the more controversial the better: the flag paintings. Feelings toward the United States were very divided in Europe; here was that controversy, that interest, which I was seeking. The show was a great success.

Loud in color, ironical, and unsentimental, the works of these young artists were bound to offend those people whose profession it was to guard the sacred altar of art. Those *grands enfants* could only view it as the art of barbarians. In the case of Jasper Johns, his flags were also considered emblems of an offensively pro-American imperialism. But in the course of the exhibition, many people came to see that these were no mere flags, but paintings of a totally new sort. At no time since then have I experienced such excitement, except with my shows of the British artists Gilbert & George in 1971 and that of the German artist A. R. Penck in 1982.

Following Johns was, naturally, a show of Robert Rauschenberg (who was to become a hero among young artists all over Europe) and after that, Andy Warhol. Then George Segal came and worked in Paris for a while before his show, and later Claes Oldenburg did the same. Roy Lichtenstein's show created a real revolution.

Jasper Johns

Flag

1 9 5 5

111

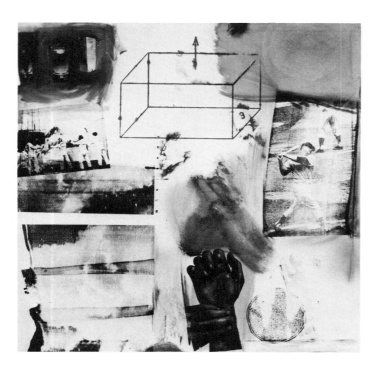

Robert Rauschenberg

Shortstop

1 9 6 2

When Andy Warhol came for his opening, he brought a whole retinue with him from New York, and we screened his films in the gallery. Soon after, Langlois showed them at the Cinématèque. There was a very interesting cultural life in Paris at that moment, a great interaction among the arts. Unfortunately, it petered out, but I think it is being revived with the Centre Pompidou and the Festival d'Automne. All the same, more interest is reserved for music than the visual arts in Paris today.

When I began showing artists like Rauschenberg, Johns, and Warhol, there were good reactions, but also a great deal of resistance. I remember one French journalist who became very upset, waving his umbrella around a great deal. But you expected that, and the controversy was very good for the artists. Even our landlady protested. She came in once to see the work we were showing, and it happened to be the day we were unpacking the Warhols fresh from New York. They were spread out on the floor. When she saw the group of Marilyn paintings she was outraged: "I forbid you to show those things on my premises. This is not art, it's necrophilia!"

During our first two years the gallery occupied a space in a hotel which had an elegant little restaurant, Le Relais Bis-

Andy Warhol

Gold Marilyn

1 9 6 2

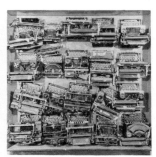

Arman

Infinity of Typewriters and

Infinity of Monkeys and

Infinity of Time—Hamlet

1 9 6 2

son. Many personalities attracted to this restaurant would come to the gallery afterward, sneaking in, so to speak. One of them was André Malraux, at the time cultural minister of France. Often he would send his people to report back on what we were doing: he was both interested and upset by it all. Miró was also very attentive to the new work from America and would stay a long time watching the goings-on and looking at paintings.

André Breton frequently passed by in those days, and unlike Malraux, he was all in favor. Good words from him certainly helped the artists we showed. When Breton and his fellow Surrealists talked about them, they of course wanted to make their own interpretations: according to them, Jasper Johns and Rauschenberg were, if not Surrealists, at least Dadaists. And when it came to James Rosenquist, he was beyond question a born Surrealist.

The Americans themselves who came over to do shows had a lot of contact with what was going on in Europe. Artists of the Nouveau Réalisme movement were intrigued with new American art. Even then the French artist Arman was a great admirer of Rauschenberg, Johns, Jim Dine, and Warhol. He, along with Martial Raysse and Tinguely, did a lot to help them by embracing them openly as the American embodiment of their "new reality."

The Nouveau Réalistes were a group of interesting young people who showed at a small but wonderfully active gallery in Paris called Galerie J. Led by the artist Yves Klein, they also included Arman, Niki de Saint-Phalle, and Gérard Descamp, a most remarkable artist who somehow got lost in the shuffle. I dealt only with Arman, whose sculptural works, which he called "accumulations," proved to be very influential. It was all a breath of fresh air.

Young European artists always wanted to meet the artists we showed. That's why we tried to bring the artists from New York for the openings. There was great excitement, and those openings were mobbed by all kinds of people — the young and not so young, cultural officials, and the general public. It was really a good time in France during the first part of the sixties. Then politics took over and people lost a lot of their interest in viewing art. Nineteen sixty-eight was a revolutionary year in France, and young people were marching rather than going to galleries, which they felt were part of the Establishment and must somehow be destroyed. They achieved it quite well, I think.

113

But we carried on. Pontus Hulten, then director of the Moderna Museet in Stockholm, came and immediately bought a very important Warhol for his museum. Count Panza, the great Italian collector, also became very enthusiastic about Oldenburg's work and afterward bought a lot of his work from the show.

In 1964, we had another show of Rauschenberg, and it became apparent that he was going to be in the Venice Biennale that year. He was producing his greatest work, and there was always a vast movement in his favor in Paris. People were coming to congratulate me, because they knew that Bob was going to be a success in Venice. They didn't know he was going to get the first prize, but they knew he was important for the Biennale.

At that point Edi de Wilde came from the Stedelijk Museum of Amsterdam, and he saw a Rauschenberg that he very much liked. Mr. Hamacher came, who was then professor at The Hague and director of the museum there; Alan Bowness, now director of the Tate Gallery, also visited, together with the critic John Russell and Bryan Robertson, the head of the Whitechapel in London. All these people wanted to see what was going on in this new, shall we say "outlandish," gallery. It was more convenient for them than going to New York; in those days traveling was not what it is today. That's why it was important to bring American art to Europe – more important, I think, than it is now.

For the same reason I show many Europeans today at my gallery in New York. Even before, I didn't think so much in terms of American art only; I never believed that art should have a nationality. I thought of the Americans as a group of people doing sensational work, work that had to be seen. Later, I began finding interesting artists in Europe and tried to arrange shows for them in New York. Again, I found the possibilities practically nonexistent. Nobody wanted to deal with European artists, young ones in particular. Paul Klee or Léger, that was a different matter. It was upsetting to see such chauvinism on both sides.

Opening a gallery in New York was really the reverse of my Paris situation, partly because I wanted Europeans to be seen here, if they were good, but also because the center of gravity of the art world had shifted to New York. We started in 1971 with a first show of the English performance artists, Gilbert & George, whom I've been showing ever since.

I am not really a dealer; I am an *amateur*, a word I use

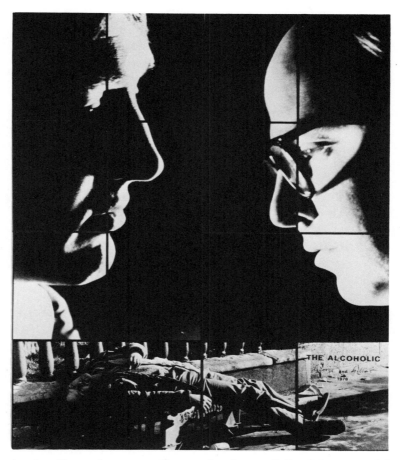

in the French sense: "one who loves." In this case, it's a love of art. Some people can only share my enthusiasms, while others can afford actually to buy the art, but my main interest remains in finding people who are as interested as I am in the artists and their work.

I show collectors what interests me at the moment, what has interested me in the past, or what I think they have missed in their collections. What I do is not at all pedagogic; I'm not trying to teach anybody anything. I do not advise; it would be very risky and presumptuous to do so. I simply present the best things I know and let people make up their minds.

Naturally, I wouldn't want to give the impression that I am not commercial, because it's not true. I like to survive and to have my artists survive as well as possible. It would be unfair to say I am a pure spirit.

I feel that one should not count too much on the loyalty

of artists, because they have needs and goals that may not always coincide with the dealer's. Artists can be very loyal, very generous people, but there are unfortunate cases where an artist changes – or perhaps the dealer changes, too. Parting ways is very painful, but it has to be done in fairness to the artist, since I work so much with my own enthusiasm. If an artist sees that things have not happened as they should, I have to admit that I cannot do much for him. We part, but remain friends.

When artists have gone through too many different galleries no one is there to maintain a level for them. I wouldn't mention the names of artists to whom this has happened, but the result is always the same: low prices at auctions. It is very unfortunate when this occurs.

I like things that make me think, that make me look for their meaning, things that force me to investigate the mental life of the artist. I am very instinctual, and I seek things that are problematic, difficult to classify on the basis of things already known.

I have a heroic idea about art. There's a heroic quality in the work of an artist like Jannis Kounellis, whom I show. Kounellis is a Greek artist who for many years has lived and worked in Rome. He is very conscious of the antiquity, of the occupation of being an artist, and his work stands in a genre all its own, relating as much to theater as to painting.

Another artist whose work exemplifies this heroic quality I have always looked for is the German painter A. R. Penck. Seeing the work of Penck for the first time gave me a great shock, the same kind of revelation I had when I visited the Lascaux caves and saw paintings thousands of years old: a similar feeling of prehistory lingers in the work of Penck. It goes beyond painting and arrives at the very source of the mystery of signs. As with the paintings in the Lascaux caves, there is a beauty but also a significance that goes far beyond esthetics. I had followed Georg Baselitz's work for a number of years, and he had a very strong showing in Venice at the 1978 Biennale. It was unthinkable not to present him in America, and I couldn't understand how no one else had done so in the last five years. After trying without success to place him in another gallery in New York, I am very happy to be able to show him myself.

I have a reputation for being outspoken. I'm supposed to be very difficult, which is not really true. But outspoken, yes. Sometimes I'm a little brutal: I had to learn how when I

Jannis Kounellis

Untitled

1 9 7 2

A. R. Penck

Am Fluss (Hypothese 3)

1 9 8 2

arrived in Paris, where women were still at a real disadvantage. It was not so easy to be a woman in the so-called business world. Many artists also thought they could maneuver women easily, so I had to be a little more blunt than I would perhaps otherwise have been. I was taken advantage of so many times by so many people that I developed a defense. It also had to do with being American; Americans are supposed to be naive children to be taken advantage of. I was a target of all this. Today I am not bothered by what could be called "reputation," nor do I act in order to be loved. Instead I prefer to be appreciated for having acted in a certain way or done certain things. You also have a lot of enemies, but you simply bear with them. Luckily, I have kept good friends as well.

Knowing the artists personally always adds to your knowledge of their work, but there is a danger of being influenced by a very pleasant personality. It's safer to know the work first. If I recognize something in a painting, find it familiar, and like it very much, if I know what the artist is doing, then I know I must beware: it is probably not very original, and probably just academic no matter how good it may be. My only rule would be not to categorize a work too easily: finding something that you don't recognize is not interesting in itself. You must find the meaning.

No dealer can project the future direction of art or the work of individual artists. One can only project, on the basis of personalities, that the work of certain people must become more recognized if they have time enough to work and to be seen. Someone like Julian Schnabel is going to get there. He has everything it takes, including the energy to carry it out. I have no doubts about him, and may be one of the few to say that so unconditionally, no matter how many followers he now enjoys.

Some artists evolve and some fossilize, not daring to evolve. I remember in Paris, when people were so shocked by Pop Art, an artist who already had a solid reputation once approached me and asked, "How should I paint now? What should I do?" I told him that if he needed my opinion, then he should just go on painting the way he had up to then.

I don't believe in trends. They are either academies or shortcuts. Labels like Pop, Minimal, Conceptual group together very different artists as a shortcut to dispense with the need to enumerate a whole list of artists.

When I set out to help the career of a young artist, I give attention to the type of shows he is in. It is dangerous for an artist to accept certain shows, just as it is dangerous to refuse. You need to find a balance. My advice to young artists who as yet have no gallery is this: they should wait; they should know that if something happens too soon, that this, too, can be a real danger; they must get to a certain level of

Vito Acconci

Installation

1 9 7 9

Anne and Patrick Poirier

The Temple of One Hundred

Columns

1 9 8 0

maturity. It doesn't have to do with age, or even with the number of years of work. It has more to do with timing and patience.

What happens today is really a little sad. Artists often have a gallery before arriving at a true body of work. Too often young artists come and show dealers three or four photographs of their work, expecting on this basis that they will find a gallery. This is unhealthy and creates pressures for them afterward, pressures that can harm the artist, that prevent him from arriving at true maturity in the work.

Since the sixties, artists have waged a kind of war against art dealers, to the point that the role of galleries has been reduced to that of simple outlets. Today it is the artists who pull the strings, not the dealers – a complete reversal from the days of Ambroise Vollard. Vollard had artists from whom he bought at a low price, promoting and eventually selling the work. All that has changed; if the dealer was once an impresario, now his gallery is little more than the commercial outpost of the artists. I don't know if this is good or bad; one can be a lot more detached today. In a sense, this development has given me a lot more freedom. If all through the seventies our job was selling the artists, in the eighties it is selling works of art. The artists are selling themselves at this point.

Mel Bochner

Syncline

1 9 7 8 – 7 9

Richard
Bellamy

Richard Bellamy (born 1927, Cincinnati, Ohio) completed high school with ambitions of becoming a radio disc jockey, but instead presided over the innovative Hansa Gallery from 1955 through 1959 and became director of the Green Gallery, funded by collector Robert Scull, in 1960. Cult figure and dealer's dealer without parallel, Bellamy devotes his Oil & Steel Gallery, started in 1981, to the painting and sculpture of artists including Michael Heizer and Mark di Suvero.

What in God's name would the reading public want to hear about the dealers? Some anecdotes? Probably. People will read about the dealers to hear about "their" artists. These come to mind: Claes Oldenburg, in about 1960, wallowing and blubbering, drinking in the mire out at Bob Whitman's place in Alpine, New Jersey; the Hansa-Reuben crowd inchoately surrounding Lucas Samaras gliding in a trance; Poons, in the days of the dots, driving a huge, rented car steady at sixty, never looking to the left or right, a concentrated mass caught up with speed.

I've been hanging around artists ever since I hit Provincetown when I came East from Cincinnati at the age of twenty-one. Provincetown is an artists' colony where Hans Hofmann lived and taught summer school, and where a historic exhibition of Abstract Expressionists was held in the summer of 1949. Clement Greenberg had written about the action painters and was already one of my heroes, through his articles in *Partisan Review*. Pollock, de Kooning, Kline, Motherwell, and Newman – seeing the exhibition was my first introduction to them.

In the early years I hadn't formed any allegiances or opinions yet, so there was no static around the art that interfered with what I was seeing. Being unpracticed, I was registering things very clearly, with an innocent eye. I had an intensity of perception, where things just got interiorized immediately.

Anyone who entered the art world at this time respected the Abstract Expressionist pantheon. I was no exception. I didn't dig Pollock at first, but de Kooning I did, immediately. I loved Motherwell's work and interiorized it from the first moment I saw it. I first saw a David Smith sculpture in the early fifties, when Marian Willard used to have them in the hallway of her New York gallery. It was not only the intrinsic quality of the work but the intensity I felt about it that made it a standard of excellence for me through the years.

The Hansa Gallery was an artists' cooperative on Twelfth Street that moved up to Central Park South in 1955. I knew a lot of the artists who showed there, and their art, but when the question of my working there came up, I never conceived of it as a career, but rather as giving a hand to some friends who were short of help. I had been doing house painting and carpentry for about a year, and had also been a radio announcer. I wanted to get a decent job that would allow me to buy my friends' art every once in a while, but I was reluctant to take a job at Hansa, for in those ragged times, art dealers were thought of as people who were always turning artists away. To me, dealers were unreachable people who rejected friends' work when they offered it for shows, so I hesitated over becoming one, or even being involved in the commercial aspect of art. It had a tainted atmosphere. It was due to a toss of the I Ching that I decided to take the job.

Ivan Karp, an art critic for the *Village Voice*, came to Hansa a year or two after that, and we worked together for a couple of years. We were making between $50 and $75 a week, plus commissions. Ivan then went over to the Martha Jackson Gallery. I stayed on, even though I had been voted out by the artists for incompetence – like drinking pints of Napoleon brandy when I got bored. My title, "gallery director," always amused me, because I just sat there, answering the phone. I never knew what it was to run a gallery, or how to sell the work.

We showed Jan Müller, Miles Forrest, Richard Stankiewicz, Fay Lansner, and George Segal, among others. Allan Kaprow, one of the founders of Hansa, had become involved along with others in the late fifties in combining theater and art into performance events to which he gave the name "happenings." He returned to the fold at Hansa in 1959, bringing with him two of his most interesting students from Douglass College in New Jersey, Lucas Samaras and Bob Whitman, just before the gallery folded. I went back to doing odd jobs, which included working for Martha Jackson for about six weeks, and, as in all the interim periods, there was Provincetown in the background whenever I could get there.

As the name implies, the Hansa Gallery artists were all ex-students of Hans Hofmann, devoted to him both as an artist and as a teacher. All through the fifties and well into the sixties, Hofmann was thought of as a negligible painter but a great teacher. I know I was repelled by his paintings the first few years I saw them. The artists who were my friends idolized him, but I still thought his paintings were just awful. It wasn't until much later that I understood his work and could appreciate its greatness. When Hofmann used to talk about color to his students, he would use this word "interval" to describe what happens when two colors meet and a light flash is created. This never made any sense

James Rosenquist

Marilyn Monroe I

1 9 6 2

to me until I had a revelation while looking at one particular painting of his at the Metropolitan Museum in New York. I actually saw color in a different way; I saw the color "interval," and I understood what he was talking about. But it was hard for me to get there, to appreciate him. It took a long time. Pollock was also very difficult for me. I was thinking in terms of validity and order, and I was totally unprepared for his pure visuality. I just couldn't figure it out.

In the early fifties we all had heroes, and my two greatest heroes were de Kooning and David Smith. I would also consider John Chamberlain one of my heroes. We met in 1955, and I went on my "foist" trip to Europe with him in 1964 for the Venice Biennale. I remember Rauschenberg's show in 1956 on Fifty-seventh Street, the "combines," and everything seemed natural to me. I wasn't taken aback by the new works that combined, or fell between, painting and sculpture any more, so that when I saw my first abstract paintings – my first de Kooning, let's say, or Mondrian – I was totally open to all these experiences; there seemed nothing threatening. Certainly I was more than curious

123

about the Rauschenbergs when I first saw them.

I also remember seeing the work of Jasper Johns, which I appreciated on an esthetic plane. I remember several years later going to Jasper's studio with Bob Scull, around 1962, for a private showing of his work that was due to be exhibited at Castelli's. There were these exquisite paintings, and I said to Jasper, "They're so beautiful. Every millimeter is filled." Johns turned to me and said, "But of course – that's the point." Today, Leo laughs at this story, saying, "I wouldn't expect him to have said anything else, because of course that is the point of Jasper's work."

Ivan Karp introduced me to Robert Scull, who wanted to open a gallery without having it known that he was the backer. We wanted the name to be as neutral as possible, and thought of names such as O. K. Harris, The Finger Lakes, and The Big Tit. We finally settled on the Green Gallery.

In 1960 I opened the Green Gallery with those artists I knew whose work I liked and who didn't have galleries. Many artists who had been at the Hansa Gallery were still looking for new places to go. We took George Segal, Milet Andrejevic, and Lucas Samaras from that group.

In the case of Donald Judd, an artist we acquired later, it was almost the reverse. He wanted the Green Gallery, although he could certainly have had his choice. I liked both him and the reviews he wrote for *Arts* magazine. I had no idea that he was an artist, but when I found out, I asked him if he would permit me to see his work when he was ready to show it. He said yes, and when I saw it I really dug it and told him he should approach Leo Castelli, since his gallery was the best to be with in every way. But Judd said that, even if Leo would want to take a chance on him that early, this first body of work still hadn't made a complete statement, and that therefore he preferred to be with a gallery that was forming, rather than starting out on top. It might have been as simple as the fact that the Green Gallery space was larger than the beautifully proportioned room at Leo's. Judd was a sculptor, and this space factor might have made a difference, but in the end I think he was sincere about entering the art world in some less-established way.

The opening show at the Green Gallery was of Mark di Suvero, whose work I had seen several months before. Mark's show got good press, but after that it was pretty much bad news in terms of public notice until the coming of Pop artists.

Donald Judd

Untitled

1 9 6 1

From late 1962 on, the Green Gallery was showing artists who were among the best of their time: George Segal, Felix Pasilis, Jack Tworkov, Taadaki Kuwayana, Pat Pasloff, and Dick Smith. A lot of attention was being thrown upon galleries and artists, due to the Pop Art phenomenon, and we certainly participated in that. We had some important shows, and several artists from the original roster were offended and left for reasons of conscience after I began to show Pop Art. Several artists protested that I hadn't sold any of their work, and they might have felt that I was disloyal to what they stood for by showing work that seemed to subvert their careers.

I resisted the idea of Pop Art well past the time it became established as a movement. For a long while I saw it merely as four or five very individual artists. I was bemused by some, found others a little bizarre, and felt in general that they related to each other only in negative aspects. In 1961 I went to the studios of Roy Lichtenstein and James Rosenquist with Ivan, and I later met Larry Poons through Rosenquist. The work of James Rosenquist struck me immediately. I felt an authentic sensibility, and that excited me very much. I was still devoted to Abstract Expressionism but certainly did not see Pop Art as a threat, as some people did, or as something innocuous, as others did. It took me a couple of years to become sensitive to the virtues of Lichtenstein's paintings. My estimation of them still fluctuates, but I certainly regard him as a serious artist.

Several months later, I saw Andy Warhol's work with Henry Geldzahler and Ivan Karp, but I disregarded it except for occasional delightful moments such as the *Pillows* shown at Leo Castelli's gallery. Warhol's premises were foreign to me, as were Roy's, but I got a great deal more out of Roy's work. However, there were certain paintings of Andy's that astonished me with their beauty – some of the *Marilyn* and *Disaster* paintings, for example.

In 1962, I began to show the work of Larry Poons, Donald Judd, Dan Flavin, James Rosenquist, Robert Morris, and Claes Oldenburg. Martha Jackson had a show called "New Forms, New Media," and Leo Castelli was showing Lichtenstein – all this was breaking at the same time. Leo attended the shows at the Green Gallery, something I think no other dealer did. He would come in with some of his artists, Jasper, Roy, whomever. Leo had a real sense of what was going on, as opposed to my very partial view. He

125

saw what was building and had the imagination to grasp the historical moment, while my vision was much more narrow.

I saw an enormous amount of work during those years at the Green Gallery. Because we were still a new enterprise and my duties were quite undefined, I felt I should look at as many artists' work as possible. I would work in the gallery all day, seven days a week, even hanging shows on Monday, the usual closing day. At night I would hang out with the artists, going to bars and visiting their studios. I landed up in the whiskey hospital more than once in 1962.

I was in my mid-thirties when the Green Gallery was in operation, but I was behaving like a twenty-year-old. The gallery was very loosely organized, and I would just take what came. I won't say it was indiscriminate, but there was no real thinking about the business aspect, or what a stable of artists means, or what a dealer does to promote them apart from sitting there and trying to sell a painting every time someone asks the price of it. If I got stuck at the end of the month, Scull would buy paintings or pay in advance for things he would eventually buy. He wanted to make it possible for the gallery to survive, but he's not an altruist. He would have wound up with fewer paintings and sculptures if other people had been buying. As it was, Scull did acquire a lot of good work, and I think many of the artists benefited.

One incident during this period that stands out in my mind involves Ethel, Bob's wife. Bob was on one of his yearly vacations in Europe, and Ethel called me out to their house in Great Neck, Long Island. At the end of the day she offered me a ride back to the city in the limousine. I sat in the back seat, and she sat up front with the chauffeur. She told me that Bob was thinking of pulling out of the gallery, that he was very grieved about it, but I was such a mess that things had become intolerable. It shook me up a little. I realized I should be running the gallery myself, considering the experience I had acquired by then. The next day I used Pledge on the desk.

Even though I managed to pull myself together some, by 1965 the gallery had run its course. It seemed to be a little superfluous, and it was too much of a burden on Bob to be responsible for this commercial gallery that really should have been carrying itself. We closed for financial reasons. Some of the artists who had been selling went on to other galleries, certainly with my blessing. I was supplying those who remained with various amounts of money per month to

Myron Stout

Untitled

1 9 5 5 – 6 8

live on. Sales were decreasing, but the artist's expenses for putting up a show were greater. I finally couldn't afford new materials and supplies for them, especially for someone like Judd, who had started to work in metal rather than wood. In short, I wasn't able to support the artists in the style to which they were beginning to become accustomed.

Noah Goldowsky, a dealer from Chicago whom I had met at The Five Spot, my jazz hangout, had a small gallery on upper Madison Avenue. He offered me the use of a room barely six by eight feet, so I packed my typewriter, filing cabinet, and bills, and moved in. Leo Castelli had also offered me some space to work out of, but I chose Noah. I needed anonymity as well as autonomy.

I was quite satisfied with the situation at Noah's when I first got there in 1965. I was learning about the trade even though there was no set program. I certainly had no wish to open a gallery again, but since my teens I had had an idea about being a businessman – having a desk, wearing a green visor on my head, and getting a lot of mail. I never advanced to Ivan Karp's stage of being an inveterate cigar smoker, although that is part of the image. Sometimes, willy-nilly, I would hang a show from what Noah had in stock, but often there would be nothing on the walls. I was trying to operate as a private dealer, which is what the space and my own inclinations were suited to.

I had no experience as a private dealer, but was introduced to the idea by Myron Stout, an original member of the Hansa Gallery. Myron had shown at the Stable Gallery before, and when Hansa folded, I assumed he would return there. Instead he asked, "Dick, why don't you just continue to handle my work?" I was taken aback, not knowing what he meant at first. How could I represent his work when I was simply adrift? The very notion of a person representing an artist without a gallery structure was something I had never thought of. It was the first glimmer of what one could do in that capacity, without the impertinences of an office or gallery, and it challenged me to think about myself in that role. In retrospect this came to bear upon a decision I made about Mark di Suvero while I was at Noah's that could be considered a major turning point in my career as a dealer.

At this time Mark had no place to work and no money to speak of for materials. One day he appeared at the gallery. I was surprised because I knew that galleries made him nervous, and that he particularly didn't like to see me working in one. At that time, apart from my physical deterioration, I would describe my overall psychic condition as cowering. Mark approached me and asked, "Dick, what do you really want to do?" With an almost-steady voice – I mean, it didn't break as in a soap opera – I said, "Mark, I guess I want to take care of your work." Although that response wasn't very strong, at least the question had been put to me, and I had to acknowledge that in fact it was what I really wanted to do.

To do this I had to move out of Noah's, but for a full year I was in a totally paralyzed, completely miserable, nothing-can-happen state. I kept telling myself, *I've got to leave Noah's,* but avoided any mention of the subject in front of him. Somehow I thought I would be letting him down, even though I knew I was a real pain in the ass for him a lot of the time. Noah had begun to charge me half the rent and insurance by then. We shared an accountant, Noah's brother-in-law Joe, and a couple of times he said, "Dick, Joe tells me you're making more money than I am!" I had been getting 10 percent commissions on private sales from other dealers, including a $15,000 Morris Louis for Andre Emmerich and five Rothkos out of Marlborough Gallery. The books reflected a profit of $40,000 that year, but, as is the case with all such profits, my bank balance was dramatically lower.

By then I was fairly desperate to leave as soon as possible, but I had to get some money to give Noah before I could go. One day when I was very glumly thinking about

Jo Baer

Untitled Diptych

1 9 6 8

David Rabinowitch

Metrical (Romanesque) Construction in Eleven Masses and Two Scales

1 9 8 0

the move, I realized that I did have one thing to sell, an Oldenburg piece that I had bought in the mid-sixties called *Ray Gun Rifle*, which I had been storing at Don Judd's since the close of the Green Gallery because the work is papier-mâché and very fragile. I was able to sell it almost immediately to the German collector Dr. Ludwig, for about $10,000. Overjoyed, I put in a call to Don to get the piece. He refused to give it up. Somehow he felt that the work had, by osmosis, become his. When I pursued the matter with follow-up calls, I was relegated to his wife, Julia. As I had a bill of sale for the work, and wanted it in a hurry, I immediately contacted my lawyer, Jerry Ordover. But, as with my accountant, there were mixed loyalties; Jerry was Judd's lawyer, too. As it turned out, Don had no legal stance, and eventually Jerry was able to return the piece to me.

Several years passed, and I was riding with Jo Baer in Central Park to celebrate her upcoming show at the Whitney. Jo is a superb rider; she does dressage and so forth. Unfortunately, I was in another, shall we say, low period, and not paying attention to what was happening. I was thrown against a tree, injuring my kidneys. The whole awful affair with Judd had stayed in my mind, and while I was in the hospital, I wrote him a letter. Apart from admiring him as an artist, I liked Don. I wrote him a note of amity, but never received a reply, which stunned, mortified, and enraged me. I will, when the mood strikes, refer to the story mysteriously. I will say that I've known a few artists in my time, but hated only one. When asked who, I will give a clue: "A short name, crowded with consonants, and hardly so delicious as the element with which it rhymes." Of course, people are curious. One day this sort of thing might get back and annoy him enough to respond to me in a forthright manner, but I don't hold out too much hope.

Alfred Leslie

First Four

1 9 5 5

In 1974, after being with Noah for seven years – at least four years too long – I opened an office on Park Avenue at Twenty-fifth Street, where I remained for almost another seven years. Although I was nominally representing Jo Baer and Al Leslie, I didn't have the will or means to run a gallery. The one exhibition I had during that entire period was a drawing show for David Rabinowitch. About a dozen people came to the opening, and exactly three more people came during the following three-week period. Nothing sold.

I opened the Oil & Steel Gallery in 1980 at 157 Chambers Street. I prefer Tribeca to Soho because there is less public contact. Solitude is more valuable to me than having a large staff. I love being here alone just shuffling things around.

There are only three artists in my present stable: di Suvero, Myron Stout, and David Rabinowitch. I gave the sculptor Richard Nonas a show when we first opened, before the walls were up. I also had a show for Manny Farber, having to do with Old-World friendship, but I don't feel that I handle his work.

The best-known artist of my present three is Mark di Suvero. Committing myself to him seemed the obvious thing to do given our so-called history, which spans more than fifteen years. It seemed that I could do a lot worse than to concentrate on him and his works, which can never be contained. When I took him on, there was nobody else in the art world who would represent him. I felt that if I were going to do it, I should do it with a sense of mission. Mark's major works are not even showable in a gallery setting, let alone salable, but in the midst of otherwise-meaningless business activities, I have never doubted that whatever I can do for him is the single most worthwhile thing I can do.

I have a reputation for getting along well with artists. I've always felt comfortable with them, and they with me. It could be because they sense I'm on the same side of the tracks, simply because they're able to impose their will and

Mark di Suvero

Foreground: *Mon Père, Mon Père*

1 9 7 4

Background: *Etoile Polare*

1 9 7 3

Michael Heizer

Dissipate—#8 of Nine

Nevada Depressions

1 9 6 8

the rigors of their vision upon me. There may also be the distorted point of view among artists that I'm not rich, or haven't made a lot of money. Neophyte artists seem to feel there's something laudable in that, although of course it's a mistaken notion.

I know how hard it is to make art because I've tried to do it myself. In the early fifties, when waiting in an artist's studio, I would pick up a brush and paint on cardboard or whatever material was handy. Once I drew on the endpaper of a beautiful book entitled *The Bitter Box* by Eleanor Clark, Robert Penn Warren's wife. My drawing was black and very "Reinhardtish." As a matter of fact, I could claim that I originated techniques generally credited to such artists as Jackson Pollock and Ad Reinhardt. In my Provincetown days, I did some all-black things that later turned out to be exactly what Kline was doing. But I had no talent, and I realized just how very difficult art is to create.

However, I know of one artist who would challenge the popular notion that I have more of a consanguinity with artists than other dealers have. In fact, I am known for the wanton destruction of his work. Recently, an English magazine published an article based on an interview with Carl Andre in which I am accused of destroying his first works by fire in the year 1960. As the tone of the piece was not attuned to the truth of the occurrence as I remember it, I

William Crozier

Marilyn

1 9 7 5 – 8 0

would like to describe some of the existential aspects of this event.

In 1960, with my wife Schyndee and our two children, I moved into a house that at one time had been owned by Frank Stella. I don't know if Stella had ever lived or worked there, but it was obvious that Carl Andre had. Left behind were several sculptures – large, pyramidal shapes consisting of interlocking blocks of wood. The building was an old brownstone on East Broadway with a backyard and a little attachment to the house that must have been intended as a sunporch of some kind, because it had a lot of windows. Even the door had windows, but not one of them shut, so there was a lot of cold air coming in all the time. Luckily, we also had an open fireplace.

It was a very cold winter that year, and I asked Carl repeatedly if he would come and remove the work, explaining how very difficult it was for us as a family to live there with these three or four very bulky sculptures. At one point, to allow us just a little more room, I did move one of them out into the backyard. My wife protested about our living arrangements, but Carl showed no interest in the topic. In fact, he seemed irked at the mere mention of the subject, and finally said we should do whatever we wanted with them, just please not to bother him about it anymore. Even so, it was with a good bit of hesitation, and with a certainty that there was some violation being done, that I would slip one or two of the blocks into the fire, very tentatively at first, on the coldest days of that winter, with the wind blowing under the windows and the kids shivering. This took place over a period of time when the cold had increased, and soon it was with *pure relish* that I overcame my scruples and built a blazing fire during the most frigid nights. I had hoped to keep a part of the piece intact, but finally it all went into that fireplace, and we survived the winter.

The subject was never raised between us, but Carl obviously repeated the story, which accounts for a certain attitude toward me on the part of some of his friends. The issue resurfaced recently when I put together a disparate group for a show called "Arp to Artschwager." I rang Carl and asked if he would participate. He never called me back.

Living with works of art does not prompt me to destroy them. In fact, the crystallization of the work of my lifetime took place during Jan Müller's exhibition at Hansa in 1956, when I was sleeping at the gallery and would wake up in the morning surrounded by the paintings. I felt I was seeing what the artist was putting down, his life going on in the work. I was able to see these paintings in an unguarded moment that art dealers rarely have.

Ivan Karp

Ivan Karp (born 1926, New York City) began his career as an art dealer at the Hansa Gallery with Richard Bellamy and later worked with Martha Jackson. He served as Leo Castelli's right-hand man from 1959–1969, establishing himself as a major force in the development of Pop Art. His Soho gallery, O. K. Harris, opened in October 1969.

My interest in art goes back to my infancy, but it became a professional matter when I was invited to write criticism on art, dance, and movies for the *Village Voice* in 1955. The editor of the paper assigned me to obscure galleries where friends of his were exhibiting, one of which was the Hansa Gallery. Hansa was a co-op gallery presided over by Richard Bellamy. At that point he was showing artists outside of the gallery belt, like George Segal and Jan Müller. Bellamy received a weekly wage of $12, plus 10 percent of work sold, which was very little. In 1956 Bellamy proposed that we share the activity of running the gallery. He had read several of my reviews about artists in the gallery and had been impressed. I was to take three days and Bellamy three days. We saw perhaps fifteen or twenty visitors in a week; we read poetry, flirted with female visitors, and did a little typing.

The art world was very small at the time, and in the throes of Abstract Expressionism: de Kooning, Kline, Rothko, and Pollock. They were a curious crowd – troubled, anxious, nasty, aggressive, even violent at times. Painters who did not work in the prevailing mode were considered peculiar and reactionary, especially the Realists, who were thought to be hanging onto a worn-out tradition.

Dick Bellamy and I had a difficult time maintaining the gallery – essentially in paying the rent. After two seasons, I was invited to resign. Immediately I was offered a job at Martha Jackson's, a ritzy, commercial Madison Avenue gallery. Mrs. Jackson was a high-strung woman, but she ran an elegant place that was active and successful. She had Sam Francis and a few other artists I was impressed with. I received a salary, plus commission. I went to Brooks Brothers and bought a new suit.

The atmosphere at Martha Jackson's was dramatically different from that of the Hansa Gallery. People came in and put down thousands of dollars for a picture. The first time I saw that happen – someone was writing out a check for $6,800 for a Sam Francis – I was overwhelmed. I couldn't believe anyone had that much in his checking account. Slowly I got used to the idea that people would pay big for fine art. I had always felt that they should, but I had never seen it happen. I was very impressed, and bought myself another suit.

I got along with Martha Jackson only because I didn't see very much of her. She showed a certain imagination and liveliness, but it was rare that I agreed with her choice of artists.

Those of us in the art world who had seen the Rauschenberg and Johns shows at Castelli in 1958 knew that these were important events. I met Castelli several times at social occasions and found him to be an affable, sincere, and totally warm-hearted character. I thought at the time that I could be comfortable working with someone like Castelli, who was showing daring and imaginative works. He didn't seem to be locked into a narrow position. And he had an elegant new space on Seventy-seventh Street.

I had my first meeting with Leo and Ileana at the Carlyle. I had never had a lunch like that before; I wore my second new suit and even ordered some wine. Castelli asked me to work for him and offered $100 a week, which was a substantial salary, so I left Martha Jackson on friendly terms.

I moved to Castelli in 1959. I thought at least two of his artists were illustrious: Johns and Rauschenberg. He had some Pollocks and some Dubuffet sculptures, really wonderful works that the gallery could survive on until the new artists made their way. Castelli's was not a famous gallery then. People went to Janis or Pierre Matisse.

Jasper Johns had already achieved some notoriety at his first show. His work was just coming into maturity. As for Rauschenberg, he was the enfant terrible. His work was considered difficult and was just about unsalable. To me, the two were heroes who had broken out of Abstract Expressionism and had introduced a fresh and provocative imagery into their art. Of the two, I preferred Rauschenberg, since he represented more of the emotional convictions I preferred in art. Johns's work was more restrained and poetic. In any event, it was because of these two that I became dedicated to the gallery, although I had rather mixed feelings about the other exhibiting artists. Some were Leo's friends. Leo had some difficulty being objective with the artists because of his personal involvement with them. He was always idealistic and rather sentimental. I believe that with Johns and Rauschenberg he saw the relationship as familial, more brotherly than fatherly, but they wanted something more paternal and strong.

There was a great pitch of excitement in those days, although our attendance at the gallery was limited – possibly two hundred a week. I saw all the artists who came in with their slides, and if I thought something was interesting, Leo and I would visit the particular artist's studio together. We made these visits every Saturday, and we enjoyed the adventure. Generally we agreed about everything we saw, which made for a sense of harmony and equilibrium. When we disagreed, Leo would say about the artist in question, "Wait, be patient. He is a very fine person, and you must allow for development. You must be considerate and nice." Even if I disagreed with Leo on various matters, in the ten years I was with him I don't think we ever had a bad word to say to each other.

Allan Kaprow at that time was doing figurative painting and was teaching at Douglass College. He called me about a colleague named Roy Lichtenstein, who Allan said did "very peculiar work." I told Allan to have him bring in his slides. But the artist apparently didn't have any slides, so he brought the paintings in on top of his station wagon.

They were indeed very peculiar pictures, like nothing I had ever seen. They were cartoons, characters with captions. There was something incredibly and brutally brash about all of what he showed me, and I felt we should keep them around the gallery for a few days just to look at. In spite of their being odd they were executed with true finesse.

When I showed them to Leo, we both felt they might upset the apple cart. We decided that they were cold, dumb, and bright, all at the same time. Other artists at the

Roy Lichtenstein

Masterpiece

1 9 6 2

gallery expressed revulsion at them, with the exception of
Salvatore Scarpitta. Roy's previous work was a kind of cartoon Cubism, and he told me that he didn't know whether
he was going to pursue this new direction or not. One of his
children had challenged him by saying that he couldn't draw
like the people who did cartoons, and in order to prove to
his son that he could, he had made a picture of Mickey
Mouse.

Another of his cartoon paintings came out of advertising.
It was of a girl holding a beach ball over her head. We put
that picture in a group show on a wall all by itself.

A few weeks later a very strange man with a terrible
complexion and mottled gray hair came in, looking for a
drawing by Jasper Johns. Although I told him they were
very expensive, $400 or $500, he asked for the drawing of a
light bulb. I showed him the Lichtenstein girl with the
beach ball, and he said his own work was similar. He then
asked me to visit his studio. I was intrigued by him and
went to his place on Eighty-ninth Street, where I saw beautiful antique furnishings alongside twenty-five paintings of
Campbell's soup cans and cartoon characters. He was playing rock-and-roll music so loudly that we couldn't really
have a conversation. One song was playing over and over
again. I could sing it to you now. It was called "I Saw Linda
Yesterday." When I asked him why he played it over and
over, he said, "The way I get to understand it is to play it a
hundred times."

I started looking at his pictures. There were two kinds –
straightforward cartoon drawings, much in the spirit of
Lichtenstein but with a more lyrical gesture, and other
paintings of cartoon and advertising subjects full of drips
and markings. I asked him, having seen Lichtenstein's
work, why he made those drips and markings, and he said
one wasn't allowed to make a painting that didn't show
poetry or expressiveness. This was Andy Warhol explaining
his respect for Abstract Expressionism. By this time I
believed I was a "leading authority" of this new style, and I
told him to forget the drips, drops, and splatters and take a
lesson from Lichtenstein, who used clear lines and primary
colors. He said that nobody would like them, because it was
1961 and people were still dripping like mad. But he was
very pleased by my response. A week later I took Morton
Neuman, a great collector, to his studio, and Morton bought
a painting for $450. Shortly after that I went to Warhol's

with Henry Geldzahler, who was a close friend working at the Metropolitan Museum at that time. Henry, who later became a celebrity in the art world, was fascinated with Warhol. In fact they were mutually taken with each other. Anyway, Henry became Andy's leading spokesman.

I then took Leo to the studio. One might say he was put off by the work, and especially by Andy, who was shy and rather eccentric looking. I expect Leo was uncomfortable since Andy was wearing a theatrical mask when we came in, and offered one to each of us. Leo thought the paintings were odd, too, but he did buy a small soup-can painting, on the spot, for $45. The fact that the work looked like Lichtenstein's was also disconcerting to him. He wondered how the idea had come to Andy and if he had seen Roy's work before he had started his own. Andy said the first Lichtenstein he had seen was in our show.

When we left, Leo said he was not about to show Warhol's work. He mentioned the similarity to Lichtenstein, but I think he was somewhat turned off by the mask, the rock-and-roll music, and the background of elaborate furnishings. Later on, Robert Elkon and Martha Jackson went to Warhol's studio and also rejected his work.

Andy himself was an engaging character. If he felt warm and affectionate toward you, he was quite open and lively. He made a good living from his commercial art, doing illustrations for department stores, and he was immensely generous.

In 1961 we exhibited Frank Stella's black paintings, a series of geometrical black paintings on raw canvas. They were controversial because when people tried to explain or interpret them, Stella would respond "What you see is what you see. Nothing more." The critics condemned the work as totally vacuous and nihilistic, but Leo was extremely responsive to Stella's work, even though he and Stella had little rapport. Although the paintings failed to sell, the gallery gave all its energy to Frank's career.

I first met Jim Rosenquist at a restaurant called Sloppy Louis in 1961. He invited me to his studio, where I saw his paintings in the style of advertising billboards. They gave me chills because here was the third artist I had seen who was working with commercial subject matter. I asked him if he had heard of Andy Warhol or Roy Lichtenstein. He said no, but that he had painted billboards, and then had begun making paintings based on those enormous images. With

Andy Warhol

Flowers Installation view)

1964

Rosenquist it now appeared that we had the foundation of a bona fide new art movement. I was so excited at the prospect that I went breathless when I spoke about it. I remained awake at night trying to fathom the implications.

During our first show of Roy's work, in 1962, a British collector came to the gallery and asked if anything interesting was going on in the art world. I took out a picture by Lichtenstein of a woman stepping on the pedal of a garbage can, and he bought it for $325. I remember calling Lichtenstein and saying, "You're not going to believe it – we sold one of those pictures." We went out to dinner that night and celebrated. Leo couldn't believe it either.

At that time we were also affiliated with John Chamberlain, whom Martha Jackson had allowed me to show in the basement of her gallery. During my year with Jackson I sold only one piece, to a man named Robert Scull, for $275. Scull, who owned a fleet of cabs, became a regular presence at Castelli and was very much taken by Jasper Johns's work. We didn't find him a very appealing person. With all his energy, vitality, and aggressive spirit, he ran over Leo like a steamroller. But Leo was pleasant and very patient, and he involved Scull with both Rauschenberg and Johns on a personal level. The Sculls would invite artists to their home, and it became a kind of family scene. It used to trouble me that Rauschenberg and Johns accepted these invitations on a regular basis from people so unlike themselves in character. I think they seized upon Robert Scull as a strong masculine presence.

Scull's negotiations were painful. He would work us over on price, and the gallery was not flourishing at the time. I will say, though, that he was truly caught up with the works of these artists and could sort out those of merit from the lesser ones. He didn't get involved with the Pop artists until their importance was established. In any event, Leo respected him for his involvement.

In the early sixties the gallery became a tumultuous meeting place for artists and personalities of the art world. I always received the young artists with courtesy, and the number of applicants continued to increase. The structure of the gallery came to mature during this period. The gallery always sustained the highest ethical standards and maintained a warm relationship with most of the collectors and artists. We never made a murky deal, overcharged for a work, or did anyone a disservice. We tried not to give preferential treatment to regular collectors, but at times it was difficult; they always seemed to know when good new works arrived at the gallery.

By 1966 the gallery had a powerful set of artists: Warhol, Chamberlain, Rauschenberg, Johns, Twombly, Lichtenstein, Rosenquist, and Frank Stella. We didn't know then that these artists would become world renowned; we only knew at that time that Johns had sold out two shows. Cy Twombly's work was considered incomprehensible and generated no sales whatsoever. Leo and I thought he was the greatest! I cut out a picture of one of his works and put it on the cover of my telephone book so I could look at it every day. I still think he is one of the best, and a fine, intelligent person as well. Ileana Sonnabend did eventually purchase a painting of his for about $450. It could be worth about $150,000 today.

By 1967 the gallery began to be identified as a pivotal place for contemporary art. We became more relaxed about the future. The major artists had been identified, and the anxiety about the Pop Art movement had eased off. Certain critics still disputed the significance and importance of the movement, and this resistance persists even today. The *New York Times* art page ran an article with the headline, "Is Not Lichtenstein the Worst Painter of Our Time?" They'll never live it down. Hilton Kramer, the *New York Times* critic, never wrote a positive word about Lichtenstein's work and rarely made any reference to Oldenburg, Warhol, or most of the others we exhibited. He believed that ours was an eccentric activity outside the mainstream of art.

During 1967 and 1968 the gallery flourished mainly on

sales of paintings of Stella and Lichtenstein. But Leo's main
affection remained with Rauschenberg and Johns. He
respected and admired the others, but I saw no real close-
ness develop. Of course, Rauschenberg always has been a
very attractive person, full of towering energy and with a
marvelous expanse of imagination. Rauschenberg was
involved with Art and Technology at that point, which was
costing him a fortune, and which I didn't believe contributed a great deal to the culture of the visual arts. I believe
his work was at its best in the early sixties, when he had
gotten into silkscreen. As for Johns, I always found him per-
sonable and extremely alert, but he is an insular person not
given to demonstrations of emotion. I expect that Leo is still
in awe of his fame and achievement even though he saw it
unfold in all its detail.

During the late sixties, I continued looking at the work of
young unknown artists, but Leo eased off this rather dis-
heartening activity, mainly to avoid the unpleasantness of
having to reject all the idealistic young applicants. I believe
he was most happy working with collectors and with certain
museum people and art journalists. The art community was –
it always will be – a small, intimate society. The imaginative
collectors of the sixties, ten or fifteen in all, are mostly the
same people he sees today. They bought advanced work
then and they are still the true tastemakers.

As for Leo's own collection, he never had any real concept of assembling an important hoard. I believe Leo
wanted to keep at least one major work of each of his artists, but he couldn't often say no to the intimate collecting
circle. And I think the only reason he has much important
work by any of his artists is that there was practically no
safe place to keep everything in the gallery and many fine
paintings went to his apartment for storage.

One day we discovered that the gallery had gotten
famous and that there were no more salable Rauschenbergs
in the rack, nor Lichtensteins, and that Johns wasn't producing paintings on a regular schedule. We had about fifteen significant artists in the gallery, but there wasn't much
to sell. Frank Stella had already divided his work with Larry
Rubin's gallery, which I know caused Leo great pain. I
thought Leo should have made a stand when Frank first said
he wanted to exhibit and sell some of his work in another
New York gallery. But the quest for fame and prosperity
can dispel loyalty at times. And I saw that this kind of thing

would become cumulative, with various dealers putting pressure on Leo to have his artists' work shown elsewhere.

There was also pressure on Leo to show artists he wasn't comfortable with. Frank Stella's wife at the time, Barbara Rose, was a strong personality with vividly expressed convictions, and she was very insistent about them. She certainly put pressure on to have the work of Robert Morris shown. At the time much of Morris's work was derived from Johns, Jim Dine, and others. There were some innovative works and a curious use of materials. But I don't believe Leo really wanted to show him. He certainly didn't ask my opinion about it. It was the first time he didn't, and the work was shown, which made me very uncomfortable. The same thing happened with Don Judd.

It appeared in the late sixties that Leo was more or less satisfied with the existing complement of artists. For me that meant that the sense of adventure was gone to a certain extent. The challenge had been to identify the best new talent from the great mass of artists who came in with their work. To exhibit artists with reputations is surely a legitimate endeavor, but for me it lacks the drama of watching a career unfold.

The final split between Leo and me occurred when he proposed to show Dan Flavin's work. We had gone to a Flavin show at Kornblee Gallery in 1967, and Leo was not particularly responsive to the work, even though we thought it stark and bold in its way. He didn't like the idea of art that derived from electric current. But in late 1968 Leo announced that he was seriously considering showing Dan Flavin, and I made an issue of it. Leo said that certain artists should be affiliated with Castelli Gallery whether we truly admired their work or not. I found out later that there were certain friends who were telling Leo he couldn't afford to reject Flavin since he represented an important posture in Minimalism. I felt that we should never exhibit what we weren't naturally responsive to. And I said that if Leo did show this artist I wouldn't feel comfortable in the gallery anymore. Leo's reply was that there were always pressures on him, and that in this case they were "interesting pressures."

Anyway, when he decided to show Flavin, I announced that I was leaving the gallery. Within twelve hours I received telephone calls from many of Leo's clients and other people offering me funds to open a gallery. Some of these offers were startling, and certainly complimentary.

143

But all the offers were tainted with the desire of the investor to play some managerial role and to have a voice in the selection of the work to be shown.

One of Leo's collectors, a warm and generous person, suggested I open an art gallery and added that he would provide the money I needed, no strings attached. It's an offer you don't hear very often.

I thought about space and rents on Madison Avenue and Fifty-seventh Street and about how much money I would have to borrow from this man. As for my own resources, I had about $3,000 and Lichtenstein and Warhol had given me some works which I might have to sell. But then how would I tell the artists that I was selling their gifts? I decided to open a gallery not in the traditional gallery districts but rather in some outpost of civilization. It occurred to me that many of my visits to artists' studios within the previous two or three years had been downtown in what is now Soho. I lived in the area myself, along with forty or fifty artists, many of them not legally in residence. Within a week I found an enormous space on West Broadway, an abandoned warehouse with seven thousand square feet. The exhibition space in Leo's gallery was about five hundred square feet, and I had always thought that substantial. I first considered that this enormous space could be divided and still be the largest gallery in the world – at less than $600 a month.

I asked Mrs. Sonnabend, who had no New York gallery at the time, if she would like to share it with me, and she said she couldn't imagine what she might do with thirty-five hundred square feet. As an act of defiance I took the whole space, financed by my generous friend. The gallery cost $44,000 to build, and the remainder of the $50,000 loan was my capital. I opened O. K. Harris in October 1969.

The name "O. K. Harris" had been devised some years earlier in a conversation with Dick Bellamy. At the time Robert Scull wanted to open a gallery with Dick Bellamy as the director, and Richard and I spent one of the more hilarious evenings of my life dreaming up names. I felt O. K. Harris was a tough, American name that sounded like that of a riverboat gambler. It would look good in print, and one could blame everything on the mystery character. Scull rejected the name and accepted "Green Gallery," which Richard said to him meant an unformed thing. I kept O. K. Harris in reserve till the moment it was needed.

Deborah Butterfield

Armor Plated Horse

1 9 7 9

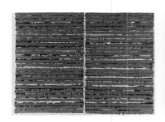

Aris Koutroulis

Untitled #4

1 9 8 1

144

Ilan Averbuch

Installation

October 17–November 7,

1 9 8 1

Kenneth Morgan

Night Flight

1 9 8 2

The opening event at the gallery was very well attended. I remember wondering whether anyone would turn up besides the exhibiting artists. Early on opening day I walked out to the street and swept the sidewalk in front of the gallery as an act of proprietorship. I had never owned a business before, and it seemed the right thing to do. I still sweep the sidewalk on a regular basis. It seems to make some of my artists uneasy.

My basic principle was to show the best new art, without any attempt to seduce artists from other galleries. There are always artists who are disgruntled with their prevailing arrangement, who have had a show that didn't go well and have blamed it on their dealer. But I preferred to exhibit only those artists whose work I admired and who had never had a one-person show. We write no contracts with our artists; the agreement is one of mutual faith; all shows are based on prevailing performance.

I continued to look at artists' work, fifteen to eighteen a day to begin with. I took it as my obligation as an exhibitor of contemporary art to receive every applicant. I still see as many as my energy allows, up to twenty-five a day. During school intersession, every instructor of painting or sculpture from every part of the country seems to turn up here with slides.

Our operation is unique in its openness to new talent. Most of the dealers I know hide away in their offices. Two artists came in recently, and when I asked if they had shown their slides before coming here, they said that no one would receive them. I feel, however, that if one is involved in a progressive aspect of art dealership it makes good sense to remain alert to the possibility that a genius may walk in, assuming one has the ability to detect one.

We begin our method of finding a new artist with evidence of his or her work, usually in the form of 35mm slides. Sometimes photos amplify the power of the work, sometimes they diminish it, and sometimes they provide only basic information. But usually there's sufficient evidence in slides to make a determination – to reject the work, to visit the artist's studio, or to have the artist bring in work for us to see.

The decision to show an artist must be based on the work of the moment. Occasionally I do feel that I can detect something in an artist that leads me to believe that he or she is committed to a consistently productive life in the studio.

145

I remember talking with Castelli when he opened the show of Stella's rather incredible *Exotic Birds*. These were a dramatic departure from his previous work – enormous, aggressive, and blazing with color. The works sold well, and I asked Leo, whimsically, if he walked into an unknown artist's studio and saw work like this, would he show it. He replied that he wasn't sure. But based on Stella's past performance, when he often surprised his audience with his power of innovation, Leo was showing the paintings on faith. Most dealers will continue to show an artist on faith and previous performance.

I tell every artist that if I don't like the work he or she is scheduled to exhibit I won't show it. Every show on my premises is a creative act for me, not just for the artist. I don't expect continuity of concept. If one of my artists changes style or format I don't find that distressing. There is always a visible thread connecting work done by the same person. Stella's work, seen in retrospect, has unity. Castelli must be given full credit for detecting this. There is sound progress, and one can see the connections. It seems logical therefore to judge any work on its particular merit. Many dealers have told me that once they have involved themselves with an artist, they remain loyal to him no matter what he or she produces. I feel this is destructive of my integrity and certainly of the artist's career. We never show

Ralph Goings

Still Life with Coffee

1 9 8 2

anything but sound, professional work. We try never to allow personal affection for an artist to interfere with objective appraisal of performance. I challenge myself to remain as objective as possible concerning each artist's achievement and fame. But I won't declare that I don't have an occasional sentimental moment. I never show a work I have no faith in, simply to sustain an artist's courage and persistence. Of course, every artist has bad moments, even the greatest. Beethoven wrote a thing called the *Wellington* Symphony, but it shouldn't have been published. Every artist falters, except perhaps Roy Lichtenstein. However, if an artist paints but five or six pictures a year, and two or three of them are bad, then he is in trouble. If you are only going to produce five paintings a year they had better be good. Jasper Johns's early production was six or eight pictures a year, all up to par. Rauschenberg, who produced about thirty a year, didn't have to have the same average. Much of his work had to be considered experimental, and it filtered down to six or eight per season that were good.

Robert Rohm

Untitled

1 9 7 5

If you operate a gallery to show new artists' work, you'd better learn to trust your own convictions about what is sound work. It's come to a point where I fully trust mine. If I like something, it's probably very good. Essentially, I look for innovation – beyond a perfected craftsmanship. In other words, I will not consider work that has not been extremely well made. Since our gallery is concerned with exploration and adventure, the art we show should contribute something to the growth of the culture. And if the work is within an established tradition it should bring at least refreshment or renewal to the concept it engages.

My gallery has been pigeonholed by certain critics and art historians as a "Realist gallery," but from the beginning the tone of the gallery was eclectic. We didn't set out to show Realism or Abstraction specifically, but just to show the best art we could find. The artist who has shown with me most frequently is a man named Robert Rohm. He does simple, strong mixed-medium constructions – a "process artist" you might call him. He has had almost no financial success at the gallery and receives almost no press attention for his shows. Yet he is an artist of consequence. I can cite a half-dozen others who remain neglected because of ignorance, art politics, or maybe our lack of advertising. Of the six or seven artists who were in my first show in 1969, only one is still with me. People like Roy Lichtenstein, with his consistency, come along once in fifty years.

Eight to 10 percent of my business comes from museum purchases, and 15 to 20 percent from corporations. Some private dealers devote all their time to buying for corporations. We don't have all that much art that would suit that particular market. Basically, corporations buy art works that won't disrupt their environment. Flower paintings and color abstraction are generally considered safe. Anything with a horizon is acceptable. Of course, all corporations are not that conservative. One major company just bought from me a painting depicting the naked posterior of a human female as the main work in the executive office. The man who bought it doesn't seem to care whether it increases or decreases his business. We prefer to believe that his business is increased. In any case, he visits all the time.

The remainder of my sales are mainly from independent American collectors, people who know what they like and who share some of my convictions. Some are old-timers and some are new on the scene. But they all have faith in their taste. And I admire them for that. They pay little homage to the art magazines and the moment's sensations. They buy what they like. They have independent judgment – a rare ingredient and valuable to me.

In terms of salesmanship, you can't actually "sell" a particular object like a sculpture or a painting that has never been seen before. I may tell the collector which of several works he or she has seen that I prefer. It is my nature to show my enthusiasm about particular works, but in the long run it's they who have to make the cash commitment, which leads me to believe that it is the collector who makes the art world, rather than the critic or the art historian or the dealer. I make the art world only to the extent that I may be aware of a significant work when I see it. But it's the collector who will put up his resources to prove his conviction.

The creative act of an art dealer is mounting a show from which you receive the plaudits of the informed, a small body of people whose good taste and judgment you respect. Hopefully, some of your discoveries come to major attention, and that's the final proof of your judgment, your track record, as it were. We have proven that you don't really need the approval of the art establishment to achieve a major position in the art world. You need not entertain extensively or attend institutional events or spend your sum-

Peter Saari

Bust with Shells

1 9 8 1

John DeAndrea

Model in Repose

1 9 8 1

John Kacere

Ileana—82

1 9 8 2

mers in the Hamptons. During its formative years Leo's gallery received very little attention from the press, except from the fashion magazines. At O. K. Harris I have had about three or four reviews in the *New York Times* in eleven years, and not all of them were friendly. Only one of the major art magazines has ever given me a cover. We put on forty-four shows a season here, and every one of those shows is of a high professional standard. They are fresh and fine and bold and provocative. We run the place like a museum facility: we have a comprehensive slide file available; we receive art societies, groups of all sorts – students and tourists – with the greatest courtesy – four thousand to six thousand visitors a week. We even have a public rest room – maybe the only one in a New York gallery. Yet we receive almost no press coverage.

It's because we don't advertise, simple as that. The *New York Times* critics cover the same galleries and artists season after season. It's considered a joke in serious art circles. At Harris we put our money elsewhere. I have the finest gallery staff in the world, and I like the idea that they enjoy their work and receive good compensation. The gallery is a family, artists and all. We pay the expenses of all shows except for advertising. The artists are free to do their own advertising if they wish.

I think it's important to explain what I believe we are doing rather than leaving the audience confounded. For me the gallery has a cultural mission. Certainly we're practical and we relish prosperity. But we're extremely idealistic, and without the feeling that we are making an important contribution to the visual arts I don't think there would be much joy in going to work in the morning.

Irving
Blum

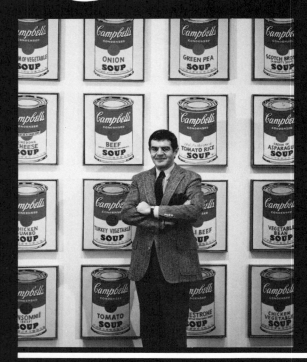

Irving Blum (born 1930, New York City) graduated from the University of Arizona. In 1958 he joined Los Angeles's Ferus Gallery, known for its exhibits of Joseph Cornell and Ed Kienholz, where he was the first to show Andy Warhol's soup-can paintings. In 1973 he returned to New York to open the Blum-Helman Gallery with Joe Helman; today Blum continues to cultivate new artists while specializing in the resale market of contemporary masterpieces.

When I was discharged from the air force I went to work for a furniture house called Knoll Associates. Part of my function was to supply various corporate accounts with paintings, so I began visiting galleries, particularly Betty Parsons, Sidney Janis, and Sam Kootz.

I found myself gravitating toward the New York art scene and becoming more familiar with it. The artist whose work initially attracted me the most was Josef Albers, because the scale and the color were absolutely right. I decided to open my own gallery when I realized that a lot of my friends were in the art world. Then Hans Knoll, the head of the company I worked for, who had been a great source of energy to me, died in an automobile accident. The company seemed to shift after his death. Meanwhile, I was getting tired of New York, and I missed the West, where I had spent most of my growing-up years, so I decided to open a gallery in Los Angeles.

When I arrived there in 1957, there were very few galleries in the city. One had been opened in 1956 by Walter Hopps and the artist Ed Kienholz. This was the Ferus Gallery, and its extraordinary vitality interested me very much. I became friendly with Walter, and he told me that Kienholz, after a year in the business, wanted to go back to making sculpture and possibly was willing to sell his share. I bought him out for around $600, which was very reasonable, and Walter and I became partners. We remained partners for about three years, until he accepted an assistant curatorship at the Pasadena Museum in 1960. I then proceeded alone with the Ferus Gallery until 1966.

Ed Kienholz was always a very perverse and provocative guy. When Walter and I were still partners at Ferus, I remember Walter coming in one day and saying he had found something incredibly beautiful which he wanted me to see. We drove out to a thrift shop in Pasadena, and he showed me a Stickley desk. This was long before interest erupted in that kind of furniture, and it was very cheap. We decided to buy it, and Walter was as happy as a person could be. We moved the desk into the office in the gallery where it shone like a beacon. It was an astonishing, astounding piece of furniture. I remember Kienholz coming in one day and admiring it. He then said, "You know, Irving, I don't really have respect for your opinion." I asked, my opinion about everything? He replied, "No, about art,

Edward Kienholtz

Little Eagle Rock Incident

1 9 5 8

and I'll tell you why if you really want to know. It's because
you like everything I do. Every time I show you something
you say it's remarkable, and since I know everything I do
isn't, I feel I can't get a straight response from you." I said
if that's what you really want, and you feel it would be useful to you, that's how we will proceed. Ed was relieved, and
said he felt much better.

Some weeks passed, and Ed surfaced in the gallery one
day with a sculpture that looked rather like a cigar box,
painted black, and with a long extension cord coming out of
one side. He set it on the Stickley desk, and I peered at it
while he said nothing. I then said, "Ed, it's silly. It just
doesn't mean anything at all. It's rather stupid." Of course,
I was thinking back to our conversation. Ed explained that it
wasn't fully operational, and proceeded to unroll the cord
and plug it into the wall. The box began to shake slowly and
hum. I watched it, and said, "Ed, it's trash. It has no mean-

ing to me whatsoever." He said, "Fine, Irving, you're being as honest and straight as you can be, and that's exactly what I wanted in terms of our relationship." He then rolled up the cord, picked up the little box, and walked out with it under his arm. He was gone by the time I noticed the three-quarter-inch hole in the Stickley desk. The box was actually a drill which had gone right through the top. Result: desk ruined. We're still friends, but wary friends.

When Walter and Kienholz started Ferus, they had a representation of roughly forty to fifty artists. I thought we couldn't deal fairly with that many, and we cut down to about a dozen. I thought that in addition to those twelve, who were from Los Angeles and San Francisco, we should have some people from the East Coast, and I chose the extraordinary, eccentric, and fascinating Joseph Cornell.

I brought in Cornell through a fortunate circumstance. In 1956, while I was still living in New York, I went to the old Stable Gallery and saw an exhibition of his, Stable Pieces. The show had an extraordinary effect on me. Eleanor Ward, the director of the gallery, had blackened the floor and hired a lighting engineer to pinpoint every single box with a beam of light. I was immensely moved by the work, the installation – in short, the totality of the show. Leaving the gallery, I passed a curio shop and saw a little card that reminded me of what I had just seen there. I walked back and got Cornell's address and sent him a little note. I put all this out of my mind until I returned to New York a year or two later, around 1959, and found that Cornell had separated from the Stable Gallery. I called him up and said, "As you're no longer with Stable, and there is no place one can see your work, may I come out and spend a little time with you?" He asked what I did, and I said I was an art dealer from Los Angeles. He said he didn't see dealers, and I responded that, after all, dealers were people, and I wasn't interested in seeing him with an eye toward buying anything, but simply to have the opportunity to see what he was up to. He told me in that case I could come, but I must remember that nothing was for sale.

I agreed to the condition, and stayed with him for about two hours, chatting on a dozen different subjects. He showed me several constructions that impressed me very much. Finally I left, and as I was walking out the door he shouted after me, "Mr. Blum! Mr. Blum!" I saw that he was waving a little card in his hand, the card I had sent him two years before. He asked if I was the person who had sent it. I found it incredible that he had kept it so long. Then he said that I could buy whatever I liked, so I bought four pieces there on the spot and carried them back to California with me. I slowly added twelve more, and then had my first Cornell show in California in 1961. Cornell had no gallery at that time, although he had shown previously with Peggy Guggenheim and Julien Levy and then at the Stable Gallery. We began a relationship that eventually led to three Cornell shows in the sixties.

The idea of working in boxes had occurred to Cornell years earlier when he left his house one day on his daily foray to the supermarket and passed a theater on the opposite side of the street. He happened to look at the box office, which was separate from the theater in the old-fashioned way, and saw a new ticket taker – blonde, blue-eyed, very young, altogether a very pretty girl. He was awestruck by this vision of a girl in a box. After a week or two of walking past this girl, he finally screwed up his courage and bought a dozen roses from a florist. When he walked up to the girl he became tongue-tied and couldn't get the words out, so he just opened the door and hurled the flowers at her. The girl screamed, and the theater manager came running out. The police were called, and Cornell was taken off to the station house, where he spent the day.

When I was in New York, which was only once or twice a year, I would always call Cornell and spend an afternoon visiting. I would leave with several works, usually in shopping bags. He was terribly poetic, private, and eccentric, and would surprise you with his knowledge of many subjects.

I began putting together artists based on the East Coast. I was very focused on what Leo Castelli was doing. His gallery seemed to have more energy than any other in New York; the people were young, and altogether his gallery seemed to me enormously distinguished. I became very close to Leo and began to have shows with his artists. I showed Frank Stella and Jasper Johns. I remember coming to New York one year and having Irving Karp show me slides of a young artist who was doing cartoon paintings. His name was Roy Lichtenstein. Ivan said they were thinking of showing the work. I said I was very interested and would like to represent him in California. In the end, I had several Lichtenstein shows.

Joseph Cornell

Central Park Carrousel,

in Memorium

1 9 5 0

Also at that time I had my first encounter with Andy Warhol. He was about halfway into his soup-can series when I visited his studio. I spent quite a bit of time chatting with him while looking hard at those paintings. I decided virtually on the spot to show them in California, and Andy was thrilled with the idea. He had no representation at that time; he sold one or two things with Martha Jackson and Allan Stone, but he had no New York gallery. We struck a bargain then and there, and the paintings arrived in California in July 1962. I showed them by encircling the gallery with the thirty-two soup cans, all of them the same size, 20 inches high and 16 inches across. I reproduced one of them on an announcement that was sent out. When people confronted these pictures for the first time, they didn't know how to deal with them. The paintings were extremely controversial. They were priced at $100 apiece, and after two weeks I had sold six at that figure. My own confrontation with these paintings was increasingly serious and intense with each passing day. After about three weeks, I rang Andy up and said, "Andy, I am haunted by these pictures, and I want to suggest something to you. I am going to attempt to keep these thirty-two paintings together, as a set." Andy said, "Irving, I'm thrilled, because they were conceived as a group, a series. If you could keep them together it would make me very happy." I said that I had sold a few of the paintings, but that I could approach the various collectors and see if I could make any progress. As soon as I hung up I called the first collector I had sold one

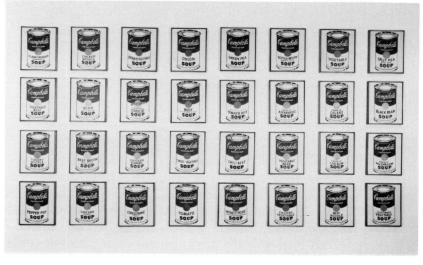

Andy Warhol

32 Soup Cans

1 9 6 1 – 6 2

of those paintings to – I think it may have been Dennis Hopper. I explained what I wanted to do, and he gracefully relinquished the picture to me. I did that six times, and when I had the complete set, I called Andy to tell him. I then asked, now that I had all the paintings together and intended to keep them, what price could me make me on the group? Andy offered me all of them for $1,000 over the course of a year, and we agreed that I would send him $100 a month.

All this was relatively easy because it had to do with the moment. A certain kind of zeitgeist either works for you or it doesn't. I was lucky enough to have it work. These people were clearly the most interesting artists at that time; they were the ones whom other artists were already focused on, and I was quick enough to get a sense of what was happening. I think the most extraordinary recommendation comes when an artist whom I admire approaches me and says he has been looking at the work of someone else, and thinks that work is worth my attention. That is a high accolade, because I think artists have the keenest sensibility, not only to their own work, but often to that of others. I rely on that extra sense of theirs, in conjunction with my own.

Joe Helman had a gallery in St. Louis while I was in California, and we did a lot of business together in the way two galleries will do when they show essentially the same material in different cities. There isn't a lot of competition, and there's usually a lot of cooperation. I came to New York in 1973 with the idea of opening a gallery here. Joe was in New York after a year or so in Italy with the same idea. We met quite by chance in someone's house and discussed our respective ideas, which were similar. Then and there we decided we could do it together. What binds us together is that similarity of vision.

What we have tried to do with the Blum-Helman Gallery is to establish a solid resale market, in addition to developing young artists. The balance of power in the resale market is complicated. I'm pretty much restricted to buying the earlier works of artists I've shown in the past. But by the time the perspective on work by Ellsworth Kelly, Jasper Johns, or Roy Lichtenstein comes up to bat, it's anyone's ballgame. By that I mean there's a great deal of competition and you have to be very sure of what you're about because the people who own the material know what they have. They want the highest price they can get, and they go to a

Andrew Lord

The Two Teapots in

Morning Light/Grey/Angled

1 9 8 1

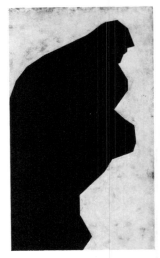

Robert Moskowitz

Thinker

1 9 8 2

great many sources, so you have to be very sharp about your own feelings and notions of the value of the specific thing you're after. Often you are asked to pay an enormously high figure and consequently must charge in turn an equally high figure, so the quality must be authentic. Leo is correct in saying it's a small pie that can only be cut in so many pieces in terms of quality, and there are a lot more people competing for the same number of paintings. I don't think it's out of proportion, but it is competitive.

The other aspect, that of taking on a new artist, has enormous risks, because the work sells very little while the expenses are constant. There is the endless problem of supporting oneself, of making the gallery go. I have as many as half a dozen younger artists who I think are brilliant. Among them are Bryan Hunt, Bruce Robbins, Stephen Keister, and Donald Sultan. No one responds to everything, but you rely very much on your own responses, and they dictate a certain look. Very often, you build up a little resistance; that is, you want to go somewhat beyond your own taste in order to do something more daring. At the end, it must have to do with one's own intuition and at the same time must transcend it.

The Pop style is an example. I saw some unfinished cartoon paintings by Andy Warhol that I didn't like very much and some much more finished paintings by Roy Lichtenstein. I was able to relate his work to earlier connections. It was reminiscent of Léger. There was no such thing as "Pop Art" when I saw Roy's work, but I knew I was onto something that I couldn't describe but that I had an intuition about. I strive to be accurate and advanced in attitudes, to be ahead of a wave.

When a style that has been hidden becomes understood by people, there is no more room for you as a dealer. The territory will be staked out, except in the resale market. This is truer today than ever before, because there are so many galleries. It's a funny condition – at a certain moment there was a real lack of interest, and today there is a super-abundance of it. One is obliged to stay alert, current, and even beyond current.

A good gallery is in a position to promote the artists it represents. Most collectors understand that; it's no mystery. A lot of collectors will buy the work speculatively, simply because a certain dealer has taken the work of a young artist into his gallery. The responsibility is enormous. You

Roy Lichtenstein

Compositions III

1 9 6 5

157

have your track record, your clientele, and you don't want
to betray them. So while a good gallery can take on anybody, if you're not effective, collectors will drift away.
Despite your track record, there's no way you can bind
them to you forever; they trust your judgment as long as
you're successful. The stakes are high, and you have to do
whatever you can as sharply as you can, because it's always
examined and speculated upon.

Taking on new artists is an enormous responsibility. It's
a long haul. A gallery first and foremost wants to survive,
and at the same time you want to do it as well as you possibly can. That means a great deal of curatorial work, putting
aside extensive files of photographs and material on the artists. All galleries should strive to do this. Castelli and Sidney Janis in his prime were great models for me. But finally,
the voyage is your own.

Doing business here in New York is very different than it
is in Los Angeles. I can tell you the difference in one word:
urgency. In California, if a collector came into my gallery
and asked me to hold a particular work for him for a week
or two, I was always happy to do it. Often he wouldn't come
back for two or three months, and the chances were that the
work was still there. That situation doesn't exist in New
York. Your expenses are too high to keep anything that
long; if you did, you'd soon be out of the game. People
understand that there is an urgency here. There are movement and activity, and they are constant. Think of how
many galleries there are doing an extraordinary business
here. That's the reason I moved from California. My personal lifestyle has diminished, but in terms of business, it's
all I hoped it would be.

The most personally satisfying thing is that it is a full-
time occupation. It's wonderful to be involved in something
to such a degree. The people you come into contact with are
bright, curious, and fascinating.

Joseph
Helman

Joseph Helman (born 1937, St. Louis, Missouri) attended Washington University and opened St. Louis's Joseph Helman Gallery in 1970. The New York partnership of Blum-Helman, formed in 1973, shows a wide range of artists from William Baziotes and Richard Serra to Steve Keister and Bryan Hunt.

I was getting a haircut in St. Louis one day when I was twenty-three years old, and I picked up a magazine. I saw a reproduction of a Jasper Johns painting that took my breath away. I turned to the barber and said, "My God, there's a great living artist. It's like history, like Van Gogh or Rembrandt."

At the time I was a land developer, working eighteen or twenty hours a day. I had started a monster development in the best location in St. Louis, two miles long and two miles wide. I was running a construction company with no help, not even a secretary. The only time I took off was to get a haircut, and the only person I talked to about anything other than business was my barber.

I had no experience in art, but I knew that these paintings were something I would like to own. The barber suggested that I go to the other end of the shopping center, where there was a small gallery/framing shop. I went there and asked if he had any Jasper Johns. He didn't, but he told me about a private dealer whom I subsequently went to see.

The private dealer said that she could get me a Johns, but she was reluctant. She would have had to buy it, and was afraid of getting stuck with it. She wouldn't even tell me where to get one, saying something to the effect that Macy's doesn't help Gimbel's.

My barber then suggested that I call the local museum. I was so naive that I couldn't tell the difference between a curator and a guard, but I called, and Emmy Rauh (later Pulitzer) came to my house. She gave me a list of contacts and galleries in New York, and shortly thereafter I bought my first painting at Leo Castelli's, Jasper Johns's *Painting with Ruler and "Gray."* I had agreed to buy it for a down payment and monthly payments of $500, but when I took the painting home, I immediately paid in full. The next month, I got a call from Castelli asking for my $500 payment. When I said that I had already paid for the work, Leo explained that if I sent $500, I would have a wonderful credit the next time I came in – and besides, they could use the money, as they were paying artists stipends. So I did. I paid Leo $500 a month whether I owed anything or not. That went on for years. I have some wonderful paintings to show for it.

In 1963 the Pop Art movement was just starting, and I was also interested in Donald Judd and Frank Stella. I'd come to New York, and Ivan Karp would call up the artists

Roy Lichtenstein

Baseball Manager

1 9 6 3

and say, "There's this minor nabob from St. Louis in town —
let's go out for dinner." For me it was marvelous to meet the
artists whom I had admired as a collector, and I remain
grateful to Ivan for involving me in that way.

Although I remained a businessman, I realized that I
was beginning to spend more time thinking about my collection than about my real-estate developments. I found myself
thinking about art all the time, the issues and the people.

In 1970, after a ten-year career as a land developer, I
opened a gallery in St. Louis. The first show was a group
exhibition of Josef Albers, Jasper Johns, Ellsworth Kelly,
Roy Lichtenstein, and Andy Warhol. The first one-man
show in the gallery was of Richard Serra's sculpture. The
show consisted of the lead prop pieces, all of which fell
over. The only surviving piece is now in The Museum of
Modern Art.

In 1972, I sold the gallery to Ronald Greenberg, who
was a long-time friend and regular client, and, with my wife
and three daughters, moved to Rome, where I lived for part
of that year and the next. Although I had no plans to leave
Rome, Irving Blum telephoned me from New York in 1973
to say that he would like to open a gallery with me if I would
return to America. I was still interested in the activity of the
art world, so I did return, and together we opened Blum
Helman Gallery on East Seventy-fifth Street in 1974. The
first show included work by Ellsworth Kelly, Roy Lichtenstein, Morris Louis, Claes Oldenburg, and Frank Stella.
Our first one-man show was of Richard Serra.

Richard Serra

Around the Corner

1 9 8 2

Some collectors can't buy anything unless they think it's a good investment, but, without realizing it, they have had an esthetic response. Other people end up with a house full of treasures when they thought they were merely decorating. I've seen others, with the most noble intentions of wanting to support the artists, who end up ten years later with a collection that proves another point of view.

Some collectors have so much money that the price itself doesn't make much difference. They may be gratified to see the work go up in value, but the real reward they get out of art is something they would never talk to you about. It's a kind of light in the darkness, something that gives them a signpost to find and measure themselves.

The financial risk for a collector who buys the work of young artists is very small. If an artist has one show in a top New York gallery, the odds are it will sell out, given today's art market. That means he will have a second show and that his prices will go up substantially. Tax laws are such that a collector will often get his money out through a donation after a brief period.

In 1981, we moved the gallery to its present location at 20 West Fifty-seventh Street. Our opening exhibition was of paintings by Richard Diebenkorn, Ellsworth Kelly, Roy Lichtenstein, and Frank Stella; the first one-man show was of Richard Serra drawings.

Bryan Hunt

Arch Falls

1 9 8 0 – 8 1

Claes Oldenburg

Giant Loaf of Raisin Bread, Sliced

1 9 6 7

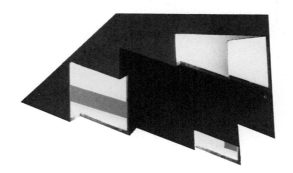

Steve Keister

USO #64

1 9 8 0

Donald Sultan

Rain, July 8, 1982

1 9 8 2

The character of the gallery has been evolving since we first opened, from a somewhat private situation in which we sold major work of the last thirty or forty years, to one that seems focused on exhibiting new work by both well-established and younger artists. In truth, I think my activity has been interpreting what I feel is an accurate art-historical continuity in post–World War II experience.

Especially since we moved to Fifty-seventh Street, where we're extremely visible to the public, we have taken on more artists and have been able to exhibit all our artists in a more substantial way. We have also been handling a much larger share of the masterpieces of modern art.

The only way to really describe the gallery's activity is by the work we handle. I made a complete list of every artist whose work we have handled in the last few years. Seeing the completed list was surprising, gratifying, and provocative for me:

Josef Albers, William Baziotes, Peter Beard, Larry Bell, Constantin Brancusi, Ralston Crawford, Jo Ann Callis, Ron Davis, Stuart Davis, Richard Diebenkorn, John Duff, Willem de Kooning, Mark di Suvero, Max Ernst, Helen Frankenthaler, Jan Groover, Hans Hofmann, Tom Holland, Bryan Hunt, Robert Irwin, Neil Jenney, Jasper Johns, Don Judd, Craig Kauffman, Steve Keister, Ellsworth Kelly, Mel Kendrick, Franz Kline, Roy Lichtenstein, Andrew Lord, Morris Louis, Robert Mangold, Brice Marden, Matta, Robert Motherwell, Bruce Nauman, Kenneth Noland, Georgia O'Keeffe, Claes Oldenburg, Jules Olitski, Jackson Pollock, Larry Poons, Kenneth Price, Robert Rauschenberg, Ad Reinhardt, Edda Renouf, Bruce Robbins, Mark Rothko, Robert Ryman, David Salle, Joel Shapiro, David Smith, Richard Serra, Frank Stella, Donald Sultan, Hap Tivey, Richard Tuttle, John Tweddle, Cy Twombly, Andy Warhol.

163

Arnold
Glimcher

Arnold Glimcher (born 1938, Duluth, Minnesota) attended the Massachusetts College of Art and Boston University's School of Fine Art before beginning his gallery on a shoestring in Boston in 1960. Since its relocation to New York in 1963, Pace Gallery has become the most imposing corporate structure in the art market, exhibiting Louise Nevelson, Brice Marden, and Chuck Close while administering the estates of Mark Rothko and Pablo Picasso.

During my first year of graduate school at Boston University, where I was a fine arts major intending to be a curator and eventually a museum director, my father died. My mother and brother and I were walking down Newbury Street seeking some sort of consolation in the art galleries when I noticed an empty store next to the most important gallery in Boston, and off the top of my head, I said it would be a great place to open a gallery. My brother suggested I do exactly that, saying that running a gallery would be similar to museum work without the restrictions. When I reminded him that I was still in school, my mother volunteered to sit in the gallery while my wife, an art history major at Wellesley, and I attended classes. Within two months I had opened the Pace Gallery, naming it after my father, Pace Glimcher.

I opened the gallery with $2,400, enough money to last about four months. At first I showed only local artists, but near the end of the first season I came to New York and asked Martha Jackson if she would permit me to give an exhibition of Louise Nevelson's sculpture. Martha was glad to do it, because although Nevelson was a very famous artist, it was not easy to place the work privately. Mostly it went to museums. Nevelson was also from New England and wanted to show in Boston.

I was at the end of my money, and if the exhibition hadn't sold I wouldn't have had the money to ship it back to New York. I called Nevelson and told her that although she did not know me, I was doing a show of her work in Boston and hoped she would come to the opening. I offered to put her up at the Ritz. She came, I gave a fantastic party, and practically sold out the show. It was the first money I made, and the fact that it was made with Nevelson was prophetic for our future relationship. It has always been a privilege to work with her. After twenty-two years, we are like family. We speak two or three times a week. She is now over eighty years old and still has an extraordinary vitality and appetite for new achievements. She continually inspires me. Every so often she will say to me, "We haven't even started yet," and I am amazed that after her brilliant career she sees this as a beginning, that she hasn't even scratched the surface yet.

The next year, 1961, I did Boston's first survey show of Pop Art, a big exhibition called "Stock Up for the Holidays"

Louise Nevelson

Sky Cathedral – Moon

Garden Plus One

1 9 5 7 – 6 0

that included Warhol, Lichtenstein, Wesselmann, Oldenburg, Segal, Marisol, and Indiana. Richard Solomon, who is
now the president of Pace Editions, was a collector and a
friend of mine at that time. His family owned the Stop 'n'
Shop chain of grocery stores, and they had a poster plas-
tered all over the store windows, an airbrushed Santa Claus
drinking a bottle of Coca-Cola and a headline saying,
"Stock Up for the Holidays." I got five hundred of the pos-
ters and had the names of all the artists printed around the
edge. This served as the announcement for the show. After
that I gave two one-man shows of Oldenburg.

At that time many Pop artists had no New York galleries; it was before Pop Art had jelled exclusively into the Leo
Castelli Gallery. Warhol and Indiana were still with the Stable Gallery which discovered them. Oldenburg, Wesselmann, and Segal were with the Green Gallery. Soon I found
that I was showing only New York art, and it became clear
that if I didn't get to New York soon other dealers would
snap up the artists I was showing in Boston. So in 1963 I
opened a gallery in New York with Fred Mueller. After a
year of spending part of each week there and part in Boston,
I moved to New York. My children were two and three at
the time, and commuting was impossible.

The stable of artists at Pace has evolved over the years.
I've taken risks on artists in my career. I've been a dealer
for twenty-two years, and there was a time when my artists
were not well known. Very few people knew who Lucas

Samaras or Larry Bell or Robert Irwin was when I gave them their early shows. When my artists became more recognized they drew other established artists to the gallery.

My taste is eclectic, so the artists who became affiliated with Pace were not from one stylistic group. I show artists who genuinely please me, to whom I have a strong response, artists who are constantly extending their perceptions and breaking new ground. At this point my artists aren't young anymore, but I feel they have the capacity to continue to grow and make new advances, to extend their careers over a lifetime, which for some reason does not seem very common among postwar American artists.

I think of my gallery essentially as a functioning, responsible, moral institution – a private museum. The history of twentieth-century American art is written in the continuing panorama of gallery exhibitions, but much of this history is lost because many great galleries didn't document their exhibitions in the sixties. That is why Pace pays more attention to documentation than most other dealers do. Today we publish the most complete and authoritative catalogues anywhere.

Agnes Martin

Untitled

1 9 7 7

We do museum-type exhibitions such as Grids, which was a survey of the use of the grid in art since the turn of the century, from Mondrian to Agnes Martin. The show cost about $100,000 to mount, and almost nothing was for sale. It is our pleasure and our responsibility to put money back into the art world as well as to take it out, in the form of subsidizing artists' projects and presenting important exhibitions. In essence, the gallery world functions as a collective museum of modern art in a way The Museum of Modern Art can't function anymore.

At Pace Gallery we provide as strong a service for our artists as possible. We have a relatively small stable of artists, only seventeen, but they're all very important figures on an international scale, and therefore they require a great deal of attention and care in every way: the presentation of their work, cataloguing, the handling of sales.

I think it's important that people who work in galleries have strong credentials in art. Renato Danese, the gallery's director, had been the assistant director of the Baltimore Museum, and Alexandra Schwartz, who runs Pace Editions' Master Prints department, had been assistant curator of prints at The Museum of Modern Art.

This kind of expertise is very valuable. Recently Chris-

Jasper Johns

Three Flags

1 9 5 8

tie's called to ask me to authenticate a "Nevelson" they were considering putting up for auction. It was absolutely *not* a Nevelson. It was the wrong color; it was the wrong wood; it was the wrong arrangement – it was as unlike Nevelson as someone else's fingerprint. Art is like handwriting. One knows the signature of a person one is very close to.

A dealer never knows what role he may be called on to play. In 1980 I arranged the sale of Jasper Johns's *Three Flags,* owned by Burton and Emily Tremaine, to the Whitney Museum. I had known the Tremaines for years, as clients and friends. Extraordinary people. Visiting their collection is like visiting a museum of modern art, and they're very generous about letting people see it. They have great paintings: Cubist Picassos, Rothkos, Delaunays, Légers. But I felt that *Three Flags* and the Mondrian *Victory Boogie-Woogie* were the pivotal works in their collection, two signposts in twentieth-century art.

The Tremaines recognized the historic importance of the Johns, too, and felt a sort of obligation that it eventually be in a museum. They told me of their past disappointment in giving works to museums and then finding them kept in storage in the basement. With good reason, Emily thought the museums appreciated works most if they had to pay for them. When the Metropolitan paid a great price for a work, people came to see it, and even if tainted by commercialism at the moment, it was displayed as a major work of art with the full prestige of the museum behind it.

I wanted very much to keep *Three Flags* in America, as did the Tremaines, and I suggested that the painting be sold to a museum for posthumous delivery. Tom Armstrong at the Whitney was so keen on the painting that he said he would consider such an arrangement. After a couple of weeks of talking about it, during which the Tremaines were psychologically loosening their grip on the picture, I suggested an outright sale. And I suggested the price of $1 million.

The Tremaines felt that if the Whitney paid $1 million the painting would get the recognition it deserved, it would be placed where they wanted it to be, and they would have no further right to possess it.

On the other side, I think it was very courageous and farsighted for the Whitney to say, "We want this painting – it's one of the quintessential masterpieces of American art – and if it costs us $1 million then we will raise $1 million to buy it." Their decision underscores their commitment to living American art, and I congratulate them for their courage. A million dollars was a world-record price for a living artist.

When the Rothko estate was deciding on a gallery to represent them – and believe me, it was their choice, not mine, as every dealer wanted the assignment – they weighed the images of several galleries before deciding on Pace. I feel it was an extraordinary endorsement of the gallery's honesty and ethical position, arising as it did from the terrible situation of the Rothko trials.

I had known Mark Rothko for about seven years prior to his death. Louise Nevelson introduced us one day at lunch, and we liked each other very much. He had been important in shaping my esthetic when I was only twenty-three and first opening my gallery in New York. I wanted to show Mark's work during his lifetime. In 1968, two years before he died, I made a deal with him for a body of work, but when I came back the next day to select the paintings, Mark seemed distressed and told me the deal was off. He said he had seen Bernard Reis, his accountant and executor of his estate in the interim, and that he just couldn't do it.

When Rothko's daughter, Kate, discovered that only three months after his suicide the three executors of his estate had secretly turned over his entire legacy of eight hundred paintings to Frank Lloyd of Marlborough Gallery, she brought suit against all parties. During the trial that ensued, the Assistant Attorney General of New York State

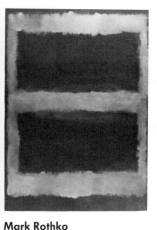

Mark Rothko

Untitled

1 9 5 8

came to see me, as he did every gallery owner in the city, asking if I had known Mark Rothko. I said that I had, and that although I never sold his work, I had made him an offer to buy eighteen paintings at $35,000 to $38,000 per picture. The Assistant Attorney General said that this was very important, as Marlborough was basing its case of paying $12,000 per picture on the fact that there were no other offers being made at the time. Indeed, there were. The international art dealer, Ernst Beyeler of Basel, who was to have put up half of the $500,000 investment in Rothko's paintings, corroborated this. We had visited Rothko's studio together that day. I said I would be willing to testify to that effect, without realizing the implications. I was there for two full days, and it was a bloody mess. The opposition tried to disqualify me, saying that I was lying and had never been in the studio, absurd things like that. At my urging, Beyeler also testified. It was a terrible attack. The image of the entire art community was wrecked by Marlborough's handling of the Rothko estate after the executors and Frank Lloyd were found guilty of misconduct. When I went to parties, people would attack me for being a dealer.

Two or three years went by, and Ed Ross, the lawyer for the estate for the Rothko children, told me they were getting ready to choose a gallery and wondered if Pace was interested. I had never met Kate Rothko, but she asked me to come to Baltimore where she was finishing her internship at Johns Hopkins. There was a fantastic rapport at that first meeting. I mean, *snap*. It happens sometimes. She knew I had known her father, and we talked about his work. When I left that night on a midnight train, I knew I would get representation of the Rothko estate. After two months, Ed Ross called and said they would like to draw up a contract. We got the estate because of that meeting and because of the reputation of the gallery, not because of my testimony; several dealers testified. The estate felt this was the gallery for Rothko, and they were right, just as it would have been the right gallery for him during his lifetime.

I recently became the representative for a large part of the Picasso estate. I met one of the children, Claude, socially, and he began asking my advice on various things. Over a period of three years we became friends, and the relationship casually evolved. Through this connection, I now have information about Picasso the man, as well as the artist, that other people don't have access to – notebooks

Pablo Picasso

La femme au Jardin

1 9 2 9 – 3 0

and verbal histories from the family. Claude Picasso told me an extraordinary story. As everyone knows, Picasso and Matisse were very close. When he was a small child, Claude was often taken to Matisse's house by his father and left there for the day. One day in the last years of Matisse's life, when he was making the *papiers découpages*, Claude was there, and as Matisse was working he gave Claude some colored paper and scissors and glue, and Claude made his own *papier découpage*. He brought it back at the end of the day and showed it to his father. He had signed it, "Matisse." Picasso said, "Why did you sign this 'Matisse'? Your name is Picasso, and that's a perfectly good name for an artist." And Claude said, "Oh, Matisse is a *serious* artist." When I asked Claude what he meant by that, he said that when he was a boy his father was very much a child to him; he would play with him, and he would dress up in his mother's slip and make masks and wear them. Matisse never did anything like that; Matisse was much more sober an individual.

I have always believed very much in Picasso's last paintings, the so-called Avignon paintings. I thought they were the coolest and most expressionistic of his career. Until 1981 they hadn't been seen in America, and I proposed to the family an exhibition which I was sure would be acclaimed by both critics and artists. Indeed, it was a tremendous success; these were painters' paintings. They were Picasso's last gift, and they were difficult paintings, impossible to fit neatly and historically into his prior body of work. Picasso for the first time used broad areas of color as form rather than embellishing lines by color, very much like Abstract Expressionistic brushwork. But if you think of Picasso as the source from which Abstract Expressionism evolved, then it's logical that he should fulfill his own prophecy. The future inherent within Cubism, passing through the next major movement of Abstract Expressionism, ends in an expressionistic way by Picasso himself at the end of his life. For me it points a finger toward the continuing history of art. The new expressionist artists in New York and Italy and Germany are the echoes and legacy of Picasso's last paintings. Leo Steinberg wrote the gallery a letter extolling the virtues of the late pictures. Robert Rosenblum thought they were wonderful, and that it would take many years for people to appreciate them. They were my first choice for my initial exhibition from the Picasso estate.

I showed Picasso's sculptures in September 1982. You know, Picasso kept almost all his sculpture. Eventually I hope to show the notebooks, which are an incredible legacy. I've seen notebooks that contain multiple studies for passages in his most famous paintings. Picasso is the paramount artist of the twentieth century. The idea that we know his mind and work is ridiculous. We know only the surface. So many of the drawings that we're bringing to light are totally unknown. Bill Rubin, the chief curator at MOMA, who is a great expert on Picasso, told me he never knew there were drawings for the ceramics, which I will show. I have the honor of helping this unfold.

My artists are my closest friends: Brice Marden, Chuck Close, Jim Dine, Saul Steinberg (a great intellectual and humorist), and the unpredictable Lucas Samaras. Going to their studios and seeing what is evolving gives me a charge to go on, to mount the exhibition, do the catalogue, call the collectors. They are my muses, and in some instances I hope that I am theirs.

Some time ago Lucas Samaras asked me to pose nude for him. I did it because he's an artist in my gallery and he was doing a series of photographs in which I strongly

Brice Marden

Card Drawing (Counting)

#17

1 9 8 2

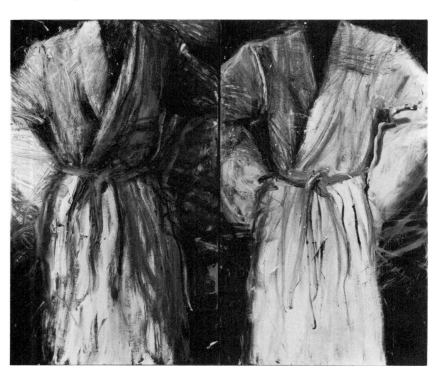

Jim Dine

Two Mighty Robes at Night

in Jerusalem

1 9 8 0

believed. Actually I think I was the second person he asked. George and Helen Segal were first. I think the model for the Mona Lisa was happy to pose for Leonardo; I was happy to pose for Samaras.

Samaras has a razor-sharp mind, and he continuously prods you to think. He is the most provocative and evocative person, insatiable for information, and also finds unexpected answers to acceptable questions. He's an extraordinary person, always assessing and reassessing answers, questions, life issues, and it's very mind-expanding to be involved with him.

More than anything in the world, I would like to be an artist. I'm a dealer because that's as close to the mark as I can get, but they are the people I admire, and theirs is the achievement which is paramount in cultural history.

Lucas Samaras

Sittings 20 x 24 (7G)

1   9   8   0

Marian
Goodman

Marian Goodman (born 1928, New York City) published limited edition prints by scores of artists such as Claes Oldenburg, Larry Rivers, and Richard Artschwager under her firm, Multiples, before making her New York gallery a bridge between Europe and America by showing European artists from Marcel Broodthaers to Anselm Kiefer.

P

rint publishing in the early sixties was an idealistic field. For many years, artists from Moholy-Nagy, Albers, and Arp to Daniel Spoerri had contended that inexpensively produced works of quality could reach beyond the world of collectors who traditionally bought art. But printmaking belonged to printmakers and to arts and crafts; with a few exceptions, it had been languishing for decades. Tatyana Grosman helped change printmaking history when she set up Universal Limited Editions in 1957. After she attracted outstanding artists like Johns and Rauschenberg, an enormous sense of excitement and promise developed.

While I had always been interested in art, my entry into the world of editions was roundabout. It began with my father, who was a collector. During the bleak days of WPA art, he had fallen in love with the vibrant paintings of one artist, Milton Avery, and collected this artist virtually all his life. Seeing the richness that art can bring into life gave me a very full introduction and led eventually to my studying art history, and to publishing a portfolio of prints for a scholarship fundraising program.

The memory of that first experience with publishing stayed with me through graduate school, and I decided to approach museums with a publishing proposal. I went to museums because I felt they would offer a better opportunity to present work by wonderful new artists of the early sixties to a young public, and I felt that with the affiliation it could all be done on a relatively noncommercial level. But the idea was premature. When nothing worked out, I decided to try it on my own in 1964, joining forces with friends, Robert Graham, Ursula Kalish, Barbara Kulick, and Sunny Sloan, to set up Multiples, Inc., with our first catalogue presenting editions by Barnett Newman, Claes Oldenburg, Philip Guston, and Larry Rivers, and graced with a cover by Josef Albers. I was very aware at the time that I would have far more opportunity to work directly with artists such as these by publishing prints than through the first few years of museum work.

It was an exciting time. Beside printmaking, artists were regaining an interest in other early techniques. We had a banner company called Betsy Ross Banner Co., started by Barbara Kulick, that produced what we called a modern-day analog to tapestry. There were wonderful works done in this medium by artists like Lichtenstein, Warhol, Falstrom,

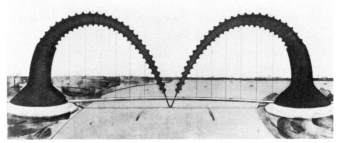

Claes Oldenburg

Screwarch Bridge, State II

1 9 8 0

Wesselman, Arman, and others. Artists also took an interest in sculpture in jewelry and furniture. We also published
phonograph records and books, among them an anthology
called *Artists and Photographs*, giving the first focused presentation of artists working with photography, many of
whom were little known at the time in the United States but
who were to later go on to show in galleries around the
world: Jan Dibbets, Joseph Kosuth, Doug Heubler, and Dan
Graham were among them. We also showed work published
in Europe by the early and influential group called Editions
Mat, and by many independent publishers in the United
States who did wonderful projects, such as Tanglewood Press.

I like to think that printmaking deeply engages artists
aesthetically as well as conceptually. An example that
comes to mind is Claes Oldenburg, who has used the
medium to demonstrate his ideas for utopian projects such
as his *Screwarch Bridge* or *Landscape with Noses*. There are
so many of his prints that are filled with wit and imagination. Then there is Arakawa, who was also interested in the
print medium for its ability to create an almost non-material
sense of space. He saw printmaking as a new way of creating textures and surfaces that could never have been done
by hand, and in a sense he has made the modern printing
press into something it hadn't been before. The examples
are endless; Robert Morris's use of lead tablets as intaglio
prints is another. The variety of ways artists have used print
mediums is as limitless as their imaginations.

Multiple editions had the air of a cottage industry in the
early sixties. There were no sophisticated shops in New
York then, only modest little places. The year I did my first
solo project with Larry Rivers I went with him on the back
of his motorcycle from shop to shop, because a different
artisan had to take care of silkscreening, collage, and fabri-
cation work. The result was an edition of a sculpture from
his Dutch Master series.

Larry Rivers

Cigar Box

1 9 6 6

View of exhibition,

"Banners"

1 9 6 6

Left to right: Robert Indiana,

Roy Lichtenstein, Andy

Warhol, Laing

Roy Lichtenstein

Huh?

1 9 7 6

Roy Lichtenstein, who was interested in sculpture of the twenties at the time, did two intricate designs for a very beautiful little cloisonné enamel pin. I found a craftsman who made enamel buttons for the army who could do the work, and we made our edition. Determined to sell them for twenty-five dollars each, so that everyone could afford one, we were somewhat dismayed to see the result of our virtually non-profit effort being bought and resold in Europe for ten times the price.

We wanted very much to do inexpensive editions of beautiful prints, and did do some with Oldenburg. We talked with Jasper Johns of doing a project where he would make a print of finest quality that would be signed, but not numbered. We would sell it for a small sum. By not signing it there would be the implication of an unlimited edition and thus it could not be exploited for profit. Many artists, notably Richard Hamilton, were also interested in exploring this direction and in trying to determine whether there indeed was a large popular audience for collecting art. We discovered that collecting was, however, still an elitist pursuit. I believe that this was the experience of many publishers, and the expansive notion of large editions was finally put to rest so that as a result, in the early seventies, the publishing world focused on smaller, and perhaps more personalized, editions.

At this time I felt it was important to encourage excellent print shops to take root and grow in New York, and I am proud to have been instrumental in initiating or helping

several of the main ones to set up. The whole process of print publishing in New York was getting more and more sophisticated, and a whole new generation of expert print-makers were not active.

Starting the Marian Goodman Gallery was a somewhat roundabout affair. My first trip to Documenta was 1968, and it was a fascinating and impressive exhibition. I saw the work of Joseph Beuys for the first time and immediately tried to arrange to have his films shown in New York. In due course it became very clear to me that there were many very important artists in Europe that were simply not being shown in New York. Opening a gallery might do something to remedy that. When I met Marcel Broodthaers I was shocked to learn that he had never shown in the United States, and I immediately set about trying to make up for this neglect.

I started the gallery in 1977; the first exhibition was a beautiful show of a broad range of work by Broodthaers — films, objects, drawings, paintings. It was designed to introduce his work to New York. I also showed James Lee

Marcel Broodthaers

Portraits

1 9 8 3

Ger Van Elk

Sketch for the Last Adieu

1 9 7 5

Byers. From that time I've gone on to build a gallery program with such European artists as Ger Van Elk, Anselm Kiefer, Tony Cragg, Anselmo, Sigmar Polke. I will also be showing the work of Gerhardt Richter, Walter Dahn, Alan Ruppersburg, Larry Bell, and, I'm sure, others to come.

I never set out to show European art exclusively, and I don't intend to. There were always certain dealers in New York who were dedicated to showing important Europeans and integrating them into the New York scene: Leo Castelli, Ileana Sonnabend, John Gibson, René Block among them. But it seemed there was still a very real need to integrate more of the most important European artists in the New York art world. I viewed the gallery I was starting almost as an alternative space.

I am interested in people who move art history along, who make the advances. There is something profoundly moving about man's urge and capacity to create. To me, that's the key, that's the reason why art is truly international. I believe that the most inspiring thing about a society is the man of culture it produces, the artist as a civilizing force in our lives.

Anselm Kiefer

Ein Schwert Verhiss mir der Vater (My Father Promised Me a Sword)

1 9 8 1

Xavier Fourcade

Xavier Fourcade (born 1926, Paris) attended Oxford University and continued studies in law, oriental languages, and political science in Paris. He joined Knoedler & Co.'s contemporary department in 1966 and opened his own gallery in 1972, concentrating on blue-chip painters and sculptors, including Willem de Kooning, Marcel Duchamp, Arshile Gorky, Henry Moore, and Barnett Newman.

All my life I have been in contact with extraordinary people, people of great creativity and talent. I knew Gertrude Stein at the end of her life in Paris.

I became a dealer in 1966 when Knoedler asked me to run their contemporary department. Again, it was the people, artists I greatly admired such as de Kooning, Barnett Newman, Henry Moore, Tony Smith, Louise Bourgeois, Dali, and others, who attracted me to this project.

Knoedler's contemporary department was a success, but when Knoedler was eventually sold, I chose not to stay and started my own gallery in 1972 with all the artists I had brought to Knoedler. They made my reputation, rather than I making theirs. Over the years I've taken on others: Michael Heizer, Joan Mitchell, Malcolm Morley, Catherine Murphy, Dorothea Rockburne, Georg Baselitz, Tony Berlant, Bill Crozier, Raoul Hague, H. C. Westermann, John Chamberlain. The only formal relation these artists have with one another is in terms of quality; they are all great individuals and exceptional creators.

I have no desire to get involved in groups or schools. I approach the work of each artist from its own unique merits. People have often said to me, "You deal with the artists nobody else can work with." Maybe they refer to artists who possess both demanding personalities and demanding ideas.

Michael Heizer was building a city in the Nevada desert. I had known his work long before 1972, when I finally met him. It creates an exhilerating feeling when his massive stone sculpture invades the space of my gallery.

Malcolm Morley called me one day in the late seventies and asked if I knew who he was. I said, "Of course. Barnett Newman and Salvador Dali noticed your work and told me about you years ago." Newman had met Morley at a restaurant where Malcolm was waiting tables shortly after his arrival in New York. When he saw Newman come in Malcolm was so flabbergasted that he dropped a tray of glasses. They both laughed, and Malcolm introduced himself, saying that he was a painter. Barney asked to come to his studio and went a week or two later. He was impressed. Meanwhile, Salvador Dali had told me about him, saying he thought Morley's paintings were remarkable.

Morley turned out to be one of the most civilized men I've ever met, exceptionally well read and very, very intelli-

Michael Heizer

45°, 90°, 180° (#2)

1 9 8 2

gent. I had trouble with the first painting he sent me. It was made of three paintings attached together, a camel and two goats. I thought it was the ugliest thing I'd ever seen, so awful that I was tempted to call Malcolm and say, "We should forget our agreement. I thought I admired your work, but I can't deal with this picture." But I didn't call. Instead, the painting went to the storage area where I looked at it every day for a week. It kept growing on me; finally I realized it *was* a strong painting, an extraordinary painting. Seeing that what at first had seemed unacceptable was in fact exceptionally beautiful, the first thing I did was double the price.

I never think of Bill de Kooning as an older man. He has a remarkable, young mind, and he's always so alive. As long as he trusts you, he in turn is the most trustworthy and easy person to deal with. Working in waves, de Kooning achieves marvelous work at certain times; at others, he is plagued by being unable to arrive at what he wants. So all his life his production has been small; until the early seventies, his whole work may have consisted of something like 200 or 250 paintings. But then in 1975 he did nearly eighteen paintings, and twenty the following year. To have such a fresh out-pouring at his age – he was in his seventies – is phenome-nal, but these late paintings were badly received by the critics. The public's reception was tremendous; his most recent show was so packed that we even required security

Malcolm Morley

The Palms of Vai

1 9 8 2

Willem de Kooning

Untitled III

1 9 8 2

guards. The public adores de Kooning.

Constant criticism of the new work of an artist is never very pleasant to accept. The role of the dealer is to hold on with him, morally, intellectually, and often financially, to support him. The main thing an artist needs is freedom from any kind of pressure, to be allowed to work in peace. That's something that a dealer, if he truly understands his role, can secure for an artist.

Sometimes I am faced with an artist's new work that I have trouble understanding and accepting. I wait and see, and it has never happened that a new direction disorients me for long: I catch up after a while. When you're in constant, almost daily, contact with artists, you follow the continuity of what is taking place in their work. By the time new work matures, you know what it is.

For many years I greatly looked forward to showing a fantastic de Kooning sculpture, a seated figure nine and a half feet high that had come into being over a period of ten years. Bill was in Italy in the summer of 1969 and spent one afternoon in the foundry of a sculptor friend. He played with clay and made thirteen small figurative sculptures, each about ten inches high. Back in New York he told me about them, and I said I wanted to see them, so we had them cast and sent to New York. Four or five months later the sculptures arrived, and I lined them up on my desk at Knoedler. I thought they were hideous. I called Bill and said, "Look, they're not good," and he said, "Of course. I don't know why you're making such a fuss. It's nothing."

Something happened the next day when I looked at them again. They were no longer *nothing;* two or three days later I saw that they were *fantastic.* I started envisioning them ten feet high. As it happened, Henry Moore was in New York for his exhibition of marble pieces at Knoedler. Moore never does anything with his own hand that he can't carry in his pocket; everything is enlarged. I don't think that any sculptor since the Renaissance had ever done big things directly. I asked Moore if he thought I was right in visualizing that very small piece of de Kooning's ten feet high, and he said it had such strength, such nervous energy, that it could be enlarged to any size.

Bill was not interested by my idea. I had the little piece photographed from two or three different angles and projected the photographs ten feet high in de Kooning's studio. It was terrific, and Bill decided to go ahead. He then

Henry Moore

Working model for a Stone

Memorial

1 9 6 1 – 7 1

decided to do big sculptures himself. He's the first sculptor in a long time to make large-sized sculptures directly. To work with clay on the scale he wanted, he had to have giant hands. The way he did it was to wear two pairs of gloves, one pair of big gloves and another pair of huge, working man's gloves over those, to give him fingers ten inches long. He left some of the gloves in the sculptures: the hand of the "Seated Woman on a Bench" is in fact one of his gloves. He was able to manipulate the clay with his enormous fingers so that he could make giant marks. It's an extraordinary tour de force. Dali, who was around at the time, suggested that Bill paint it.

Another sculptor I show is William Crozier, a realist whom the *Village Voice* recently called "Reaganite," no doubt for his blatant and therefore "non-avant-garde" realism. Hilton Kramer considered his work a break with much that has been considered significant in new sculpture for a generation or more. Some years ago he was asked to do a sculpture of Cardinal Cushing for a monument in Boston. Whoever asked Crozier to do the sculpture had probably heard that he did realistic work, but I doubt that he'd ever seen any of it. I asked Crozier what he wanted to do, and he said he wanted to have Cardinal Cushing in magnificent robes, seated in a chair, caressing the cheek of a little eight-year-old girl standing in front of him, and looking at her with very hungry eyes.

Both in terms of painting and sculpture, I have for a long time considered Georg Baselitz the most interesting artist in Europe. But I was uneasy because I did not feel that he was a great colorist, and that's something that I believe is almost indispensable to being a good painter. Then in 1980 he showed a sculpture at the Venice Biennale which was placed all alone in the big hall of the German pavillion. It was amazing – so strong, so fresh, so original, that I realized that here was really a first-rate artist, who could make sculptures of the same quality as his immensely impressive paintings. I decided to disregard whatever problems I might have had with his work, and I arranged to meet him in London, where he was included in the "New Spirit in Painting" exhibition at the Royal Academy. We made an appointment in Germany for the following weekend, but because of an airline strike, I had to postpone the meeting and go back to New York. Baselitz began to doubt me. I found out later, from a dealer in Germany, that Baselitz had even called the London airport to find out if there really was a strike. I was so perplexed with his attitude that I told his German dealer, "Fine, if he thinks I'm playing a game with him, tell him that I will come back Monday. I'll see him Monday afternoon." I saw terrific paintings, absolutely fantastic paintings, exactly what I was hoping to see – marvelously colorful, everything I had been missing in his work before. I was extremely enthusiastic, bought a group of works on the spot, and arranged his first show in New York.

I have always held the conviction that there are very few great artists at any given time. Today, it is to New York that museum curators, collectors, and dealers come from all over the world because it is here that the most interesting things have taken place in art over the past thirty years and are still taking place.

Georg Baselitz

Glastrinker (Glass Drinker)

1 9 8 1

Paula
Cooper

Paula Cooper (born 1938, Massachusetts) opened her downtown gallery in 1968, providing a rallying-point not only for Minimalist and Conceptual artists but also for performance artists and musicians. The work of painters and sculptors such as Joel Shapiro, Lynda Benglis, Michael Hurson, and Jonathan Borofsky can be seen in her gallery today.

Because I was an only child I was brought up to believe that I could do anything I set my mind to: I could be a doctor, an artist, a ballplayer, a mother. Anything went, anything was possible. I finished boarding school in three years and at sixteen went to Europe to live and study. After one year in Athens with my parents I set off on my own. I wanted to study art history, and it was in 1956 in Paris that I first saw American painting: Kline, de Kooning, Pollock. What an amazing shock. I spent all of my time in Paris looking at art, old and new, and decided then that what I wanted to do was to devote my life to working with living artists. Returning to the United States I was bored looking at slides of paintings that I knew so well, so I left school and came to New York in search of a livelihood.

In spite of the fact that I didn't know how to do a bloody thing, the first job I got was with Chanel Perfumes, because I could speak a little French. I must have had some strong feminist ideas even then, because I always refused to learn how to type, never wanting to be able to fall back on being a secretary. Ironically, I would have preferred to wash dishes rather than resort to office work. But I did take night classes in perspective and life drawing at the Art Students League. I thought it was important to have some idea of what it was like to try to make art. I also spent hours at the Museum of Modern Art.

After a year in New York I still felt intimidated by the staidness of galleries, but with the help of a friend I managed to get a job with World House Galleries, whose showrooms had been designed by Kiesler. They exhibited Giacometti, Max Ernst, Dubuffet, Morandi, Ensor, and other European artists. I became very close friends with Lee and Elsie Gatch – he was the only American artist the gallery showed. I learned everything there was to know about the different auction houses of the world, while meeting many people who were very kind and generous and still mean a great deal to me to this day, even if, in most cases, our paths in art have been very different. But most of all, it was a real apprenticeship, something I believe in still.

After marrying, leaving World House, and taking some art history courses at NYU's Institute of Fine Arts, I went to work for a young man who had just opened a gallery. I thought to myself, "I have a better eye and know much more about art than this fellow," so I opened my first gallery in 1964. It was not quite a *total* fiasco: I did show the work of Bob Thompson and Walter de Maria in that first gallery. And I had my first bad experience with the press and with a collector named Scull.

I'll never forget going with Walter to see the second exhibition of Carl Andre at Tibor de Nagy Gallery, of going to performances of Bob Whitman, happenings of Oldenburg and Kaprow, the first New York performance of Nam June Paik and Stockhausen, visiting Allen Ginsburg and seeing so much diverse good work by artists from Judd to Kelly to Johns, Rauschenberg, Rosenquist, Stella, Newman, de Kooning, and Warhol. It was a pretty rich visual diet.

I remember one student in particular who came to my gallery often, a very pretty young woman named Lynda Benglis. She was in graduate school at Hunter, and we would have long talks about all that was going on. She was very intense, very serious. At that time there were hardly any women artists showing in galleries. The dealer Robert Elkon once took me to visit John Wesley's studio, and his wife served us coffee. It was not until a couple of years later, when Jo Baer began showing her work, that I realized she was an artist herself.

The benefit I derived from that first failed gallery was learning what I didn't want to do: I did not want to have just another uptown gallery with the limitations and constraints that expressed a kind of shopkeeper attitude toward art. I wanted a vital situation. So it was very fortuitous when John Gibson called and asked me to work at Park Place, a cooperative gallery owned and run by ten artists. It was located, originally, on Park Place in lower Manhattan. Then it moved to West Broadway. The spirit of the artists, the openness, the tremendous activity, the focus on the art and not the outside world, all served to corroborate my idea of what a gallery could be. Park Place had early ideas for art and technology (remember the Nine Evenings of Experiments in Art and Technology!), and presented music also. We did two Steve Reich concerts with Max Neuhaus and Philip Glass. The whole experience gave me a new sense of things and permitted me to finish my "apprenticeship" once and for all.

I've never been drawn to one kind of art only, and I've always been interested in artists as people. Since I am not an artist myself, I never have expectations about how art should look. However, I am very slow to make the commit-

Elizabeth Murray

Keyhole

1 9 8 2

Lynda Benglis

Bijlee

1 9 8 1

ment of working with an artist. Once the decision is made, the dealer and artist are stuck with each other, so to speak. It's a relationship that must be entered into very carefully, so I always make a point of living with new work and watching it over a long period of time. There's no hurry; most often, as with the painter Elizabeth Murray, I first began by showing new work in a group show. Since then, it has been a wonderful experience to work with Elizabeth and watch the work get stronger and stronger. I never show work that I haven't been convinced about.

My approach to business is also conservative. Money was not abundant when I began, and I swept the floors myself – but of course I had to have someone come in and type several letters a week. One of the people who helped me briefly was Lynda Benglis, who needed money to be able to live and make her art. It was quite an experience having her come in. Even typing a letter turned into a comic event of some sort. She had her mind completely on her art. Lynda always wore hats as if she were trying to hide herself. She was very aware of competing in art with men, and right she was. For years I was treated in a most ignominious manner by some of my male peer dealers. When Lynda first started using glitter, everyone thought those works were terrifically vulgar, and specifically feminine. Of course things changed several years later.

189

An artist, in my opinion, should be free to concentrate
on his or her work, and a dealer, as the word implies,
should deal with business, with the more career-oriented
aspects of getting artists' work out into the world. In my
gallery we are equals working toward the same goal. But
there was a time when I was very touchy about the attitude
that many people had toward art dealers: They were thought
to be terrible people, the worst of anyone or anything associated with the art world. Artists in particular held this attitude. I remember when the Art Workers Coalition used my
gallery for meetings. I was very hurt that I wasn't personally
invited to the meetings. After all, I was an art worker, and a
damn hard worker! It doesn't worry me now. The middleman is a necessity, particularly with art. Art and money
have a peculiar relationship. There is a very fine edge
between art and money, and it is on that edge that a dealer
functions.

Jackie Winsor

Glass Piece

1 9 7 8 – 7 9

My gallery was the only one in Soho when I opened in
1968. The reason I came downtown in the first place was to
get away from the old pattern of uptown galleries: It was
moribund, too set in its ways. I wanted to be independent. I
didn't want to be bothered with all the social trimmings,
things that often counted more than the art itself. The artists themselves were very encouraging when it came to
making this break. But while there was nobody I wanted to
emulate, there were galleries I respected very much: Castelli, the Green Gallery, Sidney Janis. Ultimately, I just
wanted to do things my own way, and starting downtown
was part of that.

I did what I thought was right for the moment, which
meant a program of continuously changing group shows. But
most of the artists I knew were having a pretty difficult time
making a living, and I saw the need to show their work in a
more concentrated, cohesive way. So I switched to presenting one body of work by an individual artist. But I do love
open-ended group shows, because later I did another whole
year of them. It's true that one can manipulate work in exhibitions, but my idea is to show how different works can
clarify the information contained in each other by their differences or seeming similarities, and can introduce a dialogue. Often I show the same works over and over again,
moving them from one wall to another, from one side of the
gallery to a different side, into another context with other
works. I remember a sculpture by Jackie Winsor that I had

Robert Grosvenor

Untitled

1 9 8 0 – 8 1

190

Alan Shields

Mt. Saint Helens

1 9 8 0

on view for three months. After I moved it one day, people commented on the new piece by Jackie Winsor! They had been looking at it for three months without seeing it.

Another important aspect of the gallery, especially through 1974, was its night life: performance, dance, poetry, and films organized by Hollis Frampton, Bob Huot, Michael Snow, and others. Mabou Mines would present work that was in rehearsal and not yet ready for a larger theater audience. It was all very exciting.

In a sense, I gained consciousness growing up in the cultural climate of the sixties, and the artists whom I met during that period whose work affected me, artists like Carl Andre and Don Judd, have remained an important part of my life. People try to denigrate the seventies today, especially the more PR- and media-oriented people. They say that nothing happened in the seventies. I guess it was not for the consumer sensibility – Conceptual art (which affected the present boom in photography), performance art, video art, and land art are too elusive for the American practical ethos. But a lot of younger artists were developing and maturing: Borofsky, Murray, Shapiro, Serra, Rothenberg. Most important, women in this country crashed the barrier as artists.

It seems that things move quicker now, that it is no longer a matter of generations, but of decades or even years. Work by artists such as Judd, Le Witt, Andre, and Artschwager is still too radical for a lot of people. That's good. The work won't disappear; it's too strong. It hasn't been consumed away. Weaker art *is* consumed away. Perhaps things do happen faster today, but not to good work. It does not just come and go.

In the sixties I witnessed this same kind of revolving

Carl Andre

Shiloh, New York

1 9 8 0

door, but on a smaller scale. Many of those artists who were considered very "hot" are simply not seen anymore. They've disappeared. It's very sad, but they didn't pay enough attention to their own work. One of the most difficult periods for an artist is when he or she is just beginning to gain some kind of success. It's important to keep an even balance and regard the initial success as objectively as possible.

The decision to work with an artist takes trust. How can you really be sure? There are no guidelines other than trusting your responses. When I first met Alan Shields in 1968, he was twenty-four years old, and even in the absence of a body of work, my response was immediate. We have worked together ever since. When artists who are affiliated with other galleries call me and tell me that they're unhappy with their present gallery, I usually tell them to stay where they are, that they are fortunate. I try to make it clear to artists I include in group shows that I don't intend to establish a long-term relationship, but a group show is a chance for the public and other dealers to see their work.

At the same time, some artists are such nice people that I'm sad when I don't like their work; then, I usually also like the people whose work I do respond to. I have been working with Bob Grosvenor for seventeen years, since the Park Place Gallery; I believe in him and his work very much, and when an exhibition of his is over I feel a void. I have the same intense involvement with Alan Shields's work.

The first time I met Jonathan Borofsky was during a show that Lucy Lippard organized in the gallery in 1969; it is somehow appropriate that Borofsky first showed in my gallery in a group exhibition of conceptual art. Borofsky's work is very much like the world itself. Walking into a show of his is not so different from being out on the street. The chaos, the energy is there in the form of systems that contradict and explain themselves.

I met Joel Shapiro in 1969. He came in one day and asked me to visit his studio. When I did he showed me a large number of drawings, some of which I included in a drawing show soon after. He had his first one-person show at the gallery in 1970. He placed a series of small sculptures of different materials, each the same size and shape, on shelves that ran around the entire gallery. It puzzled a lot of people. Phil Leider, then editor of *Artforum*, used to come

Jonathan Borofsky

View of exhibition, Musem

Boymans van Beuningen,

Rotterdam, Holland

February 20–April 4, 1982

into the gallery Saturdays with his children; this time he said, "Paula, you've got to be kidding."

Working with an artist like Joel Shapiro is very different from merely dealing in art objects; you become deeply involved in the ideas contained in the work. Having represented him from the beginning of his career I've been able to see each sculpture, each drawing, as it was done. Sometimes when I go to his studio a sudden departure will take me by surprise. I always like this sort of very loaded transitional work; it captures that crucial point at which something has just been resolved, at which a concept has come into being.

I met Jennifer Bartlett in 1971, when she came in to see a sculpture by Joel Shapiro. I thought she was very sophisticated, with her makeup on crooked and her philosophical pronouncements about Joel's work. Later she borrowed our mailing list and when she was having a show of her work in Alan Saret's studio at 119 Spring Street. The first thing Jennifer did in the gallery was to give a reading, and she was hilarious. She read from the beginning of *History of the Universe,* a modest autobiography of ten thousand pages with little sketches on her childhood ambitions to be a great ballerina and a baseball player. The first time I walked into Jennifer's studio she was sitting at a table poring over huge

Jennifer Bartlett

At Sea

1 9 7 9

tomes on astrology and astronomy. Initially, it was difficult for me to accept her work because she was using arbitrary systems, systems that would break down, but the painting would continue. Her request for a reaction to all this would invariably end in long philosophical discussions about nihilism. I had trouble with the irrational element in her thinking, but I learned a lot from it. We started working together slowly, and the relationship has been rich.

The artists are the gallery; if they are doing well, the gallery does well and we can all continue to grow. It's not like any other business, not even show business!

I met Michael Hurson when Jennifer Bartlett gave her reading at the gallery. After that he used to stop by and we became friends. I began advising him, and during my first visit to his studio I noticed a group of long, narrow paintings leaning against the wall, so I asked him what they were. He became very nervous and said, "They're nothing; you don't want to see them." That was all. He refused to show them to me. Six months later, I managed to talk him into unveiling the paintings that he had been so reluctant to show me. Immediately I told him, "For God's sake, they're fantastic. Why didn't you let me see them in the first place?" They were paintings of eyeglasses. He replied, "I've been rejected so many times that I couldn't bear another negative response."

One incident like this is enough to make me wonder if there are artists as talented as Michael Hurson who never

Michael Hurson

Study for a Portrait (William)

1 9 8 1

show, who are just totally lost. Hundreds of artists come to show their work to me, but I think that a lot of good artists simply do not want to make the rounds in that manner. In the case of Hurson, those perplexing works were very advanced for the late sixties, counter to everything being done at that time. Looking at them today, one would say they had been done in the very late seventies.

There are so few people interested in art generally, let alone contemporary art, that you just adore the two people in Oshkosh who are interested. When it comes to working with collectors, including museums, the main ingredient is patience. I would actually rather see people not accept things too fast. I like to encourage collectors to look at an artist's work over a period of time, to be familiar with it and then respond to it genuinely. When that response happens, then everyone involved benefits, and an inportant part of cultural life is sustained.

John
Weber

John Weber (born 1932, Los Angeles, California) graduated from Antioch College and served as an associate
curator at the Dayton Art Institute from 1958–1960. He
also attended New York University's Institute of Fine
Arts and was director of the Martha Jackson Gallery
and the Dwan Gallery, both in Los Angeles and New
York, before establishing the John Weber Gallery in
1971.

When Tom Colt hired me as his assistant at the
Dayton Art Institute in 1958, it was my first real
chance to meet the well-known artists of the
day. Colt was a very lively museum director,
even out there in the boonies. He knew a lot of
the contemporary artists, and he'd get them to come give
lectures and teach. We mounted some large shows of contemporary art during the two years I spent there, and it
became clear to me that while museums did help establish
an artist's ego, it was the galleries that provided the more
immediate line of support. The idea of being on that first
line appealed to me, and Colt persuaded Martha Jackson to
give me a job in her New York gallery, which in 1960 was a
fairly viable, respected establishment with a staff of thirty
people.

Martha and I got along pretty well, and within four
months I was directing the place. My training in business
administration helped. I reorganized the company by cutting
back on operating expenses, reducing the staff, and elimi-
nating commissions to sales people.

Martha's heart belonged to the late École de Paris look,
artists like Fautrier, Paul Jenkins, Sam Francis, but you
could see people from the early stages of the Fluxus movement there also, that avant-garde fringe of neo-Dada, Zen,
and what have you, people like Allan Kaprow, people with
whom I was hanging around and taking part with in happenings. Somehow I managed to talk Martha into giving one-
man shows to young rogues like Jim Dine and Robert Indiana; Warhol and Oldenburg also had their first uptown
shows there. But even when Jim Dine sold out an entire
one-man show, Martha was still reluctant to promote Pop.

When Virginia Dwan offered me a job with her gallery in
California in 1962, I didn't hesitate a moment. Besides, I
was originally from Los Angeles and looking forward to
returning. Virginia Dwan was an intelligent and wealthy
woman who had opened a large gallery on Westwood Boulevard in 1959. She supported many directions simultaneously: the Abstract Expressionism of Kline, Guston, and
Reinhardt along with the French Nouveaux Réalistes Tinguely, Martial Raysse, Yves Klein, Arman, and Niki de
Saint-Phalle. Virginia had a house in Malibu where these
Europeans would live and work when they had shows; Claes
Oldenburg lived there for nine months and John Chamberlain and Mark di Suvero stopped there, too.

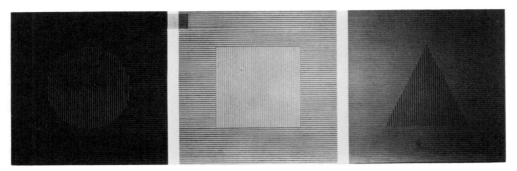

Sol Le Witt

6 Geometric Figures in

3 Colors

1 9 8 0

Our show of Ad Reinhardt's "ultimate paintings" in 1963, big, black, five-foot-square works, opened on the day John Kennedy was killed. People thought the gallery was in mourning when they saw the somber spectacle.

Virginia moved back to New York around 1966 and decided to open a branch of her own gallery there in 1967. A year later she closed the Los Angeles gallery, and I came East to assist the New York branch.

My personal direction was pretty well developed by this time. Minimalists like Sol LeWitt and Robert Ryman began gaining ground around 1966. Dwan was lending her active support to earthworks by artists like Robert Smithson, Michael Heizer, and Walter de Maria. These artists and I used to drink together and go all over the world. There was a lot of money available, and we could really do whatever we wanted: we could go out and buy a few hundred acres of land, get a bulldozer, and start moving it around – things like that.

I had tired early of Pop Art; I didn't like fast art, and Pop was fast art. I wanted to be continually informed by a work of art for as long as possible, and I found this duration of interest with the Minimal and earthwork people.

In 1968 I organized the first European show of Minimal Art at The Hague, and it was then that a group of young art dealers like Heiner Friedrich and Yvonne Lambert started up over there. In fact, there is a whole little "Mafia" of European dealers that owe a debt to Minimal Art. Why? Because they had no choice of any other American work, since Ileana Sonnabend had sewed up Pop Art in Europe and didn't want her people like Rauschenberg, Johns, and Lichtenstein to show in any gallery but her own in Paris. If a dealer insisted, she'd give 15 percent of sales, but you can't go too far on that. This left a wide breach for Minimal Art to walk through.

Alighiero e Boetti

Map of the World

1 9 7 2

Daniel Buren

"Exit" Installation

1 9 8 0

Minimalism took off like a shot in Europe. These guys were really energetic. I recommended that the European dealers work directly with the artists, so they would get the same financial break we enjoyed in New York. A support structure developed pretty fast for these artists, faster than in America. It was funny: Carl Andre was already having a retrospective at The Hague in 1969 when there wasn't one work of his in a public collection in New York.

.This period inevitably marked the beginning of widespread international travel on the part of artists, rather than the shipment of artworks. This came about because the European dealers had little money but could always scrape up just enough to bring over the artist on a charter flight. The artists would then work on location. This proved to be an idea that keyed in with the thinking of a lot of younger museum people who were doing exciting shows like Documenta in Germany and the Venice Biennale. The moving of artists rather than works of art was something we had started in California; it was easier than shipping large works of art like a Frosty Myers sculpture selling at $1,200 and requiring a $2,000 crate.

Virginia Dwan closed her gallery in 1971, and I opened my own in September at 420 West Broadway. Why Soho? For about five years the Dwan Gallery, Castelli, and Hague Art Deliveries had been renting a storage building uptown on 108th Street. Castelli had a few shows there, like the one where Richard Serra threw molten lead on the wall and all that. When this storage space was condemned by the City in 1970, Hague began looking for a building downtown. Something was found, and we all started renovating each floor. It became the 420 West Broadway building – an instant, literally overnight, success. The day we opened the galleries, twelve or thirteen thousand people came through like a swarm of locusts, stopping traffic all up the street.

My own gallery pretty much continued the programs established at the Dwan – the Minimalists and earthwork artists, at least Robert Smithson.

I began showing a lot of Europeans at the same time: Italians, French, English, all the Arte Povera people – such as Mario Merz, Anselmo, Boetti, Salvo Sorio – Daniel Buren, Richard Long, Victor Burgin, and Art and Language from England. I showed Roman Opalka, the Conceptual artist from Poland.

Critics like John Perreault and Peter Schjeldahl were

Robert Smithson

Spiral Jetty,

Great Salt Lake,

Utah

1 9 7 0

very close to the Minimalist artists and to the Arte Povera
and European Conceptual artists. You'd find almost as
many critics as artists hanging out drinking at Max's Kansas
City. If Hilton Kramer wasn't going down to Max's Kansas
City in those days it's because he was somewhat out of it.
But in compensation, his partner at the *New York Times,*
John Russell, was very sympathetic to contemporary American art. When still at the *London Times* he was already
doing a good job. There was a whole bunch of critics, but
not the Clem Greenberg–Harold Rosenberg syndrome; it
was younger people, enfant-terrible types. And artists themselves were writing: Donald Judd, Bob Morris, and a little
later, around 1974, Jeremy Gilbert-Rolfe.

Many of my customers were Europeans. Count Panza,
the great Italian contemporary-art collector, bought at least
a third of his collection through me: Oldenburg, early
Flavin, and early Bob Morris. We had given Morris a show
in 1963, and Panza bought the first Minimal fiberglass
pieces. There were six in the exhibition and Panza bought
three of them. Out of every ten collectors I was dealing with
at that time, six were European. I spent a lot of time in
Europe, living there in the summer because at the time I
was married to an Italian, Annina Nosei.

American museums weren't doing much in those days.
Alan Solomon, a wonderful person associated with the Jewish Museum, did quite a few really nice shows. But other
museums were slow to catch on. What effect did the Guggenheim Internationals really have? They always seemed

Jeremy Gilbert-Rolfe

Masurian Lakes

1 9 8 1 – 8 2

very late.

It's astounding that The Museum of Modern Art in the last fourteen years has had only three exhibitions devoted to contemporary art. With the exception of the small Projects show, which came pretty late, there was the Machine show, the Information show in 1971, and then the Eight Contemporary Artists show, in which I had five artists. And the Whitney Museum was always a sleepy place. They're like a bunch of little old ladies. The politics and lack of professionalism there are astounding.

That's why alternative spaces are very viable, the format borrowed from the European *kunstverein* or *kunsthalle*: a museum without a permanent collection or a board that came to the fore precisely because museums were rejecting twentieth-century art. This gave the raison d'être for institutions like the ICA in Cincinnati, the Contemporary Museum in Chicago, PCVA in Portland, all presenting alternatives to the very conservative attitude of museum people.

There always has been a certain chauvinistic resistance in America toward contemporary European art. Out of the three or four one-man exhibitions I did of the Italian artist Mario Merz, I sold one piece, to The Museum of Modern Art. I have never sold one piece by Boetti; I have never sold an Anselmo. After seven or eight shows of Daniel Buren, I've never sold one Daniel Buren in America to anybody, institution or private collector. There's still a very strong block.

Lucio Pozzi

The Picture Plane

1 9 8 1

Roman Opalka, on the other hand, does very well. I don't know why, unless it's because the look of his work transcends its foundation in Conceptual Art by being "beautiful." And there is a nice passage of textures in his painting, and people identify with that. But across the board there has been no support for this kind of work. I stopped showing a lot of it because it simply got to be too expensive for me to exhibit work year after year that brought in no income whatsoever. Some, like Daniel Buren or Victor Burgin, I go on showing regardless, with no motive other than the conviction that their work must be seen.

At its best, art dealing has another mission that comes before profit. A lot of my colleagues show things that they think will sell, but I never make my decisions based on that. Instead, I try to create a market, and I'm good at that. I don't worry when I take on a totally unknown artist who has not yet sold. An artist like James Biederman, whom I showed in 1981, and again in 1983, is an example. It was his first show, even though he graduated from Yale some ten years before. He's had a hard time since then, but he's still making art on an astoundingly professional level. I try to make a distinction between trends and continuity, the kind of continuity I see in the strong, hard art of Biederman.

A lot of dealers started out with money, or have all the shopping centers of the world behind them, like the Pace Gallery has. I've always wanted to be very independent, to answer to no one but myself, and therefore I've never had a backer.

It's hard to open a gallery now because the artists who can generate enough money for you to survive are already taken up elsewhere. That's why new dealers go for trends; they have no other choice. You can't open a gallery no matter how much money you have and start showing Jasper Johns. This problem has plagued Ileana Sonnabend from the time she first opened a gallery on Madison Avenue: there just wasn't anybody for her to show. When she tried to take artists away from other galleries it didn't work. Years have gone into building up her stable.

People wonder at the huge auction prices paid for one artist or the tiny prices paid for another, but it doesn't make the policies of the art world or change the reputation of an artist. If work by one of my artists goes for a good price in an auction, I'm obviously happy. But auctions are a world apart. Take their valuations of artworks, for example. When a nice piece by Sol LeWitt comes up at auction with a $2,000 valuation, I get pissed off and say, "Yeah, that's your tactic for getting people into the auction thinking they're getting a bargain." Such intentionally low prices do injury to the artist and infuriate me; they do not reflect the real world. The work in question is worth anywhere from $15,000 to $18,000. Auctions are like bargain basements really, with a lot of money and pizzazz; it's not a business I'd be involved with.

James Biederman

Untitled

1 9 8 0

Alice Aycock

The Savage Sparkler

1 9 8 1

Much of what's happening now is a rejection of the Minimalist image, although most of the artists of that group still exert a very strong influence and continue to do interesting work. For the last six years there's been a lot of floundering and experimentation, a lot of risk also, all of which I respect enormously. As a matter of fact, I take on new people on the basis of their risks, how they try to break with things rather than refine them. Alice Aycock is a good example – a unique individual who certainly cannot be categorized in any movement.

I'm not interested in artists who haven't paid their dues, who haven't survived their own particular cauldron long enough. A dealer must know that this person will go on being an artist for some time down the pike. We don't sell paintings and sculpture; we represent the artist. I don't want an artist who decides to become an architect, musician, or plumber because of slow sales during his first five years.

There are millions of artists in the world today, but only 150 artists in New York support themselves by the sale of their work. One has to be a bit of a masochist to be an artist. Still, if an artist has been around for a while, there are ways of breaking into a gallery: be very visible, get to know the right people, go to the right galleries, identify with a particular gallery that has a shared interest, and get to know some of the artists in that gallery. A recommendation from an artist is listened to closely by a dealer.

A healthy gallery balances very well-known artists with the medium-known, and then with the totally unknown. The biggies support the younger ones, thereby keeping things going. Each year I put on an invitational exhibition to infuse new people into the gallery; this is one of the major ways I make my contribution to the community of younger artists. It's an outgrowth of hundreds of hours in studios and looking at slides. I'm too young to be steamrolled; the whole trick is to keep one's mind open.

Mel Kendrick

Hucklebuck

1 9 8 1

John **Gibson**

John Gibson (born 1933, Evanston, Illinois) returned from University College in London in 1958 and worked at the University of Chicago Press and Grove Press before starting a gallery in Chicago in 1961. He then worked under art dealer Martha Jackson and at the Marlborough Gallery in New York, and opened the first gallery in Soho, Park Place, in 1965. Since that time he has raised the banners of Land Art, Body Art, Narrative, and Structure by promoting a range of artists from Joseph Beuys to Bill Beckley in the United States and Europe.

T

he solarium of an old mansion on Sixty-seventh
Street was the site of John Gibson Commissions,
and I've always thought that this one small room
was the most germinal of my many galleries.
John Gibson Commissions began in 1967 as a
gallery for new sculpture, with the idea of getting large-
scale works into public and corporate spaces. The first exhibition was called "The Hanging, Floating, Cantilevered
Show." The title came from a rather surreal dream I had,
and the announcement was a photo of myself standing cantilevered off the wall into the gallery space. The show contained unusual sculptural ideas: Warhol's silver pillows
floating around the upper space, and a drawing Carl Andre
made for the ceiling, even though he is known for his floor
pieces. There was a wall relief by Sol LeWitt and one of the
first boxes of Donald Judd. Christo suspended the model for
his 1968 Documenta project – a 280-foot-high package –
upside-down from the ceiling. To celebrate the occasion he
also made a thirty-foot package filled with balloons which
hung from the window just above the heads of pedestrians.
There were also works by Claes Oldenburg, Robert Smithson, Mark di Suvero, and others.

The first truly successful one-man of Christo followed
that same year. This exhibition of projects, drawings, collage and scale models for large works sold out. We took it
down, put up another and sold out again, extended the exhibition and then put up a third, and sold half of that. The
first year I represented Christo we sold fifty works of art in
the form of models and photographs. It was a great, much
deserved success.

Christo's great outdoor projects have always been his
best work. My favorite large-scale work is the famous
"Wrapped Coast," one million square feet of coastline in
New South Wales, Australia. The goal of this concealment
is to create a sensation of mystery. When Christo wraps a
building, it's no longer a building: it's a sculpture.

The collector Vera List and I were having coffee one day
during the 1968 Documenta, the international exhibition
held every four years in Kassel, Germany, and she
remarked that she would like to have a large outdoor work
by Christo for her sculpture garden. I suggested a wrapped
tree. She agreed, stipulating that it be no more than twenty
feet long. That fall, Christo and I went looking for trees near
Greenwich, Connecticut. A new road had been dynamited

Christo

Wrapped Coast—Little Bay,

Australia

1 9 6 9

out, and Christo fell in love with an enormous fallen oak tree; it must have been at least fifty feet long, but he had to have it.

When the bulldozer loaded the tree onto the truck I had ordered, the truck proved far too small, but somehow we got it on, balancing precariously, and we began the ten-mile drive back to Greenwich. Christo and I followed in a car, and by the time we rounded the first curve we saw that the tree was sweeping all the approaching automobiles right off the road. For the rest of the trip we were in a state of hysteria, crying with laughter until we got to the List estate. It was an experience out of an old Buster Keaton film.

When we returned, Vera List was sitting in her study, absorbed in a great pile of art mailings. I told her, simply, that the tree had arrived. Without going out to look at it she suggested that we dump it by the side of the garden. The next day, completely nonplussed by the tremendous size of the tree, Vera ordered a crane to lift it onto a site overlooking Long Island Sound and ordered a concrete base to be built for it. Over the next several weeks, Christo wrapped the branches in plastic and the roots in burlap, and then polyurethaned the trunk.

Ten years later, visiting the List collection, I noticed that the Christo tree had vanished. I asked where it was. Vera told me that it had attracted all the neighborhood dogs so her husband, Albert, had cut it up for firewood.

In early 1968, I was hanging around Max's Kansas City and happened to hear about two young artists who had plans to do large outdoor landscape projects – they were Dennis

Oppenheim and Michael Heizer. I went to see them both, was extremely impressed by their work, and decided to show Dennis Oppenheim.

The first exhibition to present the idea of land art took place at the gallery in the spring of 1968. It was Oppenheim's first one-man show, and he introduced into the gallery scale models for the vast terrestrial projects which he has since carried out all over the world. The models themselves were alive: he had plants growing in them to represent hedges, flowers as ground cover, and water. Drawings corresponding to each project were displayed on the wall. This first show was terrifically exciting, and generated a great deal of interest for large outdoor projects in general.

Nineteen sixty-eight was one of the most important years in the history of art. That October I decided to do the first group show of artists who were using new and unusual materials: Ryman, Tuttle, Hesse, Serra, Saret, Sonnier. It was called "Anti-Form," and corresponded to Italian *Arte Povera*. Leo Castelli did a similar show that included Robert Morris and Bruce Nauman some months later. The Whitney Museum did another exhibition called "Procedure and Process," and that same month, October 1968, my sister gallery, Virginia Dwan, did her famous "Earthworks" exhibition in which two of my artists, Oppenheim and Peter Hutchinson, were seen. It was a great moment to be involved with advanced art.

The pace of events did not slacken, and in December Gerry Schum came over from Germany with his *video gallerie:* artists executed works of on-location, performance-related art especially for Schum to videotape and then display not only in museums but also on nationwide German television. Oppenheim took him to the Canadian border in Maine where Oppenheim proceeded to do his famous snow projects: "Annual Rings," "One-Hour Run," and "Time Line." We showed the resulting photographs of these snow projects in his "Below Zero" exhibition in January 1969.

Oppenheim's "Annual Rings" was made on the frozen St. John River between the United States and Canada. Oppenheim took the schemata of growth rings from a tree trunk and enlarged it enormously, at the center of the river where a change of time zones occurs, snowplowing half the lines of the rings in the United States and half in Canada. The resulting form of "Annual Rings" was a configuration of repeated concentric circles.

View of exhibition,

"Anti-Form"

October–November

1 9 6 8

Dennis Oppenheim

Annual Rings

1 9 6 8

Richard Long also had his first exhibition in America at my gallery. He showed land art works such as the large X he had made by walking through a field of daisies, and the "Journey out and back, from London to the Summit of Ben Nevells in Scotland," which he had done, in his own words, simply as a walking sculpture: He took a photograph of the sky and the ground from wherever he happened to be each morning at eleven o'clock. Richard Long also did the first outdoor land art work in New York City, which was accomplished in Battery Park with the cooperation of the Parks Department. This untitled sculpture was made by removing the sod in a long rectangle and replacing it at different levels.

It is important to understand and accept the fact that these projects were made in order to be photographed. The resulting photographs were the works of art. This concept had been realized already in the early sixties when Robert Rauschenberg sent a telegram to Iris Clert, an art dealer in Paris, which read: "This telegram is a work of art if I say it is." Many of the new artists took the same tack when they declared that the photographs were their works of art. Scores of Europeans collected these photographs as art.

Peter Hutchinson achieved his dream of working on a live volcano as a way of merging art and nature, and in January 1970, the gallery made a show of his great volcano project, which was accomplished with the sponsorship of Vera List, Virginia Dwan, and *Time* magazine. Paracutin is a volcano in the Uropan Province of Mexico and was, at the time, the world's most recent active volcano. The artist organized bands of Taraskan Indians who carted his gear up the mountain on the backs of small burros. Arriving at the crater edge, he was so excited that he dropped a rope ladder into the volcano and began climbing down. Peter didn't realize that toxic gas was still being released and after one whiff he almost passed out and lost his life.

The correspondent for *Time* drove out with three hundred loaves of Super Wonder bread. The bread was brought up by burro, and Peter made a line with it along the natural clefts and faults of the volcano's rim. The line extended for one hundred yards and was covered with plastic to create a kind of outdoor greenhouse. He left it to develop mold for five days, with the idea of reintroducing organic cells back into the totally dead environment of the volcano. Hutchinson photographed the work from various points, including a small airplane. As they were leaving the volcano site, black ravens came and ate the bread. The photographs appeared in the next issue of *Time* magazine.

Again, when we showed these photographs in the gallery, we were not dealing with paintings of the landscape sites; there were no painted deserts or oil-on-canvas icebergs. The works were color photographs of the sculpture in its location, in this case, Paracutin volcano.

In all, I've done nine exhibitions for Dennis Oppenheim, and the third one concentrated on his now-classic land art projects for vast terrestrial spaces, beginning with the "Directed Seeding/Cancelled Crop," in which he planted wheat seed in a field in Holland with the help of an art-involved farmer. Two months later he came back and harvested the wheat in the form of an *X*, taking the wheat to be processed and packaged in plastic containers as an edition of signed and numbered fine art multiples.

Oppenheim had begun doing some of the first works of body art at this time. By working in a solitary uninhabited

Dennis Oppenheim

Parallel Stress

1 9 7 0

place, Oppenheim had become very much aware of his own body in relation to the space around him; his own subjectivity became very vivid and important to him. He began using his body as the subject of his works. Some of the earliest works in this vein were his attempts to do all the Olympic games he could, as works of art. He did the one-hundred-meter dash and afterward cast each footprint, and piled up the casts as sculpture along the gallery wall below photographs of the run.

Another work, *Standing Broadjump*, was performed in the gallery. Oppenheim placed sections of two-by-fours filled with powdered cement and jumped into them as far as he could, leaving the physical imprint of the jump behind.

Doug Davis, an art critic and an artist himself, wanted to write a piece on Oppenheim for *Newsweek* during this show. Dennis decided to do a special work, so the three of us, with a photographer, went to Brooklyn, and Dennis built two temporary walls of cement blocks on the shore beneath the Brooklyn Bridge. He hung from his hands and feet between the two walls, after I had lifted his feet to the second wall. It was an excellent example of the thinking at this time: art was a bridge of life, and the artist's poetic conception of that life had become the subject for his art.

The last show in the gallery on Sixty-seventh Street was the first one-man show of Vito Acconci. It was an installation in which Acconci confined a cat in a large plywood box. The artist came every day to feed the cat and give it affection. The gallery closed after that exhibition: one month with a cat on my back.

I moved the gallery and the performance series to Berlin for the art fair that year, where I turned my space into a kind of Kino-Kamp. The space was wrapped in black plastic with films projected on one wall, a kind of theater space with chairs, where recent works of Christo, Oppenheim, Graham and Acconci were shown. In the midst of an erstwhile art fair, the event was a sensation. Joseph Beuys invited me to do a program of his work in the Dusseldorf Kunstakademie similar to what I'd done in Berlin. In Germany, when Beuys and his friends in the German avant-garde turn out *en masse* for an event there is an unmistakable sense of occasion: this is exactly what happened in Dusseldorf. The European press gave it heavy coverage, and I met many of my peers, the young art dealers of Europe, who were extremely receptive to my program and

Peter Hutchinson

January from "Year Series"

1 9 7 8

wanted to introduce these artists at their galleries throughout Europe.

I met Joseph Beuys for the first time at the 1968 Documenta. One of the most impressive experiences in my life was to walk into the large room of sculptures by Joseph Beuys. I thought that after Marcel Duchamp I was finished with heroes. But seeing the work of Beuys, I was astonished. There were sculptures in felt, copper, wood; real objects – electrical and chemical; tables covered in copper, corners with felt; abstract objects – long beams of wood in different formations, again covered in felt. It was a revelation.

For my own reference I photographed every detail of each work. Beuys was standing by, surprised and bemused by the detailed nature of my study. When I published the photos in London as a box of color slides, he was very appreciative. It was the beginning of our professional friendship.

I visited Joseph Beuys at his home in Dusseldorf in 1971. He decided that since I had already demonstrated an interest in his work, I should undertake a thorough collection of his multiples and prints, because, as he put it, this was the best information one could have about his work while still being, in itself, art.

Marcel Broodthaers was also present at the 1968 Documenta, and the spectrum of objects and editions instantly suggested to me the persona of a Mallarmé; I was fascinated to find something as unexpected as the origins of French Symbolist poetry being put to use in the work of this Belgian artist.

All this was the beginning of my ten-year career as the wandering American art dealer in Europe. I had a new gallery locked in the trunk of my car: portable and accessible works of art in large black portfolios. I was astonished at the interest and acceptance of the new American art by European collectors, dealers, and museum directors. It was possible to sell art several times a week, if not every day in Europe. I went directly to the collectors, visiting their homes with large amounts of the artists' work. More often than not, something would be bought, something would be left behind. That way, over the years, there were hundreds of works by American artists that went into significant European collections.

European dealers would never have dreamed of doing

Marcel Broodthaers

Museum

1 9 6 8

what I did. Among American dealers, I was the one to travel in depth around Europe: that gave me the choice of the best European artists such as Beuys and Broodthaers, the French artists Robert Filliou and Jean le Gac, and Ben Vautier, the French Fluxus artist and unofficial leader of the École de Nice group.

Joseph Beuys

Felt Suits (Installation view)

1 9 7 0

By the time my second gallery opened on West Broadway in 1972, I had a complement of older famous European artists to show, as well as a new generation of American artists including David Askivold, Bill Beckley, Robert Cumming, and Roger Welch. The gallery opened with a huge show of the multiples of Joseph Beuys. The New York public was stunned by the five oversized felt suits hanging on the wall, along with the famous sled. It was a European imagery unknown by the American audience at that time. The purpose of the first exhibition was to begin building an archive of the multiples work of Beuys in America, as I also did with Broodthaers, and through their works to heighten our awareness of the activities of European artists then working. With the younger Americans and the older Europeans together in the new gallery I had, as Ben would say, all my guns together.

I have shown the comic art of Ben several times in New York. Headquartered in the hills overlooking the Mediterranean and Nice, the city of Apollinaire and Yves Klein, Ben has executed a wide range of provocative and subversive works with such captions as "There is some pleasure in putting one's finger in butter," or "Suicide: right way, wrong way," accompanying a photo of the artist with a shotgun. But as Ben himself has said in another art work, "It is only a joke."

The dominant art form of the seventies was Narrative Art, a term which arose from exhibitions in my gallery of art works comprised of written texts accompanied by photographs as a form of storytelling, mostly personal stories told

Ben Vautier

I reserve the right to consider this text as interesting in the future as it is in the present.

1 9 7 1

Bill Lumberg

Detail from *Charades*

1 9 7 6

William Childress

One or Two True

Testimonies

1 9 7 8 – 7 9

by the artist. Whether unusual and disquieting or mundane and understated, these statements serve as the actual content in their work, becoming the work itself, something uncommon to the preconceived notion of where the boundaries of art leave off and the real world begins. In 1973 I did a show entitled "Story Art" with Askivold, Beckley, Cumming, Le Gac, Hutchinson, Bill Wegman, and John Baldissari; thereafter, we had one such show a year, and each time I would change the title to avoid any didacticism: the next show, in 1974, was entitled "Narrative II."

The Palais de Beaux Arts in Brussels did a major show, "Narrative Art," at that same time, again illustrating how rapid communications can be when a major new group of American artists emerges and a year later are given an exhibition in an important museum in Europe.

The art of the eighties really started in the late seventies with the "Structure" group: Bill Lundberg, Bill Childress, James Carpenter, Janet Rifkin, Leandro Katz, Noel Harding. This group of artists has arrived at an expressive kind of realism by appropriating various techniques from technology to use as a transparent filter for their ideas. The work takes on the form of installation sculpture and employs photographs, projected film, sound, and language, structured as sculptural elements.

There is a terrific intelligence informing this work, and at the same time a great accessibility in its form. The advance these artists have made doesn't lie in the discovery of new mediums, but in the use of existing ones: the technology they put to use is by now a familiar part of our lives, and the Structure artists handle it with a clarity that will make its mark on the decade ahead.

I'm reminded of a marvelous Bruce Nauman piece from 1967, a neon sculpture in the form of a circle, a form which the work of many artists has taken: Smithson, Oppenheim, Long, Hutchinson. In this work, Nauman wrote around the circle, "The true artist helps the world by revealing mystic truths." Artists turned to photography, film, and language as forms of expression, not from a desire to be photographers, film makers, or writers, but as Valentin Tatransky says, from "a desire to make art whose raw materials would be located in the real world."

The true artist reveals mystic truths: the spirit of this work is what I always look for, and go on finding, in the best work of the artists in my gallery.

Ronald
Feldman

Ronald Feldman (born 1938, Bronx, New York) left a
law career in 1970 to enter the art world, eventually
gathering together Joseph Beuys, Buckminster Fuller,
Arakawa, and others in his Soho gallery.

I was never satisfied with the practice of law, and Saturdays I'd run off to art galleries. I was driven to know how artists balanced elements, how an art work was constructed, and most of all, the reason behind its creation. I found myself reading art books and magazines instead of the law journals.

A week or two after becoming a partner in a law firm in 1970, I came home and told my wife, Frayda, that I was going to Europe the following Monday. I was going to become an art dealer. She didn't flinch, and she told me that she hadn't married a lawyer. I appreciated her support.

During my trek across Europe, I hardly slept. Not having much capital, I bought whatever I liked and thought I could sell. I came back to New York with an inventory of Miró, Picasso, Chagall, Giacometti, Rouault, and other artists who were strong on the fine-print market. More affordable than paintings, quality lithographs and etchings had been almost overlooked up to that time.

I had no idea that running a gallery was going to be a twenty-four-hour-a-day job. During our first month, I'd come home and marvel that people had actually walked in. How did they find the place? I was learning that there is a large number of people interested in art. This is one of the ingredients that makes New York so vibrant.

A gallery is an information center. The best galleries in the world are really contemporary museums, only self-funded. Some visitors actually call before a show and ask us if there is an admission charge. It's absolutely amazing – what can they possibly think we could be charging?

My attention focuses on artists who take an interest in the world about them, who tackle various disciplines and bring that information into their art, transforming it. Touch and depth of content are paramount.

The German artist Joseph Beuys is such an artist. The first show with Beuys consisted of the gallery without art objects. We were the art. People would say there was nothing there. Beuys would tell them over and over again that it was his first social sculpture. "Don't you feel it?" he would ask. Some knew immediately what he meant. Others still thought of him as a charlatan instead of a shaman.

Beuys was written up by a Wall Street newsletter as blue chip, the Picasso of our time. I received calls from all over the country asking what the paintings looked like. I told them Beuys doesn't paint. Those people hung up very quickly.

Beuys is acutely aware of media and public relations as a means to further his ideas and his art. He can handle a cigarette in the course of a conversation so that it becomes like a dance. He knows exactly when the cameras are clicking. He has a hundred different poses, which are absolutely beautiful to watch.

Beuys granted many interviews during this first visit. Because of the antimaterialist nature of his work, everyone wanted to know if he was a "Marxist"; the question was always about the economy. He struggled with this, giving several variations in his answer. Finally, Janet Malcolm from *The New Yorker* asked the same question. He replied, "Money should flow through the society like blood through the body." It is a beautiful metaphor.

I have walked along beaches and marshes with Beuys, and he knows each plant and its uses, the names of birds and water creatures and what they are called in different parts of the world. He blends this knowledge with philosophical insights. Declaring himself King of the Animals is a simile for his ecological concerns. He sees himself as a rabbit, the hare.

At the end of this century, we are going to see a whole reappraisal of what went on in the arts. One of the questions is going to be, Where was the fine cutting edge – in the sciences or the arts?

Science and technology are often viewed as the enemy of art. It is said that artists work metaphorically and that scientists work with facts. But, as Todd Siler indicates, at the moment of creation, the moment of intuition, they are as one. In our expanding society, artists are also dealing with unexplored content and different disciplines. They must create metaphors on a very high level.

Many years ago, I realized that several artists, like Arakawa and Kowalski, were turning to science and many different disciplines for subject matter. If I were going to make a context for them, it was important for me also to work with Buckminster Fuller.

One day Tatyana Grosman of Universal Limited Art Editions rang me to say that she was planning to do a lithographic book with Dr. Fuller. I readily agreed, at her request, to have an exhibition of this book, *Tetrascroll*. It took almost two years before we were able to celebrate its

Joseph Beuys

Evervess

1 9 6 8

Joseph Beuys

Without the Rose, It Doesn't Matter

1 9 7 2

completion with an opening in the gallery. Before Dr. Fuller
came in, I asked Ed Schlossberg, who had written the epi-
logue for *Tetrascroll*, "How do you address Buckminster
Fuller?" He said, "You give him a hug and call him Bucky."
That's exactly what I did. We embraced and became good
friends.

The gallery went on to do a second show, fifty years of
Bucky's drawings. When Frayda was organizing it, many of
the younger members of his staff couldn't believe that the
things that had accumulated in his drawers and files had
esthetic value. The exhibition was an enormous success.

When I met Tom Shannon through another artist in the
gallery, David Smyth, I recognized that Tom is a truly
visionary sculptor making beautiful drawings. In 1982 all the
artists in my gallery made a record album called *Revolutions
per Minute (The Art Record)*. Tom's song on the album is
absolutely amazing. "Smashing Beauty" is very much what
his work is all about — space, dreams, and our relation to the
universe.

We recently sold a sculpture of Tom Shannon's called
Compass of Love to the Museum of Modern Art in Paris. It
consists of a twenty-two-foot needle that floats above its
curved base without actually touching it. It is not hooked up
to any electrical outlet and will float that way forever. It cost
a fortune to make, and no one got rich when it was sold. But
all along I felt it was something that just *had* to be done.

A dealer definitely can guide a collector, but it doesn't
always work as one would hope. A banker once called me

about a man who had just deposited a check for $35 million. He was a retired seller of surplus government materials, and he told the banker that he wanted to get some culture. He came to the gallery with a list of pretty Fifty-seventh Street/ Palm Beach artists, the ones who look like Impressionists but aren't. I told him he could have a much finer collection, and I arranged for a private lecturer to take him and his wife to all the museums. First his wife dropped out. She had made all her beauty-parlor appointments to coincide with the museum visits. Finally he too had had enough. I asked him what his thoughts were. He pondered my question, and then told me he still wanted to buy second- and third-rate Impressionists. He still liked them and just hadn't known what to call them before. The last I saw him he was headed toward Parke-Bernet, catalogue in hand, to one of those afternoon auctions where they try to sell everything that no one wants. Can you imagine him commissioning a building by SITE?

On the other hand, we recently had a show of the highly political British artist, Conrad Atkinson. There were red hearts drawn on the walls with controversial information simply and ingeniously placed in the middle of them. When-ever we got a request, which was rare, from someone who was interested in pricing them, my staff would immediately notify me. Only daring collectors are interested in buying work on hunger, nuclear warfare, peaceful use of the atom, asbestos, or many of the things that are the subjects of Con-rad's art. These people are very special to me. In this case, we were successful in selling three of Conrad's pieces. He wrote me that I was now his best dealer. I'm still his *only* dealer.

In the beginning, I felt enormous pressure to produce money for the artists. I think they were counting on the fact that I would; and in many cases, such as Komar and

Conrad Atkinson

Northern Ireland 1968–

May Day 1975 (detail)

1 9 7 4

Eleanor Antin

Eleanora Antinova

reminiscing about her life

with Diaghilev

1 9 8 0

Melamid, I did. But in many cases I couldn't. There just wasn't an audience to buy what they were making. In the beginning, Chris Burden made nothing to sell, and Hannah Wilke's vaginal sculptures, Margaret Harrison's rape paintings, and Mierle Ukele's touch sanitation pieces are admittedly difficult art. I would not drop an artist because I was unsuccessful in selling the work. That is not the criterion. Sometimes it takes several shows before the audience realizes what the artist is doing and can appreciate the aesthetic.

Eleanor Antin's rich layering of personalities and Les Levine's complex use of media are not easy to grasp in one look. Why should they be? Helen and Newton Harrison's ecological/philosophical work is an evolving story, like chapters in a book. Doug Davis's movies and videos are the same. It is hard to catch a ghost. Terry Fox's work is very subtle, almost elusive. Like all good art, it is poetic, magical, seductive – just like the poems in Arakawa's paintings or Agnetti's beautiful voice juxtaposed with sounds from his bathroom and kitchen as recorded in his *Revolutions per Minute* composition.

The real problem is that we have many people in positions of power in the art world who have no idea what art is about. Unless the quality of the dialogue improves, we will see many of our best minds withdraw from what we call art and go about their business elsewhere. Everything opens up if we use Beuys's definition of art as a general guideline: "Art equals creativity."

A museum curator was once discussing the work of Arakawa and said he probably would not show it because it comes out of Duchamp and "he's passé now." There was nothing to say to this individual. Two brilliant artists were dismissed ignorantly and arrogantly in a misguided understanding of the roots of art. It is another thing for Beuys to state that "the silence of Marcel Duchamp is overrated" and then go on to pursue, actively and publicly, intellectual and political ideas. That is like Rauschenberg "creating" a work of art by erasing a de Kooning drawing, as he did in 1951. It's part of an important art dialogue, not merely a changing fashion. Art is an enormous game that we can play. It is certainly a lot more interesting than Pac-Man.

Daniel
Wolf

Daniel Wolf (born 1955, Cheyenne, Wyoming) studied with the photographer Minor White and graduated from Bennington College. An avid collector himself, he opened a gallery in 1977 that continually displays the full and varied range of photography, from nineteenth-century masters to contemporary innovators.

I began taking photographs at fourteen under the influence of Minor White. Working with this old, already mythical figure with gray hair made a lasting impression on me. His sense of mission, of total belief in his art, was contagious. First of all, he really conveyed his concern for the fine print; technique meant everything to him. At that young age I couldn't fully appreciate the almost mystical state of heightened awareness that he encouraged when looking at nature or at the resulting photographs themselves. These elements of his teaching struck me only later.

Still, as I watched Minor White photographing a tree, I knew even then that he was not merely interested in the thing itself; he was interested above all in the experience of looking. This search for the visual metaphor of the tree was carried out with such intensity that I've never lost the impact of his approach to imagery. But technique was always stressed. Today, because of White, I find myself taking artistic vision and technique into account equally when I look at contemporary photography. A good photographer usually takes his working process very seriously.

I was already collecting in college, and every time I discovered a photograph it was like finding a treasure. In some cases it was exactly that. During the early seventies, almost any photograph you bought in the Paris bookstores was a rarity. And you can find them today, too, but instead of paying $5 you'll be paying $5,000. Still, I don't mind. They're worth the price.

When I began to buy photographs, only a handful of people showed any interest. There wasn't the focus, the press coverage, and there certainly weren't the buyers we see today. Although the market remains small in relation to painting, sculpture, antiquities, decorative arts, and books, photography has been accepted as a fine art. It's difficult to say what brought about this increased attention; partly it was because photographs were inexpensive and available. Then too, we had seen the end of Abstract Expressionism, the end of Pop Art, and the heavy sense of detail and the objective reality in photography became attractive to a lot of people.

Precedents did exist for dealing photography as an art as far back as the 1860s, when Julia Margaret Cameron had shows in London. Photography had always been collected by farsighted curators, but the market broadened as photo-

Harold Edgerton

Shock Waves from Impact

1 9 6 5

graphs became more widely recognized as collectible.

Even before becoming a dealer, I knew intuitively that I could sell a photograph. But there was more to it than that; for one thing, photography did not yet enjoy the enlightened media exposure that painting and sculpture galleries take for granted. I knew the quality of my material but also recognized the vital contribution of the press to help the public navigate the uncharted waters of photography.

Looking at it from an economic or accounting point of view, in photography one deals with more units of art. A painting dealer might sell a few major paintings per month, even per year, depending on their value; given the nature of the photography market we do sell major $15,000 photographs to keep things going, but we also sell a lot of $300 photographs.

Since photography is a young field, the most difficult aspect of it is probably other dealers; everyone is trying to make the same sale to the same client. I've always found dealing photography to be like politics, learning to deal with people. Also, photography dealers frankly do not make enough money yet. Bitter competition arises at times.

Financially, photography dealers can make it or break it

at auction. You have to be really sharp. An auction is a dealer's territory; it's like the futures market in Chicago. You make decisions in a second that will make or lose a lot of money. Besides keeping up in New York and California, I go to auctions in Europe three times a year. I can go to an auction and not spend a dime yet walk out with anywhere from $2,000 to $3,000 by buying and selling within the auction.

Before entering the auction I know what certain people will be looking for, so I sometimes bring them together; often a flip of a coin prevents dealers from bidding against each other. You can also be paid not to bid on certain things or to bid on others. When I feel that people are bidding me up because it's I, I can have someone else bid for me at a certain point. Taking long pauses between bids draws attention to the bidding or suggests that there may be a question in your mind as to how far to go.

The photographers in my gallery fall into two categories, one of well-known masters over the age of fifty and the second of young photographers in their thirties. I use the same criterion for both, looking for the cutting edge, the unique. I have no time for work that is good merely by virtue of resembling someone else's image.

Eliot Porter, at eighty, is truly a master, a Renaissance man. When Alfred Stieglitz showed so much enthusiasm for his work, Porter left his career as a scientist at Harvard, where he taught medicine, and devoted himself to photogra-

John Coplans

Mummer's Parade,

Philadelphia, 1982

1 9 8 2

phy. He developed his own method in the highly complicated area of printing dye transfers, involving processes like
making matrixes and separations. The resulting photographs, primarily color landscapes, remain one of the great
enduring bodies of work that we have.

Art Sinsabaugh, who died in 1983, worked with a twelve-
by-twenty-inch camera to make black-and-white contact
prints. He was a master as well, a meticulous printer and
craftsman. I've gone on expeditions to the Grand Canyon,
Monument Valley, and Maine with him, roughing it and taking photographs all day. I always looked forward to those
trips. It's beautiful watching him work, seeing how he mar-
shals years of experience with a camera. He's satisfied with
nothing short of perfection.

A new addition to the older generation is John Coplans.
He is a curious figure in the art world, having been a
teacher, then editor of *Artforum,* and head of a museum in
Akron, Ohio. Three years ago he took up photography, and
after about a year I began to see his tremendous knack for
black-and-white portraits. He works harder than anyone I
know, and his first show was a great success, moving from
the gallery to the Chicago Art Institute. Although one of the
things I must cope with early in a photographer's career is
difficulty in sales, I'm patient: in the future the work of
Coplans should be widely recognized.

Out of the several hundred photographers I see each
year only three have come to my gallery out of the blue:
Sheila Metzner, Michael Geiger, and Jed Devine. Sheila
came in unannounced, during a period when I was less
interested in contemporary photography, and said, "I'd like
to show you my work." I told her I wasn't really looking, but
she insisted. Minutes went by, and after I had looked at her
portfolio I found myself saying, "I'll give you a show."
Sheila was my first contemporary, and she has always
worked in a soft-focus style with a certain Art Deco influence. She can fill a rectangle better than almost anybody I
know.

There also have been photographers I passed up
because I was not astute enough at the time or simply not in
the right mood. Jed Devine's work didn't knock me out at
first. I liked it, though, and called him back to have a second look. The longer I looked, the more I saw; finally, I told
him we were on. His subject matter varies from portraits
and landscapes to still lifes and architecture.

Sheila Metzner

Turquoise Vase—Painted

Gladiola

1 9 8 0

I was very lucky to get Jan Groover when she left the Sonnabend Gallery. To get an idea of her work, imagine two or three color photographs placed side by side, taken from the same point but with slight variations. Think of a city building with the light of a sunset against it: this is the general backdrop for one segment of Groover's work, and against it we may see a passing car or a pedestrian, or even just a shadow as it changes. Put together, they tell us about the passage of time.

Another area Jan Groover explores is the still life. Imagine you've just washed the dishes and put them in a pile to dry; cut out a rectangle very close up and focus on the corner of a pan, a dish, the handle of a spoon: the result is a very concentrated space. Groover also employs platinum prints, a technique that Jed Devine taught her, an example of the crossfertilization that can go on in the art world. Jan's work reflects a keen intelligence: the colors she gets to reflect off a simple kitchen knife are extraordinary.

It's not the easiest thing in the world to be a young photographer. Few live from the sale of their work and many teach. Although some try, very few are involved with commercial work. Generally a commercial photographer doesn't make a good art photographer, but an art photographer can make a very good commercial photographer. This is not to

225

say I don't enjoy looking at commercial photography as an
art form. Today at least, it's different from art photography.
The line was thinner in the thirties, with photographers like
Man Ray, whose work crossed over. That doesn't seem to
happen today, or maybe it's because the work is too new.
It's easier to look at a commercial photograph of the thirties
as art across the distance of time.

There is more than one category of photography to collect; there are levels of old masters and even contemporary
old masters. There remains a wonderful supply of photographs, but this will all change, and that will affect the market. The collector today who can afford to spend, let's say,
$100,000, which is not a lot in terms of buying art, can still
put together pretty much the finest collection in any area of
photography he chooses to concentrate on. The fact that
this possibility exists, now that so many other areas of art
are nearly closed to collecting, makes photography an
attractive field.

Right now $200 to $600 will buy an excellent contemporary photograph. While many collectors have thoroughly
concentrated on the nineteenth century, on the twenties,
the thirties, or the fifties, no one has stepped in to focus on
young photographers.

I am waiting for that person, for that visionary collector
with a great eye for contemporary photography who can see
where things are going. Five years ago I'd tell people to buy
nineteenth-century photography, and they wouldn't. They
missed it. Then four years ago I said buy nineteenth-century
albums, and they missed it again. Now a collector should
buy contemporary photography. There's fun in timing things
correctly. It's a game; there is a general game plan, and as a
dealer I have to be ahead of it.

I usually buy beautiful photographs every week, and I
enjoy seeing a client take home something really important;
dealing is also teaching, not just making a sale.

Photography is all about art, the eyes that relate to it,
the soul that relates to any art whether it be nineteenth-
century photographs from Burma, German architectural
details, Javanese terra-cotta, or ivories from Bali. That's
why I'm not only a dealer, but also an incurable collector: I
love to look at beautiful things.

Max
Protetch

Max Protetch (born 1946, Youngstown, Ohio) graduated from George Washington University and received
a master's degree in International Relations and Political Science from Georgetown University. In both his
galleries on Fifty-seventh Street and Lafayette Street in
Soho, Protetch attempts to bridge the gap between art
and architecture by representing such artists as Scott
Burton, Richard Fleischner, and Mary Miss, and the
architectural works of Frank Lloyd Wright, Michael
Graves, and Robert Venturi, among others.

As long as art is the beauty parlor of civilization, neither art nor civilization is secure." These words of John Dewey are written inside Siah Armajani's large-scale outdoor piece called *Meeting Garden* at Art Park, the sculpture garden in New York State. Siah is an idealist. That is not a popular position to take today, but art galleries betray economic theory. Most businesses research a market and work toward supplying an existing demand. It's just the opposite in dealing art. The serious dealer looks for art he likes and tries to convince the world of its importance.

One of my main goals is providing a bridge between art and architecture. I show architects' drawings, architectural photographs, and commissions for architectural sites, just as I show painting and sculpture. Both my Fifty-seventh Street gallery and my large, six-thousand-square-foot space on Lafayette Street are places where the art and architectural communities meet and see each other's work. Many shows center on sculptural commissions, and a great number of the sculptors in my gallery have architectural concerns. Mary Miss, for instance, is very interested in the space her sculpture will occupy; she wants to be part of the design process.

The architect Robert Venturi has on more than one occasion referred to himself as an artist; I think this enters into the discourse my gallery is trying to make. That's why Scott Burton and Armajani and Fleischner are essential figures in it. It doesn't mean that they are my favorite artists, or architects, or the best; but they are in the center of this discussion.

I exhibit the furniture of Scott Burton, an artist, and also that of the architect Frank Gehry. A show on Bauhaus will be followed by a sculpture show, and after that, architectural drawings. Work such as Armajani's fit into this spectrum, which can, and does, cohere in my gallery. It is my task to bridge the gap between disciplines that couldn't be further apart in terms of audience. Still, I see the worlds of architecture and art closing in on one another.

I never doubted that showing architectural drawing was right and would ultimately be successful; what surprised me was how quickly it happened. I thought it would take years, but now I realize that I was slow in coming to it. Obviously, I wasn't the only one who recognized that the modern movement had ended, or that the moment was almost as explosive as it was in the art world when Abstract Expressionism gave up its grip on painting.

Drawing is a very important part of architecture, and we understand some great architects such as Frank Lloyd Wright and Le Corbusier more through their drawings and writing than through their actual buildings. There used to be a taboo among modern architects against making their drawings precious; it was part of the modernist's revolt against the Beaux Arts tradition. It was all right to donate drawings to museums as archival documents, but it was in bad taste to show or sell them as if they were art. Architects don't think that way anymore. Young architects save every scrap of paper. I once asked Richard Meier if I could show some rough sketches on yellow tracing paper that I had seen and liked even more than his finished drawings. There was almost a tear in his eye when he said he'd thrown them away.

At first many architects were reluctant to have shows in my gallery. Michael Graves was the first to show, not only because his work is so strong, important, and timely, but because he was willing. He was clear as a bell that showing

Michael Graves

Garden Facade, Plocek

House, Warren, New Jersey

1 9 7 7 – 7 9

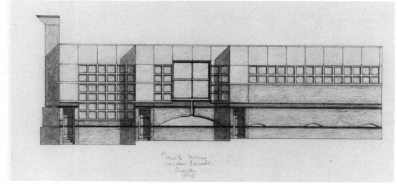

Michael Graves

Preliminary Street Facade,

Plocek House, Warren,

New Jersey

1 9 7 7 – 7 9

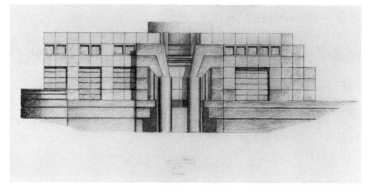

Richard Fleischner

Untitled

1 9 8 1

was the right way to make sure his work was understood. Contextually his murals are architecture and physically they are painting, and I don't care what label is put on them.

I felt similarly about showing the works of Ezra Stoller, the father of architectural photography and the first to make it a legitimate endeavor. He never thought of himself as an artist, but his work is so good, and he advanced the craft so far, that I felt very good about having it seen in a gallery.

I suppose that the two areas most important in the theoretical world these days are represented by those architects who are interested in the architecture of the city, like Aldo Rossi, Leon Krier, and Rem Koolhaas, all three Europeans, and those whose major work was formulated around the architecture of the house, like the Americans Michael Graves, Robert Venturi, Frank Gehry, and John Hejduk.

Because they are so clearly separate, I can represent many points of view without internal conflict in the gallery. But, trained on competition and criticism, architects are much more difficult to work with than artists. The architectural world is so vicious it makes the art world seem kind, cozy, and supportive. Good friends are constantly pitted against each other, scrambling to get a plum of a commission that only one can win. I admire architects and have never met a group that worked harder, or had to wear so many hats.

Sculpture is exciting on many levels. The role of the sculptor is changing in society. Its break with painting has been clear since David Smith. One can't use the language of

Siah Armajani

Closed Door—Open Door

1 9 8 1

Scott Burton

Concrete Tables

1 9 8 1

painting or architecture to describe sculpture; it is inventing its own language, one that speaks of scale, site, placement, and the role of the viewer as active participant.

The sculptor is becoming more integrated into society, far less of an outsider who shocks and upsets the viewer, but a participant whose ego is sublimated to the need of society. Much of the new work functions in very pragmatic forms. Richard Fleischner's Seattle strip-mine reclamation proposal included an apartment complex, and though his other work is less directly pragmatic, it usually involves the use of urban spaces that serve some functional public purpose. Aldo Giurgola finds Fleischner a "problem-solver" for spaces in his building projects that seem to defy typical architectural solutions. I. M. Pei and Edward Larrabee Barnes have worked successfully with Fleischner on the new M.I.T. and Dallas museums.

Many works of Armajani, Scott Burton, Jackie Ferrara, and Mary Miss are "sited" and involved with the notions of use, appropriateness, and active participation. Their work isn't an encroachment on architecture or landscape architecture but a complement to it. To say that sculpture conflicts with architecture today is as fallacious as the old architectural dictum that there is something wrong with a wall if you have to put a painting on it.

The area I find most troublesome at the moment is painting. I certainly don't believe that painting is dead, but I do see very little that I think is good. I got excited when I was very young about Abstract Expressionism and Pop Art. I began my gallery in Washington, D.C. with Pop and Minimal art. But I think the market is now forced, and like the political mood at the present time, I'm conservative. I'm not

Jackie Ferrara

Gray Gazebo

1 9 8 2

at all convinced by David Salle and Julian Schnabel.

The media, like television and movies, has a stranglehold on sensationalism. The market for painting is stronger now than ever, but I don't trust it, at least at the popular core. Style is important but transient, and there seems to be a great deal of pandering to the public. As the stakes got higher, the way paintings were sold changed, and some galleries have had more painters leave than stay. The revolving-door approach to selling art is more like the fashion industry's way of marketing clothing. The immediate future does look brighter, and younger artists seem more serious, but I'm finding more pleasure in old favorites like Golub, Mangold, LeWitt, or some new people, like the sculptors I've mentioned or Barbara Kruger, who use a new medium.

The art that moves me transcends style and its times. I

hope that the art I'm involved with will continue to have that quality. I'm not denying my interest in the business of dealing art. In fact, I find that more intriguing all the time. This is the last bastion of pure capitalism, as our product, at its introduction, has no intrinsic market. It is the role of a good gallery to create an "art market" of quality. The best artists have taught us to see. It seems logical that the best dealers could lead the public to that art.

Mary Miss

Veiled Landscape

1 9 7 9

Holly
Solomon

Holly Solomon (born 1934, Bridgeport, Connecticut) consolidated her avocations in theater, alternative-space sponsorship, and art collecting when she opened her Soho gallery in 1975. She broke new ground in the seventies by launching a movement called "Pattern and Decoration" and exhibiting artists such as Robert Kushner, William Wegman, Laurie Anderson, and Judy Pfaff. She and her husband, Horace, continue their partnership in the Holly Solomon Gallery, now located on Fifth Avenue and Fifty-seventh Street.

I n 1963, for our tenth wedding anniversary, I told my husband, Horace, I wanted a portrait by Andy Warhol and we bought the commission from Leo Castelli, with Andy's consent. He agreed, and I met Andy at a photo booth on Forty-second Street. I must have had ten dollars' worth of quarters, and he left me in the booth to do the photographs by myself. When I was done I had hundreds of pictures. I gave them to Andy but didn't hear from him for a long time. Finally Andy called one day to say he had done several portraits and that Horace and I should come over to choose which three panels we would like to acquire. When we got to the studio, eight paintings were spread out on the floor. Horace and I went over them all, telling Andy which ones we liked and why. Finally Horace asked if they were dry. When Andy said they were, Horace exclaimed, "I'll take all of them!" We were stunned.

It is interesting how many people have subsequently informed me that I don't at all resemble Andy's portrait of me. I am different from the smiling young woman in the flip hairdo. In a sense, during the heyday of Pop, I was camping. Horace and I collected, but I wasn't an important collector of the stature or seriousness of a Mrs. Tremaine or a Mrs. Bagley Wright. I was just young, spontaneous, and pretty. I played at being a little girl, the Pop Princess. The role threatened no one, and I played it everywhere at that time. Andy saw this.

Actually, as a little girl, I had two ambitions. One was to be an actress, the other to collect art. When I was a young woman, the theater was my first passion, but after a discouraging day of making the audition rounds, I would visit the museums and galleries. I began to find a new world there that came to be as rich and imaginative to me as acting. At Vassar I had seen a very fine collection of work by Calder and Arp at the apartment of one of my professors, Miss Barber. It taught me that you didn't have to be either immensely wealthy or terribly powerful to collect art. Intelligence and taste are the critical factors in collecting. This observation made me bold, and it was not long after that I walked into the Sidney Janis Gallery and asked to see a sculpture by Jean Arp. I didn't buy one, but Mr. Janis was perfect – gracious and informative. I've always felt that meeting Sidney Janis was an auspicious introduction to so much of what followed over the next twenty years. And it

Andy Warhol

Holly

1 9 6 6

wasn't too long before I did buy a piece from Dick Bellamy's Greene Gallery, a Dan Flavin in 1961 or 1962.

At first Horace wasn't interested in contemporary art. I did the collecting. But one day I brought home an object that intrigued him, a Brillo box by Andy Warhol. He decided that it was time to take a closer look. One rainy Saturday in 1962, Horace walked into a Lichtenstein show of cartoons at Leo Castelli's gallery. He thought it was sensational – the seamless continuity of the paintings and the absolute beauty of the women in them – and he bought a painting called *The Anxious Girl*. That was when we began collecting *together*, not expensive things, but beautiful things.

In 1969 Horace and I opened the 98 Greene Street Loft as a combined exhibition, performance, and poetry space. We funded it with our "collecting money" – instead of buying art, we were able to maintain a space where younger artists could work and get more public exposure than they did in a studio, but with none of the commercial pressures of a gallery. Somehow it all worked. Under the guidance of the poets Ted Greenwald and Peter Schjeldahl, and the late sculptor Gordon Matta-Clark, 98 Greene Street flourished with a spirit of brilliant improvisation. Gordon was the real catalyst: he brought people together and animated every moment.

Throughout the years, however, I've always brought something of the theater into my involvement with art. I've been drawn to "happenings," performance art, poetry-and-art projects, and of course sculpture, which I especially love; simply presenting it can become an event.

I was able to perform my plays in the studio; I guess they'd be called "conceptual plays" today. I remember showing them to Lee Strasberg, who asked, "What is this? Whatever it is, I don't want any part of it." I replied, "But this is the future. We have to stop thinking in theatrical clichés. We have to start breaking things down into *nonnarrative* plays." Lee thought I was an idiot child.

Ninety-eight Greene Street was very important for me creatively. I made a movie with the cinematographer Burt Spielvogel called *98.5*, which captures and celebrates that time. The movie was a five-part anthology about five different artists. Each segment was metaphorical. One showed George Schneeman painting two poets in his studio on St. Mark's Place. A segment called "Clay Pit" had Charles

Simonds building a house on a woman's stomach. Another, called "Windows," was about Susan Hall, a young artist, coming to New York from San Francisco. "Interview" was a satire of a television talk show with Ed Baynard, Patty Ast, and me. The fifth, Gordon Matta-Clark's piece about a garbage dump, was called "Freshkill."

The artists whose work I was seeing then believed in the active powers of art, in rituals of reuse and regeneration. In 1972 I went to Robert Stearn's studio to see the performance "Robert Kushner and His Friends Eat Their Clothes." At the end of the performance the cast and audience ate the costumes, which were made of fruits and vegetables. There was nothing fetishistic about it. It was an artist's feast, an event of great humor and style.

So many of the young artists who were coming of age at this time seemed to be motivated by a personal sense of political activism. The artists worked with a sense of the diminished powers of technology. Limitations and relative poverty were approached creatively. I was seeing it in conceptual art, and I was seeing it in artists whose work would later become associated with decoration, such as Tina Girouard, Robert Kushner, and Thomas Lanigan-Schmidt. There was a political basis to all this work, but it wasn't talked about much. They were afraid that by talking too much about it, they would neglect to do it.

Soho was like a little college town then, with the artists sitting in the Spring Street Bar and patting each other on the back. It was more damn fun than I can tell you. It was a little elite. But the day comes when the artist must break through to his audience and deal with the real world, when he can no longer gain satisfaction just from his little clique. If no one can pay the rent for his loft, where does that lead?

It was Gordon Matta-Clark, along with Richard Nonas, who encouraged Horace and me to open the Holly Solomon Gallery in 1975. I became a dealer only because I felt it was needed at the time. There was a growing number of artists that needed commercial representation, and as I knew their work best and felt capable of representing it, it was almost a fait accompli.

When I opened the gallery, the ground-floor location was a deliberate choice, as were the large showcase windows opening into the street. The windows could accommodate a painting or a sculpture, a performance or a dance. Everyone understood that the gallery represented a breakthrough. We

Thomas Lanigan-Schmidt

The Siberian Monk and the Philokalia

1 9 7 8

237

were not denying the past; we were including it. People were surprised to find that the artists were already mature, that they were not bumpkins. They had been working underground for the past four or five years, undiscovered.

The first one-person show at the gallery was by Brad Davis. I felt that his work was particularly representative of the significant change taking place in painting. It seemed that he was working from new sources, specifically Oriental and Indian, expanding them as an American looking at his heritage and coming up with a new form of decoration filtered through these cultures. It seemed to be the beginning of a movement, which later became known as "Pattern and Decoration."

Decoration has always been particularly despised in art discourse. In 1976 artists like Valerie Jaudon, Joyce Kozloff, Robert Kushner, and Mimi Shapiro were meeting and beginning to articulate their ideas about decoration. The ideas had been operative in their art and in the work of others since the beginning of the decade, but no one had identified them except the late Amy Goldin, who was an extraordinary teacher and writer. In the fall of 1977, John Perreault curated his "Pattern Painting" exhibition for P. S. 1 (the Institute for Art and Urban Resources' outpost in Queens) and wrote about the related artists in *Artforum*. In the early seventies it seemed that all the art shown in every gallery had to look alike. It was thought to show a purity of thinking.

In 1977 I presented a group of my gallery artists under the title "Pattern and Decoration" at the Basel Art Fair. The show was immediately controversial – a bit like the child everyone beats over the head when he's got nothing better to do. Because it seemed so audacious, Pattern and Decoration became a political issue. But "P and D," forging through the rag-and-bones shop of traditional decorative motifs, was simply challenging the prevailing narrow Conceptual and Minimal dicta of the seventies that decorative art could not be "serious" art. After a while, the collective phenomenon gave way to the work of individual artists. Decoration was seen as a context, not a movement. I think its lasting value has been a critical factor in the search for new imagery that has characterized the art of the last decade. Decoration was instrumental in opening art again to the richness of its visual vocabulary.

Kahnweiler is one of my models. I had the idea, from his

Robert Kushner

Mixed Emotions

1 9 7 9

Ned Smyth

Study for floor mosaic

1 9 8 1

example, that you find an artist, put the work on the wall, get a chair and sit down, and wait for people to walk in the door. They come in and either they like it and buy it, or they walk out. Again, it can get a bit more complicated than that; but it has been our experience that, by and large, collectors find us.

Years ago I was told that a great collector is very rare, and the statement shocked me. I couldn't understand it, possibly because collecting came so naturally to me. Now I agree with that appraisal. It takes more than money; in fact, some people with a great deal of money buy very foolishly.

I look upon collecting as a kind of record of one's thoughts at any given time, a journal of one's life. The passionate collector loves, of course, to proselytize his passion. Sometimes, not infrequently, he manages to convince his friends. I must say, however, that I shy away from collectors who move in packs. I tend to suspect consensus opinions. I do see these perfunctory and "correct" collections — but those people do not buy from me.

This gallery has one important function above all others: It guarantees the artist's artistic freedom. I never dictate to an artist, and I will show work even if I think it unsalable. For example, when one of my artists, Nicholas Africano, told me that he would like to do a series about rape, called

Kim MacConnel

Greek

1 9 8 0

"The Battered Woman," I said, "Oh Lordy! Do it. I don't know if I will be able to sell it, but I'll try." When you're dealing with art, you're dealing with unpredictability. Ideas emerge cumulatively from a body of work.

I never know what any of my artists will produce in the future. I don't even know what the next painting will be like. When I walk into an artist's studio, I look at more than the art. I look at how the artist lives – his books, his records, the objects he chooses to live with. I must judge his character and how he lives and how he perceives his career. It doesn't mean that I have to love the artist, or even like him, but I must respect him, which is a much bigger thing.

Judy Pfaff

Magic

1 9 8 1

Nicholas Africano

The Body and Soul II

1 9 8 2

In many ways, Laurie Anderson epitomizes so much of what I like to think the gallery is about – the personalization of one's material, and extending it to a broader audience. This is illustrated by two of her songs, "White on White" and "It's Not the Bullet that Kills You, It's the Hole." In the first song, which refers to a painting by Robert Ryman, she is rejecting art about art, and in the other she is celebrating art about life. Her metaphors are about herself and her audience's personal lives, filled with emotional content but *not* sentimental.

At every step in an artist's career there are problems, and a good artist should be able to deal with them all. I want to see the professionalism of an artist, not only in the studio but in a clear space. I also want to see how the artist conducts his affairs, how he deals with his space and his audience.

If a piece of work makes me change my perception of art and of my life, if it makes me feel that I'll never again look at a building in the same way or ride the subway in the same way, then I know the creator is a great artist.

In 1983, after fourteen years in Soho, Horace and I decided to move uptown to 724 Fifth Avenue. When we began, we weren't known by either museums or collectors, but we have long since achieved that goal. Now we want to bring some excitement uptown to a different audience.

Leo Castelli once told me he thought that my gallery had a feeling of "family" about it. I think the relationship between the artists and the gallery is a bit more complicated, but I appreciate the observation. My association with artists over the last twenty years has become the fabric of my life. They represent a kind of organic history for me, just as the gallery traces the course of our lives.

Joe Zucker

Ivan Koloff vs. Executioner

One

1 9 8 1

Charles
Cowles

Charles Cowles (born 1941, Los Angeles, California)
followed his family's publishing tradition when he
became publisher of *Artforum* after graduating from
Stanford University. A collector and former curator of
modern art at the Seattle Art Museum, he began his first
gallery enterprise in January 1980.

I started collecting art when I was about eighteen – odd things like prints by Braque, Picasso, and Cézanne, together with street-fair art from Greenwich Village and North Beach. My parents are collectors, and my father, Gardner Cowles, has been a trustee of The Museum of Modern Art for thirty years, so I was regularly exposed to the art world at an early age, as well as to the world of publishing.

When I first got involved with *Artforum* in October 1964, I was finishing my journalism studies at Stanford University. I was interested in art, and I loved California; I naively thought at the time that this was a perfect situation. And yet I still realized that if I wanted to have a *great* magazine the original objective had to be rethought – and the best way to accomplish that was to change locations.

In the summer of 1965, we moved *Artforum* from San Francisco to Los Angeles, with the idea that eventually we would go to New York, possibly to Europe. While Los Angeles was certainly booming at the time, we felt the magazine had to be in an international art center. Nicholas Wilder's gallery was across from our office on La Cienega Boulevard, and Irving Blum's Ferus Gallery was downstairs, so we had a wonderful little clique going there. We would lunch together every day at a sidewalk café with collectors and curators to discuss the facts of life and love in the art world.

Shortly after I took over as publisher of *Artforum*, I ran into Leo Castelli and Roy Lichtenstein in the transit lounge at Heathrow Airport in London, where we were all waiting for the flight to Venice for the Biennale. For the next two weeks we traveled together. It was magnificent the way Leo took me under his wing, making sure I met everyone and saw everything – in short, that I was properly introduced to the art world. Leo wanted everyone to be aware of the future potential of *Artforum*.

In 1967 the magazine finally settled in New York, where it is today. Phil Lieder was the editor who contributed the most to the magazine's quality and growth in those early days. Ed Ruscha, one of the most prominent artists on the scene in L.A., had done the magazine's design for us when we were there and agreed to come to New York on a regular basis to supervise.

After ten years with *Artforum*, I felt it was time to explore other things. Virginia Wright, then one of the most important collectors west of the Hudson, asked if I would consider moving to Seattle to start a modern department at the museum there. My initial reaction was negative, as I did not want to leave New York, but Jinny insisted, and I finally decided it might be a good idea: I could use the opportunity to rethink what I had been doing with *Artforum* and involve myself with a worthwhile project in Seattle.

The Seattle Art Museum had been a very private, one-man institution for many years. The real thrust of the museum was the Fuller Collection of Asian art, in which I had developed a growing interest. There were several important collectors of modern art in the city – most notably the Wrights, the Richard Langs, and Richard Hedreen. There was the small nucleus of a modern collection in the museum, although a wonderful Jackson Pollock donated by Peggy Guggenheim was, unfortunately, stored in a broom closet. Ann Gerber had also given her collection to the museum, which included Paul Klee and Willem de Kooning. In addition, there were about three thousand people in Seattle who considered themselves artists, creating an active if somewhat provincial scene. Mark Tobey and Morris Graves had long before moved away.

I moved to Seattle in March 1975, with the idea that I would stay for five years – a time limit set because I didn't want to lose touch with New York and the other major art centers. As it was, I insisted on taking monthly trips to New York. When you are a curator of modern and contemporary art, that firsthand view is indispensable.

Seattle was a wonderful experience, and I have no regrets. Working at a museum and being part of the staff dealing with the public was something I had never done before. What finally bored me, though, were the committee meetings. But we did very well with our limited acquisitions funds. We bought everything, from the "classics" like Roy Lichtenstein, Andy Warhol, Ellsworth Kelly, and Joseph Cornell to young Seattle artists. I felt it was important for the museum to continue to buy local work, but even more important was bringing major national artists to the Seattle community for exhibitions and lectures.

In Seattle, I learned that the Art Museum Directors' Association says that you should not collect in the areas in which you are curator. I agree; there should be no conflict. However, when I submitted a work to the museum collections committee and saw it turned down, I felt perfectly free to buy it for myself. I also started to collect in other areas,

Manuel Neri

Penance #3

1 9 8 2

particularly photography and Japanese and antique American pottery, where there was no conflict at all with my museum acquisitions.

There are two ways to run a museum – as a dead institution that accepts art and occasionally dusts it off, or as a pacesetting institution that encourages growth in a community through its exhibitions and collecting process. The latter is what we tried to do in Seattle. My experience there made me realize that I had to be more aware of the public, but by then I also knew I was more interested in private enterprise than in public service.

The day I told the Seattle Museum that I was leaving, I called André Emmerich, who had two galleries in New York, and told him I would like to buy his space at 420 West Broadway. He readily agreed, noting that he would be happy to consolidate uptown.

Having my own, fairly extensive collection gave me a good starting inventory when I opened my New York gallery in April 1980. Nevertheless, every time I've sold something from my own collection, I have conscientiously tried to buy another work by the same artist. At the time I opened the gallery, there were several good locations uptown. There has always been a certain wealthy clientele that buys art on Fifty-seventh Street. They tend to go shopping after lunch, and if they happen to shop for art rather than gloves, it's because gloves are out and art is in. The people who care about contemporary art go to Soho. I feel very comfortable downtown. It's a dynamic, growing area, and it will continue to grow. I believe that you can't sell what you can't show, and that's why I prefer the larger spaces of Soho to what is available uptown. I think that Soho will be the center of the art world for the next ten years.

I intentionally chose the European artist Mark Boyle for my first exhibition, because I did not want to be classified as a California gallery. Mark has a fine reputation in Europe, and I had worked with him on a museum tour; therefore it was logical for me to offer him his first gallery show in America.

I then made a list of the most important artists in America. My question was, which of them are not represented by New York galleries? I love Roy Lichtenstein's work, but he had been with Leo Castelli for so many years that I wasn't about to try to steal him away. Thus, I continued to cross off the artists who I knew were entrenched in other galleries.

Besides, there were too many good artists around who were
not represented. Therefore, I decided to show those artists
who needed to be seen in New York – Nathan Oliveira and
Peter Voulkos, for example.

One thing I would never do is take an artist into the
gallery who demanded resale royalty rights, where an artist
gets a percentage of the profit if his work is resold. It's a
one-sided situation that stifles and limits the market.
Ninety-five percent of what is sold as contemporary art does
not go up in value. Does that mean the artist is going to
reimburse me? No, of course not. Not being in California,
where the artist's royalty on resale has been enacted into
law, I'm not directly involved in the issue, but I am strongly
opposed to it in principle.

I have a different working relationship with each of my
artists. Some I represent exclusively throughout the world,
others throughout the United States, and others I represent
only in New York. It is the hope of an art dealer to build the
artists he represents into major figures. Contrary to what
many people think, there is no single critic who can make or
break an artist, although they certainly think they can. Nor
do I believe the old Hollywood saying that any publicity is
good publicity. If a serious critic is interested in an artist's
work, I will do everything I can to get him the material he
needs – but I do not believe in courting critics.

Technically, a gallery is a business, and the business
should make money. Before I started my gallery, I knew I
should have enough money in the bank to operate for three
years with no sales. The Art Dealers' Association does not
consider a person for membership until he has been in business for five years, because ninety-five percent of all galleries – and this is a statistic quoted by the Art Dealers'
Association – go out of business in under five years.

An art dealer should project honesty and sincerity.
Whether he is clean-shaven every day is another matter.
There are certain dealers who always wear a dark, pin-
striped suit, and there are certain dealers who are as
disheveled and disagreeable as possible. I think it's best to
present an individual image. Still, because my name is on
the door, my presence is often required, and I try to look
decent and be available as much as possible. However, if
one of my assistants has started to sell a work, I will let him
carry on, but usually at some point I do walk over, say hello
to the client, and introduce myself.

Peter Voulkos

Untitled

1 9 8 1

What is the dealer's obligation to the collector? It depends on the circumstances. Certain collectors purchase for investment, which I do not feel is the correct way to buy art. Recently a man came in and made no secret of the fact that he was going to buy for investment. I tried to explain to him my feelings on the matter. He was so cheap that he didn't even want to buy the frame the picture was in, so we removed it. Six months later he returned and asked our advice on how to frame it. At the same time he asked if he could sell the picture back to us for a profit! I of course refused and recommended the original frame we had removed.

The collecting scene is changing. There are the well-known collectors who come around to look but don't buy. They may feel that their collection is complete, or that their home is fully decorated. Then there are new, young collectors who appear on the scene daily and who are not necessarily from New York. The older collectors have long ago established their pattern of collecting, but the new collectors are open to new ideas.

An amazing amount of work is sold to people who walk in off the street. I think that is very healthy. These are people who have heard about Soho and who are interested in art. My hope is always that they will develop into serious collectors.

Unfortunately, we also get lots of these dreadful tours that come through the gallery every morning – forty little old ladies who don't understand art, don't care, and have no intention of understanding it. They're just occupying their time and paying a tour guide a fee. In September 1980, I showed the English artist Richard Hamilton, one of the most important artists alive. On that particular Tuesday morning, the tour guide told her group of ladies, "This is a young artist from Seattle." It wasn't worth my effort to correct the error. The ladies were chatting and not listening anyway.

It's rare, but sometimes there are thefts. We lost two small watercolors by Nathan Oliveira to the well-publicized art thief from Philadelphia, Dr. Waxman, who was discovered to have pilfered hundreds of small works of art from New York galleries. I wasn't aware of Waxman ever being in the gallery, nor of the things missing until sometime after they disappeared. Somehow he had gotten into the inventory room, which is most unusual. When the story broke about him in the papers, we called Philadelphia and asked,

Nathan Oliveira

Figure Six

1 9 8 3

"Do you have . . . ?" and they said, "Oh yes, we were wondering who owned those!"

The only other incident we've had of that kind was during an exhibition of Dale Chihuly in 1982 when four pocket-size pieces were taken. It was most disturbing, and finally we had to hire a guard to sit by the entrance. Luckily, both Dale and I were aware before we opened the show that the pieces were small and stealable, and we had decided they should not be signed. We also had taken photographs of each piece and recorded them with the FBI and the Art Dealers' Association. If they ever surface, we can easily claim them, but so far there's not a trace. These thefts happened shortly after the Waxman affair, and were surely influenced by his success in remaining undetected for so many years.

One of the biggest problems that all dealers have is discounts. Recently a lot of young collectors have come to

Dale Chihuly

Untitled

1 9 8 1

expect a discount and don't want to buy unless they receive
one. I price my artists as fairly as possible. If a collector
asks me for a discount he is asking me to take money out of
my pocket, or even worse, out of the artist's pocket. It's
dishonest, ultimately, to the artist.

At present I have twenty artists in the gallery. Having a
gallery offers me, in a sense, my own museum. I can show
anyone I want without asking the permission of a committee. I love the fact that the ultimate decision is mine alone.

Brooke
Alexander

Brooke Alexander (born 1937, Los Angeles, California) was educated at Yale University. His involvement with prints and graphics began at Frank Lloyd's Marlborough Gallery, and he served as director of the American branch of the British publisher Editions Alecto before opening his own print gallery in 1968. In 1975 he expanded his business and shifted the emphasis to the painting of emerging artists, including John Ahearn and Judy Rifka.

Alex Katz

Self-Portrait

1 9 7 8

At the end of the sixties a lot of artists were making prints. There was rather a boom, based on the work Tamarind had done on the West Coast. Then there were Gemini and Tatyana Grosman, naturally, who set the quality and esthetic standards. Suddenly prints became a respectable thing for good artists to do, and there was an expanding market for them. A print is a replicated image that is a real work of art, and its value is dependent upon the painting and drawing reputation of the artist. There's no point in doing them for very young artists, as it's such an expensive process.

My wife, Carolyn, and I began our print business in 1968. One of the first portfolios we published was based around an exhibition in Milwaukee called "Aspects of New Realism." I put together six artists who were in that show: Philip Pearlstein, Alex Katz, John Clem Clarke, Malcolm Morley, Bob Stanley, and Jack Beal. The kind of realism in their work had previously been overshadowed by Pop Art. By 1969 Pop Art was well established and it seemed, to me, to have shaken itself out. Anyway, I was interested in these artists who are what I call "painterly realists" and began to publish them.

Five years ago I started doing catalogues of prints that were more or less equivalent to those you would get from old-master print dealers. I would list the edition, dimensions, and medium together with a reproduction of the print. In a sense this institutionalizes the work and puts a serious stamp on the modern-print world since, aside from an occasional publisher's catalogue, there's nothing like this around. Yet in the old-master print world or twentieth-century masters area, great catalogues do exist. Doing catalogues is the responsibility of a serious modern-print dealer. I have done catalogues for Robert Motherwell, Jasper Johns, Sam Francis, Philip Pearlstein, Alex Katz, Joel Shapiro, and Neil Welliver. A catalogue is not just a sales tool. When a show is gone no one would know of it without reproductions and a small essay to preserve the occasion.

Our emphasis slowly but progressively changed from prints to paintings. I began seeing the work of a lot of young artists who were not ready to make prints, but who were doing interesting paintings. Around 1975 we started representing artists such as Martha Diamond, Margo Margolis, and Rodney Ripps, and we moved the gallery to a larger space on Fifty-seventh Street.

251

Fairfield Porter

Rocks and Shore Growth

1 9 7 5

When I began showing paintings, they were by artists whose prints I had previously published. We had published almost all of Fairfield Porter's prints, and Carolyn had noticed that every time we did one, he had made a wonderful watercolor study for it. No one had seen his watercolors for years, so we asked him to do a watercolor show. We had a magnificent exhibition of Porter watercolors in 1975, six weeks after he died.

I have a great deal of confidence and enthusiasm for the artists in the gallery, and Carolyn and I feel a very serious responsibility to the artists we represent.

Many artists fall by the wayside between the ages of twenty-five and thirty-five. A young artist whose work has interesting qualities may grow and come to fruition, but he may also become interested in something else or find that painting is too hard and give it up. It's really a roll of the dice, and one never knows what is going to happen. One mistake can be showing an artist too early. The work may be there before he is ready mentally, and if he has some success at that point he may become afraid to take chances and to explore his images fully. On the other hand, sometimes with a little encouragement an artist can burst wide open and expand his expressive range: look at Julian Schnabel – he is a young man who has had the encouragement and the energy and ambition to follow it through, with the result that he has opened up a very wide spectrum for

Martha Diamond

Façade

1 9 8 2

252

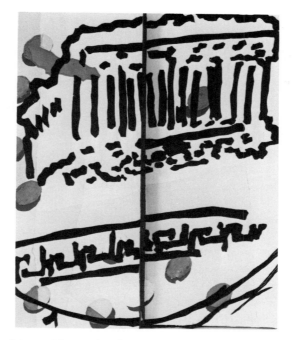

himself in which to make works of art.

It is the responsibility of a dealer to be straight with an artist about his work. He must represent the eyes of the world; he must offer genuine encouragement and also be able to tell an artist that something isn't up to standard or that he's been goofing off and must get down to it and do better. All the while the artist must know that the dealer is 100 percent behind him. The sympathy of mind and community of interest between artist and dealer must endure above all else.

I try to monitor what's going on, scouting the alternative spaces like White Columns, P. S. 1, or Artists Space. I have an endless number of announcement cards with notes and names scribbled on them, which I occasionally review in order to remember the names. I looked very hard at the Times Square Show in 1980. There were many interesting artists who at the time were not necessarily ready for anything more, but I've stayed in touch with them because I liked the energy and thrust of that show. Even if artists are not yet ready for commercial galleries, one can often see a glimmer of things to come in those early stages.

I am now involved with three artists who have emerged in this way: John Ahearn, Richard Bosman, and Judy Rifka. I became aware of Judy Rifka through the Times Square

253

Show and her association with Colab. I first saw her work on Eldridge Street, where she was living in what I would call her "deep bohemian phase." I mean, the place was not what you would call comfortable. I was very impressed with her because she said, "I've had it with this stuff; it's time for me to get serious." I said, "That's great, but I don't really connect with the work yet. Let me see what happens next." Three weeks later she called me and said, "I've done a new series of paintings I think you'd like to see." There were twelve of them, and they were terrific. Only much later did I learn that she referred to them as "the Labors of Hercules."

From her early promise in 1973–1974 when she showed at the Bykert Gallery, Rifka had decided to do what I'd call basic investigation on herself. Once she was asked to do an issue of *Art-Rite*, a short-lived magazine published by Walter Robinson and Edit de Ak. Rather than do something for reproduction, Rifka did two thousand drawings, and each copy of the magazine was unique. It took six months of steady work. Edit has a few copies, but nobody knows where the rest are. I was enormously impressed by her ability to stick to a project like that. That basic material is something she's drawn on subsequently. Having gone inward and now outward again, she's really ready to take on the world. Discipline is crucial. If you look at the concentration of Jasper Johns when he's working on something, it's unbelievable. I've seen him working on prints, and his attention, in the maelstrom of activity – people proofing things, changing colors, doing all that – is absolutely extraordinary. He's totally focused on the object at hand.

When I first went to Richard Bosman's studio, I found the work interesting, but not in a form I could show. Sometimes you like an artist's turn of mind more than what he does. I went to his studio eight or ten times over the next two years, and each time the work had changed. All of a sudden, at exactly the point I thought would be the final visit, he turned out something that was fascinating: it was a series of little linoleum cuts he'd printed very crudely on cheap paper – absolutely extraordinary and very personal. I said, "These things have such great feeling to them, such power." He said, "Yeah, well, I've done a couple of paintings like that, too." He brought them out. Six months later he was in the Illustration and Allegory show.

A great collector, Morton Neumann from Chicago,

became interested in Bosman's work and was thinking about a picture with a polar bear in it, but couldn't make up his mind. I became impatient with him and pressed him for a decision which he wouldn't make. I then sold the picture to someone else and he was furious. He said, "Around 1952 I passed up a Picasso still life with a lobster in it and was so sick about it afterward that I couldn't eat lobster for twelve years." I said, "Well, Morton, not many people eat polar bear these days." We worked it out, though, and he got a terrific painting from Richard's next show.

One's perception of things keeps changing. What I may have thought outrageous in 1967 I might find totally passé at this point. But I think it a good thing for people to have a violent reaction to new work they are seeing for the first time. If they react that way, it means the work has taken hold, whereas thinking that the work is *nice* is usually a dismissal. If you have a violent reaction, either hate or rapture, then you have something you can work with.

For example, Paula Cooper and I put together a collection for a law firm, a mixture of paintings, sculpture, and prints. Paula's and my sensibilities work well together; there is a large spectrum where we agree, but there is disagreement at both ends, something I prefer to total likemindedness when working with another dealer. We learned a lot from working with a committee of partners from the firm. Part of their profession is to reason and to refute, and they spend their time either in litigation or in constructing complicated deals for taking over companies, and I found it a challenge to present them with something unfamiliar. It threw Paula and me back on our own resources, and we came out the better for it. Most of them were not unfamiliar with art, and in general they were sympathetic. We were showing them what we thought had merit and quality. Many times they would reject a work initially and approve it three months later when we showed it to them again. Sometimes by the time they came to appreciate a work they had initially been skeptical about it would be gone, but we did sell them a wonderful and important Donald Judd sculpture which they accepted after seeing it several times.

Dealing with a private collector is different. Corporate committees have rules concerning what is appropriate for offices (no nudes, for example), but the private collector can be a little more lively and can get into something more risky or problematic.

Richard Bosman

The Kick

1 9 8 2

255

Patrick Lannan was a collector with an incredible enthusiasm for younger artists. He's about seventy-five years old, a self-made man from Chicago, a boxer in his early days, on the board of I T & T, a former publisher, and a great patron of poetry and the arts. He even established his own museum, the Lannan Foundation Museum in Lake Worth, Florida. In 1980 Patrick and I went to the Times Square Show together. Both of us were fascinated by the work of a young artist named John Ahearn. He has a very serious social commitment to the people of the Bronx, where he lives and works out of a storefront studio. He makes plaster casts of people's heads, and often hangs one of the heads outside the store. People walk by, blacks and Hispanics, and ask him, "Hey man, how do I get one for me?" and that is the beginning of a dialogue. He makes two casts, one for the sitter as a portrait and the other for some project of his own. As part of the process he also takes a Polaroid picture of the subject, and after the cast is made he paints it based on the Polaroid. He has likened himself to the itinerant portraitists of nineteenth-century America who traveled from town to town.

Lannan badly wanted to acquire a whole installation of Ahearn's work for his museum and asked for my help. He also wanted to see the work where it is made. Although he

John Ahearn

Louis with Bite in Forehead

1 9 8 0

256

didn't feel well, Patrick insisted on making the trip to the Bronx, and John started hanging casts on the wall. Patrick loved them, and he told Ahearn, "I want to buy six of them, and I want you to do your own installation." Ahearn was not sure that Palm Beach was the context his casts of blacks and Hispanics should be seen in, but Patrick explained that the museum was primarily educational and that the Foundation provides bus service and tours to school districts in the region. We described the collection, which Lannan had been assembling since the early fifties, from a wonderful early Calder and several Morris Louis paintings to a great Judd box and the first piece that Joel Shapiro ever sold. John was still reluctant to make the commitment, and as Lannan left the studio, he said in an ironic tone, "Grant a dying man his wish." John eventually went down to check out the situation for himself and felt his art would indeed be well placed there, and he designed his own installation, to everyone's satisfaction: the artist, the dealer, and the collector.

I'm in the process of getting together a stable of new, young artists. I want to put together a cohesive group of painters, integrated into what I show already. Paula Cooper and Leo Castelli each has a group of artists whose energies support one another, bounce off each other, and look great in one room. When the work of Johns, Rauschenberg, Stella, and Judd is seen together, there's nothing passive.

A lot of voices have a chance to be heard in the eighties, and people's minds seem to be wide open. I don't like the word "pluralism," because it implies that anything goes. Things that seemed to be problematic and out of favor five years ago look pretty worthwhile now. There's an atmosphere today in which many different kinds of talents can flourish, and you find a lot of different energies. It's a real challenge to the younger artists who are coming up, as well as to the older ones at whose heels they are nipping.

When there was a hegemony of Minimalism in art, there was a sense of repression that came with it. There was a seriousness with no place for humor or violence. The spectrum for expression had narrowed to what I would call airless high art. But I've always thought that art and life are the same; one wants a bit of the fabric of the real world. You find that with great novelists, so why not with artists?

Patricia Hamilton

Patricia Hamilton (born 1948, Upper Darby, Pennsylvania) graduated from Temple University and received a master's degree in art history from Rutgers. After apprenticeships at the Clark Institute in Williamstown, Massachusetts, and the Whitney Museum, and a brief period as managing editor at *Art in America*, she opened her own gallery in 1977.

If I hadn't become an art dealer I think I would have been a vicious attorney. I would have been a great litigator. Instead, I decided to take my masters degree in thirteenth-century Italian painting.

When I arrived in New York in 1971 to look for a job, a friend who worked for an art dealer advised me not even to try breaking into the New York art world: it was so small, so exclusive, that I would just be wasting my time. But I did my best to ignore this friendly hint, and in the end my idealism, or naïveté, landed me a job at the Whitney Museum. The curator I worked for, Robert Doty, was doing exciting shows of artists like Lucas Samaras. He let me do things that underlings never get a chance at, and I learned a lot about caring for art and the installation of shows from him. I loved working at the Whitney, but who can live in New York on $7,000 a year?

If there ever was a person who shouldn't be a magazine editor, it is me. But that was my next job, at *Art in America*. Editors have to be meticulous, and after six months we all admitted it was a mistake, and I left. I didn't want to leave New York, so I found a position with the art dealer Andrew Crispo. I am still very proud of the exhibitions I mounted there, such as "Ten American Masters of Watercolor," for which I sorted through hundreds of watercolors to arrive at a show of Avery, Burchfield, Demuth, Hopper, Homer, Marin, Pendergast, Sargent, and Wyeth.

Then with Jay Gorney, who is now my associate director, I organized at Crispo's the first Matta exhibition New York had seen in years. It was a whirlwind show put together in three weeks, catalogue and all.

More and more the idea of dealing pictures appealed to me. I decided to get involved with corporations on my own and also organized exhibitions for museums outside New York. I put together a drawing show that went to six museums and got a National Endowment grant for a sculpture exhibition.

A lot of artists I knew kept telling me to open a gallery; I was about twenty-five at the time. One night I sold a $60,000 Burchfield watercolor, and that made me think more seriously about what I could do with a living artist I really believed in. But I had to figure out a way to finance a gallery.

Galleries financed by one backer are a disaster. One

fight and it's all over. So I decided to have a bunch of backers and raise money as you do on Broadway, by playing a little song from the show. I went around with a slide show and a letter of intent from each of the artists that stated, "If Patricia Hamilton opens a gallery on Fifty-seventh Street in 1976 I will be represented by her exclusively."

The next step was to look for a space, and I had a whole psychology in choosing to be uptown: the artists I wanted to show were all at the uptown stage in their careers, and a lot of collectors don't make it downtown. When I saw a space on Fifty-seventh Street, the Maximillien Fur Storage, I knew I had made the right choice.

A seventy-five-page prospectus came next, listing the artists, indicating what they had sold the year before, what I expected to sell, what my expenses would be, cash flow charts, rent, utilities, trucking, insurance. I stated my reasons for locating on Fifty-seventh Street, including an article by John Russell. There was a lot of legal mumbo jumbo concerning limited partnership, which my gallery is.

Around Labor Day I started raising the money. I did it in a remarkably short time, although for me it was sheer hell. Very simply, it involved asking people to put capital into a high-risk investment. Many trusted my eye but had doubts about my business ability. Some prospective backers wanted me to cut back to 33⅓ percent, but I kept 51 percent of the gallery. Any time there would be a vote about gallery policy, I wanted to know who would win.

By February we were open. My initial shows were the first clues that the year would be hell. Clement Meadmore and Deborah Remington, the two people I had thought were going to be my big sellers, didn't do as well as I had hoped. I had fifteen backers calling me every day to ask what I had sold. My social life was nonexistent. It took me about two months to get really scared: I didn't know if I could do it.

Our group shows for the first year were museum quality. One called Sculpture in the Constructivist Tradition had large blow-ups on the wall of Rodchenko and Tatlin works, with the sculpture of Sidney Gordin, Clement Meadmore, Robert Murray, Snelson, di Suvero, and Witkin. The next year David Hare, a gallery artist, was shown at the Guggenheim, and we started selling a lot of paintings. Then Robert Murray had a successful show.

I was inclined to show artists with safe markets. I didn't take any real chances and couldn't relax until the following

Austé

I Look at You

1 9 8 1

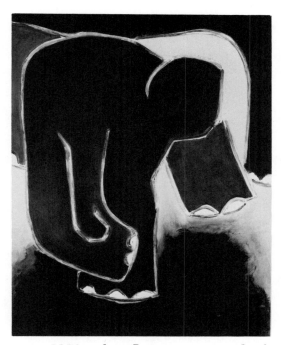

David Hare

Elephants and Violets No. 5

1 9 7 9

year, 1978, when I went out on a limb with a show called
"Color and Structure," paintings that are not just two-
dimensional but contained sculptural elements coming off
the wall. From then on there was a whole different feeling in
the gallery. By the time I started representing the painter
Ron Gorchov I began to understand the phenomenon of the
hot artist, the hot show. A new breed of collectors started
coming in, and that's when I knew it was going to happen.

I grew to like tougher work, wanting to be more challenged by what I showed. I found artists like Rafael Ferrer,
who were doing more outrageous work than I had considered in the past. The sculptors were weeded out to only
those who were having a great deal of success, and most of
them are now on waiting lists. I stopped showing the sculptors with whom I was having no success.

I've worked a lot with outdoor sculpture commissions for
parks and public grounds. Uncle Sam should get more
involved the way museums do, trying to make the public see
that this is good art. That's no easy task. Then sometimes it
works out very well. The Rafael Ferrer piece in the Bronx
has been one of the few sculptures with no graffiti because
the people love it.

Since the sixties there have been so many different
movements, and I saw that an eclectic gallery would fill a lot

Richard Hennessy

Stay of Execution

1 9 8 1

of gaps. My motivation was to give a second chance to people whose work I believed in. In the seventies, photographs, film and other media came into their own, as art was redefined to include a wider range of activities. But one thing that has come back is painting. Painting is alive and well.

I think a lot of young artists started with Surrealism and are expanding that vocabulary. I see a movement toward Surrealism in the whole figurative scene, of which David Salle is an example. But presenting only one cultural viewpoint can limit clients and sales. Some galleries have a very strict dogma, but I don't want to be limited to a particular movement. I chose to show an artist like Austé because I consider her the best of a particular movement.

The artists I showed initially were in midcareer but as yet not blue chip, due either to a bad experience with a dealer or just to being in the wrong place. Sometimes a good abstract artist like Richard Hennessy is showing in a gallery that only shows realist paintings. You have to have the right artist for the right gallery.

I don't show many artists who haven't shown before, so there is a history already. Still, I talk to critics before an exhibition, write a good press release, call the *New York Times* and ask them to see the show. I talk up the artist to my best collectors six months ahead of time. If I'm trying to sell you a picture, I better know that it's more than merely beautiful, and many times they are not pretty pictures. In those cases I provide the collector with the reasons why that painting will compel him to look at it for twenty years; a merely pretty picture loses its interest within a year.

Since most artists I show came to me with a market value already established, I increase their prices a little if I can say that the work is a bargain. I thought Hennessy's paintings were wildly underpriced, so when I first took him on I increased them 10 percent and still thought they were low. I sold quite a few, then for his first show I increased them another 10 percent. I've been telling collectors that he is a very good painter, underpriced because he hadn't been exhibiting, and that what I'm giving them at this point is a bargain. You can be piggy about it, but if you have people beating down the door at $10,000, raising prices to $15,000 is not a problem. You raise it to $15,000 and some will resist, some won't. If he's hot, he'll hold. Generally, I don't

Joan Snyder

Symphony V

1 9 8 2

like to raise prices over 50 percent in one year. For that huge a jump I need people who are screaming for pictures.

I give a pretty good pitch on investment and understand what an investment means, how easy a turnover it is. I can tell a collector that something is a good investment, but I can't say that if he gives it back to me on a Tuesday, he'll have his money on Wednesday. You do not always get your money back quickly, but you can do very well. You can double your money, though sometimes it will take time to sell. Of course, if collectors are standing in line for a painting by an artist like Joan Snyder, you could have your money the next day. That's rare. It's never happened in my situation. I try not to lead collectors on, and I don't want a work bought only as an investment. I discourage the purchase if it will just be stuck in a closet. I want them to like the painting.

Martin Silverman

Passion

1 9 8 1

Michael David

Between Seduction and

Subversion

1   9   8   2

For years, I stole mailing lists everywhere I worked. But I don't think that you can choose your collectors. As far as I'm concerned, if the check clears, they're wonderful. Anyone can buy something from me as long as they pay. I'm not snooty about saying you're not ready to buy a Rafael Ferrer. Anyone willing to pay the price is ready. On the other hand, where a waiting list is involved, museums get first preference.

With corporate collections you deal with a panel, and they all have to decide. A private collector can make a fast decision, and generally pays faster than corporations. Sam Hunter is an example of an art consultant who is doing his job with style, but in his case he is the only one who selects. That's the ideal situation. Mary Lanier also buys for corporations, and when she makes a decision, it's sold. It's done very well, but again, there are exceptions to the rule.

There weren't many powerful female dealers when I started; I thought there was room for a woman, and I wanted to be big bucks as a female dealer. Virginia Zabriskie was not as big as she is now, Holly Solomon had just opened, and Paula Cooper is so understated that I wasn't aware of how important she is. Mary Boone wasn't around at all. So most of the women dealers I knew, no matter how great, like Betty Parsons, were not major league. I thought there was room for a woman in the major league.

I have a good reputation for working with other dealers and sharing artists. A commission is allocated to the other dealer, 10 percent if you have a really hot artist and you're doing him a favor, 20 percent if it's an artist you can't sell yourself. But I have a mean, nasty temper when somebody doesn't abide by his agreements, doesn't pay, or damages work. I'm not a nice person to fight with.

I have dreams about paintings. Sometimes you can't stand it, you want to collect the art you show. From Labor Day to Memorial Day you are an art dealer every day of the week and every night; you'd become a phenomenal bore if the only thing you're interested in were art, but there are worse occupational hazards. When I see a painting that I cannot stand another minute without having, all I can do is convey that feeling to others. If someone else starts losing sleep over it, then I know I've succeeded in what I set out to do.

Miani Johnson

Miani Johnson (born 1948, New York City) began working soon after her graduation from Barnard College at the gallery founded by her mother in 1938. Gradually assuming the directorship of the Willard Gallery, she added new artists such as Lois Lane, Susan Rothenberg, Ralph Humphrey, and Kenneth Price to a roster that includes Morris Graves and Mark Tobey.

My mother, Marian Willard, started the East River Gallery in 1936. She showed, among others, Paul Klee, Lyonel Feininger, Alexander Calder and David Smith. In 1940 she moved west on 57th Street to Madison Avenue and changed the name of the gallery to Willard. Mark Tobey and Morris Graves, whom we still represent, joined the gallery in the early 40s. For thirty years the Willard Gallery presented solo exhibitions of these and other artists as well as a diverse range of thematic shows, among them Japanese screens and early American folk art.

Nothing was ever said about following in the family art business, but the whole incarnation of my mother's gallery left its impression; it was all around me, and even though I eventually showed art from a different time, my mother's influence was always there.

I started work in the gallery after college. One thing was clear: I would give myself five years to see if I wanted to be an art dealer. My mother was very generous and gave me an open hand, and by the time five years had passed I was so totally involved with the artists and gallery that there was no looking back.

Morris Graves

Bird Masking

1 9 5 3

First, I wanted to find artists from my own generation. I gradually started meeting painters and sculptors my own age, finding out about the contemporary downtown scene by visiting studios, as well as alternative spaces like 98 and 112 Greene Street and Artists Space.

As I explored what the new artists were doing, we continued to show artists from the old days like Morris Graves and Mark Tobey. Morris Graves is best known for using the bird as a personal metaphor. He is a very private man. He lives on a lake in the redwoods of northern California, and visiting him is like going back to seventeenth-century Japan. Since the early forties he has done paintings of nature with oriental and mystical overtones. His recent still life paintings are celebrations of the many species found in the virgin forest where he lives in the Pacific Northwest. My mother helped to prepare the catalogue for a retrospective of his work at the Phillips Collection in Washington, D.C., in September 1983.

By 1976 I had already had one-man shows of John Duff, Ken Price, and Susan Rothenberg. I was beginning to see that very much in isolation, almost secretly, various artists who had been doing abstract work were using imagery

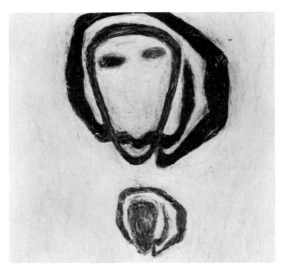

Susan Rothenberg

Untitled #147

1 9 8 0 – 8 1

again, each in a different way. It was taboo at the time to work representationally, but these artists felt that they could use recognizable images as formal devices without losing those images' evocative qualities. In spite of the diffi-culty, and the danger, of categorizing artists, I did a show in 1976 called "Abstract Images", which included Lois Lane, Susan Rothenberg, Neil Jenney, and Joel Shapiro.

I remember my shock when I first found myself attracted to a painting with an image in it. It was when I first saw Susan's work. I was totally prejudiced against "realism" and considered only abstraction to be "serious" art. However, when I saw the way Susan was using the horse it made sense to me that an artist could take an extremely familiar image and use it to make paintings about space, light, flatness, and surface, plus offering the viewer an intense emotional experience. Over the years Susan has explored these same ideas, while constantly evolving and changing her image. The horse was gradually taken apart, its place taken up by abstracted heads, hands, figures, sail-boats, swans.

Lois Lane's work, which uses images like trees, snakes, and birds, was even more perplexing to me. It took a full year of being bothered by it to get me back to her studio. Lois is a Brontë-type character with little need for the out-side world and a very full fantasy life. For this reason her paintings often puzzle people until they see that they are not symbols so much as emblems, personal abstractions of her private experiences. Rather than yielding a specific mean-

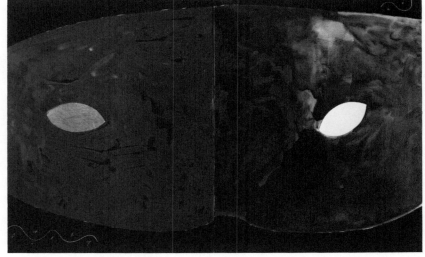

ing, these abstractions, in fact, often work somewhat like a Rorschach test, often revealing more to the viewer about the viewer than about Lois.

Quite a number of the artists I show make objects, either free-standing sculpture, or sculpture which attaches in some way to the wall. Robert Lobe carefully selects a site and pounds aluminum over the formation of rocks and trees. He then removes the "rubbing" and reassembles it, in or out of doors. Barry Ledoux, who admits to being influenced by Joseph Beuys and Joel Shapiro, uses lead and copper to build his body/clothing metaphors. He uses lettering, wax hands, insects, day-glo paint, and lead gloves in his assemblages to convey very specific bits of information about very personal emotions. His work is a sculptural embodiment of the current expressionism that has so far been seen in painting. He also uses clothing as a base, but from a totally different starting point. Judith Shea began making wearable clothing and has gradually become more interested in how clothing-derived images look without the body. Her sensibility is cool, classical, and geometric. In her most recent work folding, primary color, and basic geometry are now giving way to moodier, muddier, more three-dimensional forms. One of the sculptors I show uses clay. Ken Price began making clay sculpture in the late 50s in California. In recent years he has worked in two very different ways. One, "Happy's Curios," based on a Mexican vocabulary, has literally hundreds of scene-painted pieces set into cabinets he calls "units." His single geometric pieces—the other mode—are

269

highly colored, planar, cubistic, even architectural statements.

I like the fact that the artists in my gallery range in age from their late twenties to their early seventies. The youngest artist I show is Tod Wizon. His work relates to the early twentieth century American artists such as Dove and Hartley. He paints in small format, using acidic colors and visceral forms which can be read in a number of ways: highly charged landscapes, anatomical forms, or as pure abstractions. I have found that ambiguity of this sort is an element which I look for in art. It allows the viewer to use his own imagination, expanding the experience of the work and making it constantly provocative and interesting for repeated viewings.

The closest objective source of judgment that I have is my memory: if I'm still thinking about the work I saw in a studio two days after a visit, I find it a very good indicator that something's going on there. Perhaps it's because memory is such a close neighbor of the unconscious.

You never know which phase of an artist's output is most important until you can look back. Five years ago a particular painting by Lois Lane seemed out of place to me, an oddball picture; now I can recognize it as the beginning of an important phase. There are times when the most unpopular painting in a show will be hailed by critics at a later date as the important one, or at least the most transitional. Then how can a dealer price work? I feel that new work can be priced only by size in the beginning: you cannot price according to quality because there is no way to know what will be, someday, the most coveted. I always tell my artists to keep back enough of their own work for themselves as the only alternative in the absence of re-sale laws.

The position an art dealer places himself in is never a question of taking sides, or choosing between artist or collector. No matter how different their lifestyles and expectations may be, artists and collectors are not in an adversary relationship. The demands made by these two sides, each wanting something from the other, define the space within which every dealer works.

Everyone sees what he or she wants to. Susan Rothenberg's paintings are almost coincidentally identified with today's attachment to Expressionism. There could be so many other ways of viewing her work. I think there's going to be another, cooler phase coming along soon, not the

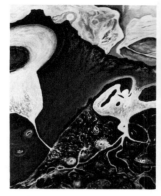

Tod Wizon

Gradient

1 9 8 0

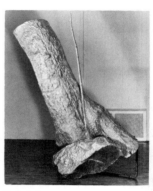

Bob Lobe

Trees

1 9 8 1

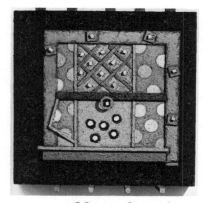

Ralph Humphrey

Ground Control

1 9 8 1

return to Minimalism, but something less narrative than a lot of the work we are seeing today.

In some ways the strength of recent figurative painting points up the even more difficult challenge of making convincing abstraction. I have always maintained an interest in abstract works, even more strongly in recent years. Joan Thorne and Harriet Korman have consistently adhered to abstraction. Ralph Humphrey's latest three-dimensional paintings sum up two decades of exploration of virtually every issue of abstraction, and his way of combining an Abstract Expressionist approach to surface and color while imbuing the paint with light has been very influential on a younger generation of artists. The hardest thing to do at this point, as before, is to make a truly convincing abstract painting.

Joan Thorne

Zamba

1 9 8 2

Mary Boone

Mary Boone (born 1951, Erie, Pennsylvania) attended
Rhode Island School of Design and worked at Klaus
Kertess's Bykert Gallery before going on her own in the
1977–78 season. Her small stable of thirteen artists
includes many of the leading painters of the early

Historically there are two kinds of art dealers: the kind I call the Kahnweiler type, who discovers artists when they are just starting out, as Kahnweiler discovered Picasso, Braque, and Léger; and the Duveen type, who deals with either very established artists or their estates. Today, these two types are most clearly realized in Leo Castelli and Arnold Glimcher. Since I began with young, mostly unknown artists myself, one can say that I see things from the Kahnweiler viewpoint.

It's curious how people become art dealers in the first place, because there are no formal parameters that dictate how it should be done. My studies in art had concentrated on the Italian fifteenth century, but while I like detailed information, I was never well suited temperamentally to being an art historian, spending hours and hours in the past. I attended the Rhode Island School of Design to make art, which at the time was what I thought I was going to be doing. But at the ripe old age of sixteen I realized that what I loved most was talking about art; I loved putting ideas together and seeing where the new tendencies in art were going.

When I went to work for Klaus Kertess at Bykert Gallery in 1973, I still had no idea that I would end up a dealer myself. Klaus Kertess is a special kind of art dealer; he is an art historian himself and always stressed that aspect at Bykert, sometimes to the point that business suffered; yet Klaus discovered people like Brice Marden, Chuck Close, Dorothea Rockburne. There were a lot of young artists coming through the gallery, Ross Bleckner among them. It was a very exciting place.

By the end of my second year at Bykert, I had stopped making art altogether. I realized that my job as an art dealer was in fact consuming my life. I left the gallery in 1975 to take as long as necessary to decide whether to be an artist or a dealer, but within three months I began to miss working in the gallery; in the end, dealing art won out.

I knew that the life of an artist in New York takes place in a more hierarchal structure than anywhere else; most of his dealings are with his gallery, and he seldom knows more than a narrow range of collectors. It's really the art dealer who has contact with both the art world and the world outside. I realized that the public role was the perfect one for me.

Anselm Kiefer

Ikarus I

1 9 7 6

The next decision was the question of opening a gallery or working for someone else again. People offered me jobs, but by this time I had very definite ideas about what kind of art I wanted to be associated with. I had been involved with artists like Sol LeWitt, Robert Mangold, and the reductive, intellectual strain at the Bykert Gallery, and now that my tastes were even more defined, I found no gallery where I'd be able to stand behind the work completely.

In deciding to go on my own, I wanted to create a gallery space that had the humanistic feeling of the art that I liked, humanistic not only in terms of how it was made, how the shapes, forms, and textures were generated, but also in size. In 1977, I took a space at 420 West Broadway.

Dealers in the 420 building all had started with artists at the outset of their careers, following the Kahnweiler format. It made a neat package when I moved into a building where Castelli represented the sixties; Sonnabend the sixties primarily in Europe and the European counterpart of Pop, Arte Povera; Emmerich the Greenberg group of the early sixties; and John Weber the Minimalism of the seventies. My gallery happens to feel very youthful and exciting right now because I show more unknown artists.

I had witnessed the rise of Minimalism in the mid-sixties, but ten years later Minimalism had become clearly fixed historically. People were itching for something new, and the most interesting young artists were not third-generation Minimalists. They were artists making a direct reaction against many aspects of Minimalism, doing something very smart, very intellectual, while at the same time very emotional, totally opposed to the austerity of the period just before. The work was very *made*; you felt the touch of the human hand again.

While I'm of the youngest generation, I think that the method I use to pick my artists differs very little from that of my elders. Not having had the scouts like Dick Bellamy or Ivan Karp, whom Castelli consulted, I went to studios myself and looked at all the work I could, listened to everything, and found I was being led by one new artist to another.

I had met Ross Bleckner while I was at Bykert. I went to his studio in 1975, and he interested me from the start. Since then, his work has changed radically, but what I originally saw was quite allusive, with almost formal tendencies. I was beginning to sense that the new art was moving in a direction of psychological narratives. Even in the abstract work of someone like Bleckner, there was a psychologizing of shapes; I can't call them images, but they were forms one could name, as opposed to pure abstract painting.

Through Ross, I met Julian Schnabel, who was keeping a low profile in New York and spending a lot of time in Europe and Texas during the mid-seventies. But when I did see his paintings for the first time I was immediately captivated, almost to the point that I didn't trust my own judgment. That first visit to Schnabel's studio had a staggering effect on my perceptions of art. What I saw was totally opposite from the antiemotional work of the most applauded

Julian Schnabel

St. Francis in Ecstasy

1 9 8 0

David Salle

Cut Out the Beggar

1 9 8 1

artists of the time, people like Brice Marden with their cool, reduced surface. Schnabel's painting was figurative and awkward, going against every current view of what was "beautiful." The raw, physical canvases were almost badly made; the stretchers didn't have the right corners, and the pictures themselves were ungainly and garish, to say the least. They were totally outlandish.

That same year I met David Salle. I was very ambivalent about his work when I first saw it at Artists Space. Salle tends to do figures that are overlaid on a background of other figures. There is a lot of pentimento in the paintings, and they are very thinly painted but have a clear physicality. I had very strong feelings about his work, but they weren't completely positive. Yet Salle's work confused me enough to want to keep going back; it piqued my interest.

It was four years later, in the spring of 1979, that I went back to see David Salle at his studio. It was getting close to the edge. I knew I was about ready. By September the paintings he had produced really began to interest me. He had always used one skin of paint and then painted over that; what he had added now was a second color, putting a

Gary Stephan

Century

1 9 8 3

frontal figure over that second skin. It changed the impact totally.

I really loved those new paintings. We started talking. He had a semiprivate show with Annina Nosei, who wasn't sure she would open a gallery. After that show, Salle came to my gallery. He was good friends with Schnabel, Bleckner, and Gary Stephan, and felt he would be comfortable in that company.

I have no prerequisites when looking at new work. Even though I see a correlation among all artists I admire, I don't go in looking for pattern painting or figurative painting. All the work I like proffers an emotional response as well as an analytical one. This usually means figure-ground relationships, which is not to say the work has to be figurative; it can be something as abstract as Gary Stephan's clear spatial relationships. It's only in looking at work in retrospect that I can see any connections.

The correlation between my background interest in fifteenth-century Italian art and contemporary art is fairly oblique. I may see the connection, but it's rare that others do. The early Renaissance saw the first introduction of space and a very special use of lighting from several sources. Because the use of space was still fairly unsophisticated, with single or double perspectives, it tends to be on different planes, very much like David Salle's work today. Architecturally during that whole period, things looked a lot like Gary Stephan's. Because they're dealing with psychology, a number of these artists also are involved with a certain spirituality. Looking at Julian Schnabel's paintings we recognize that they have a spiritual nature, and an allegorical aspect just as Medieval and Renaissance art introduced a narrative for the viewer.

The eighties have already taken on a different tenor than, say, the sixties. People had a lot of fun in the sixties, but it was a period of great prosperity. We now live in a highly inflationary time which makes people think they're richer than they are. I think that there is an undercurrent of conservativism, which in art is seen as the intellectual element. Instead of dealing with all-out humor and parodying things, using worldly, mundane objects as reference points the way Pop Art did in the sixties, artists today are using forms of narrative psychology and internal musings as inspiration.

Today, the work of artists like Susan Rothenberg, Joe Zucker, Robert Longo, and David Salle could be mislabeled as having a relation to Pop. It can be accessible, even joyful; it has humor; it's colorful, emotional, exuberant. But it also has one thing that Pop did not: a highly psychological element. These artists have been through the whole intellectual gambit of the seventies and have decided to settle on the most humanistic aspects of Minimalism; they've gotten involved with the psychology, the study of why people do the things they do. This element becomes a trigger for the viewer who confronts their work.

One interesting result is the large numbers of people involved with art today, as opposed to the seventies. That's always more fun, whether they are buying or looking. More people are looking and getting something out of the experience. And the visual arts have points of reference in other art fields today. Music is one important counterpart, as we have seen in the theatrical collaborations of Phil Glass and Robert Wilson. And all my artists seem to listen to new-wave rock when they're working in their studios, although I don't know precisely how it relates to their work; maybe it's rather like Jasper Johns listening to the Beatles.

I never think of myself only as a person who sells art. Fortunately, I'm very verbal and people can pick up on my enthusiasms. I have never had the presumptuous attitude that my gallery was going to fill a need; I thought there were certainly a lot of very good young artists whose work I liked, but most of them would easily have been shown in other galleries. It's very common for more than one dealer to look at the work of an artist when it starts to crystallize. Annina Nosei was there to show the work of Salle; Holly Solomon was going to Schnabel's studio and offered him a show before I did. Looking back on it, Artists Space, which was run by Helene Winer, had been a hotbed showing practically all the artists in my gallery with the exception of Gary Stephan and Julian Schnabel. It's remarkable that Matt Mullican, David Salle, Ross Bleckner, and Troy Brauntuch all had some contact with Helene.

It's flattering to think that artists come to you because they like you, but most are attracted by what a gallery represents. I happen to have a rigorous and professional attitude about what a gallery should do for an artist: I think it should do everything, and I try to do just that. But artists come to me because of the other artists. During the early sixties, Castelli had a lot of the artists that were of a certain

Troy Brauntuch

Untitled

1 9 8 2

cartoonish, frontal, accessible mentality that came to be called Pop. When an artist came out of that milieu, Castelli was where he wanted to show.

I have cultivated American collectors because I don't want to have the kind of situation seen with Impressionist painting, where all the best work went to the other continent. But Europeans do play a hefty role in getting out the work; the Europeans have a tradition of buying in volume, something that seldom enters the American collector's thought processes.

I prefer to work with a small group of collectors so that I have the feeling that I am helping to build each collection. Although several of my artists are very prolific, making between twenty and twenty-five paintings each year, for many there is never enough work to go around. I'm therefore not only very interested in where the work is going but what the other work around it will be.

There are collectors who buy early and collectors who buy late; I deal with those who buy early. It makes more of a demand on the collector's own commitment as well as on their faith in the dealer. It's altogether different from asking Arnold Glimcher to help you pick out a Rothko.

To me, the best collectors are those who historically have collected young artists, who tend to be involved with the world of art per se, and who can meet the artist's temperament half way. I am not speaking of the collector who comes into an artist's career when the work is already selling for $60,000. Collecting young artists requires a sense of adventure and a knack for being in the right place at the right time. It should not be surprising that many people who now buy from me are people who bought from Leo fifteen years ago. A gallery's role is to present the present, and with hope, the future. When Picasso told Gertrude Stein that he was to have a show at The Museum of Modern Art, she replied, "No museum can be modern." A lot goes into an artist's career before he arrives at the museums, and much of that takes place in a gallery.

Not every collector responds to all the artists I represent. I don't stress that they should. You can go to homes and see an Arnold Glimcher collection in which literally everything on the walls came from Arnie. I would much rather emphasize that the collection is the collector's, and that there will be things I show him that maybe he's not going to like: David Salle because he's too literal, perhaps;

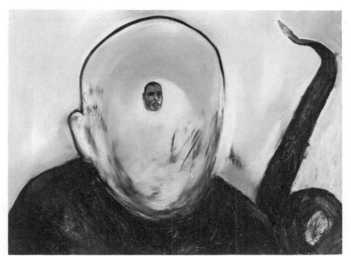

Francesco Clemente

Sound Point

1 9 8 3

then he will love Julian Schnabel, or maybe go toward more abstract work. I don't think it's important for collectors to accept it all.

There are certain dealers with whom I've asked to share something who have been possessive of their artists and refused. By making my pieces available in another gallery, I get involved with a different audience. Also, there are certain galleries that cross even larger boundaries: Annina Nosei, as an Italian, enjoys a very large European following, and through her David Salle's work has been seen by a whole new group of people.

One of the nice things about showing with galleries outside New York is not only that you find a regional difference in terms of audience, but also that a lot of people simply don't come to New York. Also, by showing in another gallery you're showing your artist with a whole new mix: I showed Gary Stephan with Margo Leavin's gallery in Houston. It is wonderful when she has a drawing show for there will be Jasper Johns, Robert Mangold, Lucas Samaras, and Gary Stephan. This way the art has a chance to be seen in a context that is viable and important, since all these artists are represented by different dealers.

The art world is very small, but on another level, work can be sanctioned in different ways; Leo Castelli has been the pioneer in this by allowing other galleries everywhere to show his artists over the past thirty years. In that way, I think his generosity has paid off with exposure for his artists. Already I've felt it. It means you cannot be possessive about something like art.

Annina
Nosei

Annina Nosei (born Rome, Italy) began working at Ileana Sonnabend's Paris gallery immediately after receiving doctorates of Literature and Philosophy from the University of Rome. She came to the United States to teach at the University of Michigan-Ann Arbor and UCLA. Her own gallery opened in May 1980.

Y

ears ago I was having lunch in Rome with the artist Franco Angeli and the great star of the Italian avant-garde, Piero Manzoni. Suddenly Manzoni offered to sign us both as his works of art. Franco thought more quickly than I and had him sign his shoe. Manzoni did sign my hand, however. What was I to do? I've been stuck from that day on: I am an artwork by Piero Manzoni. I still have the certificate of authenticity, but after all, I have since found a job for myself.

As a student at the University, I studied with the art historian Argan, and never dreamed that I would one day apply what I was learning to something like the gallery business. At the time my studies had no aim other than my own pleasure. Professor Argan was a sensitive teacher and saw where my thoughts in art were leading, so he encouraged me to write my thesis on Marcel Duchamp, whose example more than any other transformed the way we see art. Since his influence was strongly felt in the United States, I devoted a chapter to new American art, which in Europe was often termed the New Dada.

For anyone who wanted to see the latest from America in the sixties, there was no place in the whole of Europe like the gallery of Ileana Sonnabend. So before completing my thesis I went to Paris to meet the woman responsible for introducing so much American art. I liked her immediately, and after graduation I began working for Ileana. There was little pay but a great deal of learning, a chance for close study of great shows by Warhol, Rauschenberg, Chamberlain, Pistoletto, and so many others.

My first opportunity to experience American culture directly came in 1964, through a teaching grant at the University of Michigan in Ann Arbor. I previously had met John Cage and his legendary Once group, an avant-garde performing company with whom I began traveling and participating in happenings. Later that year I accepted an offer to teach at UCLA. Before I started out to the Coast, Rauschenberg, whom I knew through Ileana, told me to look up John Weber when I got to Los Angeles. I did, and eventually we were married.

In Los Angeles I witnessed the beginnings of Minimal Art in shows my husband organized for the Dwan Gallery: Dan Flavin, Sol LeWitt, Dan Flavin, Carl Andre, Kenneth Snelson, the first works of Robert Smithson. Helping install

Carl Andre's Negatives show was an unforgettable experience. We also took airplane excursions to Nevada with Michael Heizer and Walter de Maria to locate land for their earthwork projects. I will always look back on that time with intense nostalgia.

It is never a type of art but a type of *authenticity* that attracts me. In the future much of today's art will look alike; only something completely different will stand out. So I kept all possibilities in mind: I organized a show of Minimal Art for the St. Louis art dealer Ronnie Greenberg in 1975, while already working with Mimmo Paladino and Sandro Chia and looking at another Italian painter, Francesco Clemente. But at the same time I was also interested in the monochromatic work of Olivier Mosset, a direction totally different from the Italians.

In a semiprivate loft on West Broadway in Soho, I began showing younger artists like David Salle, whom I exhibited in October 1979. For one year, in preview shows, I mixed the work of young artists like Donald Newman, Troy Braun-

Mimmo Paladino

Porta (Door)

1 9 8 0

Sandro Chia

Kangaroo Boxing Match

1 9 7 7

Donald Newman

The Drummer

1 9 8 1

tuch, and Richard Prince with Stella, Judd, and Twombly.

Conceptual artists who come from the radicalism of Ad Reinhardt always attracted me. Joseph Kosuth, with his fantasy and energy, is as real an artist as any painter even though he has gone far beyond brushes, paint, and easel. But after Kosuth, post-Conceptual artists never interested me. I began looking for artists who dealt in ideological concerns with conceptual strategies, so that when I showed David Salle it was not with the thought of specializing in painting; I acted on my interest in his ambiguity of image. I also like the work of Donald Newman for the way it incorporates photographs to make them pictorial again; I never considered him a traditional painter, but like Salle, an artist establishing new emotional ambiguity between medium and image.

Besides the challenge of making discoveries, I also was faced by lack of the finances and, therefore, the power necessary to approach well-known artists, and this led me into the open field of the new Italian painters and the new Germans, including Hödicke and Koberling from the older gen-

Mike Glier

The Glory of Crispus Attucks

(Monuments Lie)

1 9 8 0

eration, as well as American artists whose work was widely labeled Neo-Expressionism, New Figuration, Anxious Figure – call it what you will.

What struck me most in the work of the Italian painters was their subject matter. The morphology of this work is founded on Italian culture, full of poetic images developed through sentiment. Remembering that the Futurists stressed emotional tension brought to a high pitch, I now saw the new Italians making their own synthesis of past and present culture. I liked Sandro Chia's paintings, which seem more rooted in subject matter of the thirties and forties, not unlike de Pisis and Rosai. Chia uses a repertory of earthy imagery found ready-made in Italian visual culture.

The Germans, such as those from Berlin, are real painters dealing with questions of paint, color, subject matter. If their work often resembles prewar Expressionism, there is also a new sense of protest that comes close to the freedom and intensity of performance art.

The Americans seem more analytical. Still, it's not a movement, since the work is not based on theory or developed out of Minimalism or Conceptual Art. I liked David Salle's work from the first painting I saw. It is challenging in an intellectual sense and introduces a new type of relationship with reality.

I see few strong connections between the European and American artists today, although Julian Schnabel may be an exception. While lacking the regional identity of the Europeans, he too has a great interest in subject matter, the synthesis of a collective epic. I was among the first to buy

K. H. Hodicke

Potsdamer Strasse

1 9 7 9

286

Berndt Koberling

Wingspan

1 9 8 1

Schnabel's work, at the time seeing the influence of the German painter Sigmar Polke, but results closer to Paladino. Both Schnabel and Paladino deal with objects in space, exploding and continuing the concept of collage.

When I first encountered the large drawings of David Deutsch, recommended to me by the artist Bill Wegman, they struck me as the work of a real intellectual. I saw a curiosity, a sincere research toward some dream, some ideal, that went far beyond the mere announcement of an esthetic position. This is what I am always looking for in art, not the object itself but the laying open of truth and morality through art.

My taste is difficult and extreme. I always advise collectors to buy works of art that demonstrate extreme fantasy and extreme sensibility. Before I opened my gallery, a collector once came to my house and wanted to buy everything I owned. I was flattered in a way, but advised him on other works instead, as I do with all collectors, since collecting must be an individual procedure.

Dealers must know instinctively who to sell an artist to first, and when. I saw Jean Michel Basquiat as an exciting addition to my gallery, and for his first exhibition I priced the work very low, selling to the most intellectual collectors, those who got excited immediately. At the time, I was putting together major sales to important collectors who were buying, for example, the Germans. I told them that they should have a work by Jean Michel Basquiat also, for $1,000 or $1,500 more on the bill of $25,000 they had already run

David Deutsch

Untitled

1 9 7 9

up. This worked quite well: these collectors gained an early commitment, told their friends, and all of a sudden Basquiat's paintings were found in collections beside more well-known artists, as the youngest of all. When a European collector bought a Paladino, I encouraged him to take a drawing by Basquiat for around $900; later when I show paintings for $2,000, the improvement in that new work confirmed the small commitment already made. A community of interest has grown around it.

The best advisor for a young artist is usually another artist. When Sandro Chia saw the work of Jean Michel Basquiat, its vivacious quality somehow summed up for him the American scene today. Sandro thought that if I gave a chance to so young an artist – which meant money – he might make more paintings and develop quite soon. I made the commitment, and the results were astonishing. Soon I was not alone in seeing Basquiat as one of the few Americans capable of handling urban subject matter, quoting without restraint, as de Kooning himself did.

Sandro Chia displayed that vital instinct by which artists are able to catch on, before anyone else, to important changes in art. Dealers need to possess this artist's instinct

Jean Michel Basquiat

Mater

1 9 8 2

themselves if they expect to make true discoveries. If I trust an artist, I prefer his confirmation over that of a critic. Also, it enlarges my appreciation for both the older and the younger artist in question.

It's part of my cultural nature to promote ideas all the time, with collectors, writers, friends; still, the real promotion of a new artist is to sell his work, to present it to the right collector or the right curator at the proper time. Yet when artists jump galleries, I often think their decision is dictated by a false idea of career. It can be confusing and disappointing. I feel that artists should remain faithful to the ideas in their work and, finding a dealer who understands those ideas, stick with that gallery. The other strategies all fail.

This needn't mean staying with a gallery that has no money, of course. It is worth a minute's thought to consider why art dealers have chosen their profession. People tend to think dealers are parasites in it just for the money. But let's remember that dealers such as John Weber, Mary Boone, Joe Helman, or Marian Goodman all could be making much more money in other fields. John Weber could be a top executive in a large corporation; Joe Helman could be a major figure in investment. These people chose to make art their life's work more out of dedication than motives of profit. Many artists recognize this. Others do not. My years of study were not to learn about money. The gallery business itself, the economic aspect, is creative only in a relative way; the redeeming factor remains the idea behind the art itself.

Helene
Winer

Helene Winer (born 1946, Chicago, Illinois) graduated with a degree in art history from the University of Southern California, and worked at the Los Angeles County Museum and London's Whitechapel Gallery before becoming director of Artists Space, a New York showcase for unknown artists, in 1975. She opened Metro Pictures with Janelle Reiring in 1980.

Janelle
Reiring

Janelle Reiring (born 1946, Los Angeles, California) received both bachelor's and master's degrees in English and history from the University of California at Berkeley, and learned the art business by working for five years with Leo Castelli. She opened her own gallery, Metro Pictures, with Helene Winer in 1980.

I never thought of opening a gallery of my own during most of the five years I worked for Leo Castelli. That was my first involvement with a commercial gallery, and to me his always seemed the ideal. What other single gallery could bring together such a group of artists? The most remarkable thing about Leo, and also Ileana Sonnabend, is that they continue to be actively involved with new art. Certainly Leo could have limited his gallery to Johns, Rauschenberg, Lichtenstein, and Warhol and still been extremely successful. But instead, while remaining supportive of his early artists, both the stars and those whose careers took longer to establish, he showed the best artists of the most important new movements as they arose. Each generation of artists reacts to the one before, and there are sometimes abrupt changes in style or content; it's not that easy for the dealer to make that jump.

Helene Winer and I opened Metro Pictures in November 1980 because we both felt very strongly about the work of a group of young artists who were not represented by any gallery. Because Helene had spent five years as director of Artists Space, she was absolutely invaluable to the early success of our gallery. She had in fact spent five years looking at new art, exhibiting it, and following the development of the artists she found most interesting. These artists, such as Jack Goldstein, Robert Longo, and Cindy Sherman, were beginning to receive some critical attention and some interest from dealers and certain astute collectors. It is very important for young artists in New York to gain an audience for their work through peer support, alternative spaces such as Artists Space, White Columns, P. S. 1, and group shows before they exhibit in a commercial gallery. I think it is almost impossible for a commercial dealer to show a young, unknown artist who does not have this solid basis to their career and arouse interest in the show and the work. Our job is to capitalize, exploit, and enlarge an interest that had already begun, not to create that interest.

Another important factor in our decision to open a gallery at that time was the realization that the art being done by this group of young artists was accessible to a much wider public than the art of the seventies. These artists were released from the prescriptive, hermetic tenor that had dominated the art world in the recent past. In some respects this can be viewed as a reactionary period; some of the most

Jack Goldstein

Untitled

1 9 8 3

effective young artists today are exploiting very traditional modes of painting and sculpture. But I think it has given the artist greater freedom to use the most effective visual medium to present an idea, whether it be painting, sculpture, photography, or drawing.

The first season of Metro Pictures came at a very particular moment. When a new phenomenon is first identified, everybody looks for similarities and generalizations to explain it. And they *are* there when you're dealing with artists of roughly the same age who exist in the same culture and have the same art history to build upon and react to. Since Metro Pictures was new and each artist was having his first one-person show in New York, this identity as a group probably played too strong a role. And sometimes when the idea of an art movement is talked about, with everyone looking for similarities, people forget that the artist goes about his work in his own way and that eventually it is the differences from other artists that are seen as important. We certainly don't want the gallery to be viewed as

Cindy Sherman

Untitled

1 9 8 3

Richard Prince

Untitled

1 9 8 2

John Miller

Untitled

1 9 8 3

programmatic in the art it shows. I always dread it when an artist approaches us, or someone recommends an artist, with the phrase, "I think the work will really fit in the gallery." I'm almost sure I won't be interested in it. We're really looking for something we haven't seen before, in our gallery or any other. The two younger artists we have taken on most recently, Mike Kelley and John Miller, are of a very different sensibility and their work takes a very different physical form from what we have shown before. We are also representing the Eva Hesse estate with Donald Droll, which adds another dimension to the gallery.

As we have started out with artists at the beginning of their careers, we want to continue with them. Obviously there are changes. A dealer has to perform well. I don't think contractual agreements are of any use. What dealer is going to sue an artist? And then there are situations where the dealer simply has to admit he made a mistake and a particular artist's work just doesn't have the interest or potential he thought it did. And without a continuing sincere belief in the work, a dealer can't do much for an artist. Artists are in a very strong position today vis à vis dealers, which is a major change – and a healthy one – in the New York art market. Before the arrival of so many new galleries, there were many good artists without dealer representation. Now the galleries are competing for them. New artists are given shows just to see if they'll catch on, so it's no longer possible to stand back and follow an artist's development before acting; the luxury we had of watching our artists for several years before opening Metro Pictures is a thing of the past. But I do think this relationship is cyclical. If the next generation of artists produces difficult work that doesn't elicit easy public acceptance, there will be fewer galleries anxious to show that art.

In today's art world, there is a large number of young artists receiving an extraordinary amount of attention and financial support compared to five or ten years ago. There is a lot of criticism that this success is based on hype and that artists are overly ambitious, which I don't agree with. Ambition is an element I look for in an artist, and I certainly have ambitions as a dealer. I guess most of us are involved in this activity because of certain romantic views about art and artists. But once we're in it, it is a practical, functioning world; it is a business. The same sort of drives and ambitions and instincts function for an artist as they do for other professionals. I don't think there are good artists out there in obscurity who will not be discovered eventually. The undiscovered genius has become a myth.

There's also talk about the effects of sudden success and overexposure on the work of young artists, but I don't think any artist will fail *because* of success. It's most damaging to the artists not currently receiving that success. They see it happening to other artists and they know it's a possibility, and they want it. Theoretically all the artists we opened with started out on the same level – having their first New York shows. But very soon one artist isn't getting as much attention as another in the gallery. It's easy to blame the

Mike Kelley

Cross-Cultural Development

1 9 8 3

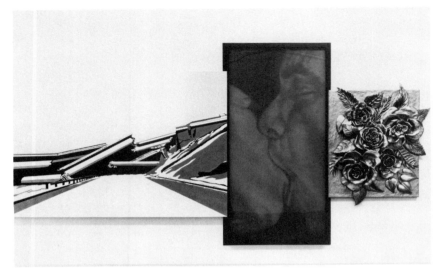

Robert Longo

Ornamental Love

1 9 8 3

dealer, but it's not that simple. The nature of the work, the personality of the artist, how the work reproduces in print – many factors are involved as the dealer tries to get the work across to the public. That's why the dealer must treat each artist differently. Persistence is a key quality – if you believe in the work of an artist, you persist. I think there are many artists capable of doing one or two good shows, but the dealer must be certain that he knows what he's showing, that the artist has a deep belief in the art he makes.

Though I won't deny the pleasure and economic necessity of selling art, it really plays a relatively small role in the activities of a dealer. We certainly spend as much time with critics and curators and attending to the basics of an artist's career – disseminating information, arranging exhibitions at other galleries, making loans to museum shows – than we do actually selling work. But of course it is all those other things that "sell" the work, not a sales pitch from the dealer. And a lot of time is spent with the artists. Though it often takes a social veneer, it's very complicated and intense. Many of our artists have faced extraordinary changes in their lives. For instance Robert Longo received a great deal of attention and success after his first exhibition at the gallery. His became a problem of too many offers and wanting to do too much. And as he's also interested in music, performance, and film, and collaborating with other people on projects, it was largely a matter of helping him to sort out what shows or activities or people were really important to his work and career. There's a delicate balance

Walter Robinson

Willie's Girl

1 9 8 2

between overexposure and capitalizing on the existing interest. Robert did not have a one-person show in New York last year. Since his first show, he's become involved in very technically complicated large-scale work. The first completed piece was shown at the 1982 Documenta, and this series of work culminated in a very large show at Metro and Leo Castelli in 1983. Certainly Robert's success has affected his work, as he is now economically able to produce work that he could not have before. Cindy Sherman's success came about more gradually, and her reaction to it is very different. She proceeds with her work unaffected by what is happening around her in the same way she always has done. We just returned from the opening of her exhibition at the Stedelijk Museum. To coincide with the exhibition, a book was published that reproduces almost all the work she has done since 1977. Though she is very happy with the exhibition and the book, I know Cindy feels a bit uncomfortable with the rewards of her success – personal attention, critical evaluation, money, and with each new series of works she attempts to work against the praise she has received for the last series.

Ultimately a gallery is only as good as the artists it represents; thus it must constantly prove itself useful to them. It may sound ridiculous, with a gallery as young as ours, to say that we hope to be able to stay on top of what's going on. Dealers constantly try to sort out what will happen next, but all you can do is to wait for the artists. I am even more in awe of Leo Castelli now than before: I don't know how he was able to stay in there, group after group, and continue to take up the best of the new.

Thomas Lawson

To Those Who Follow After

1 9 8 3

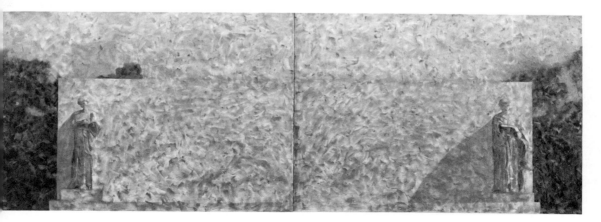

Tony *Shafrazi*

Tony Shafrazi (born 1943, Abadan, Iran) began his studies at Hammersmith College of Art and graduated from the Royal College of Art in London in 1963. After a short period teaching and lecturing at the Manchester College of Art in England, the School of Visual Arts in New York, and other institutions, he then set out on his own career as an artist in New York, until choosing in the mid-seventies to devote more time to the work of others. Shafrazi's quest for undiscovered talent led to the opening of his gallery in Soho in 1981.

Long before I started studying sculpture at the Royal College, I knew that art was going to be my whole life. London was a fabulous place to be in the early sixties, a lot like New York is right now. I can still picture David Hockney as a second-year student, running down a dark corridor of the Royal College with his hair not quite dry after being dyed blond for the first time. It was just before he left for the United States.

The thought of America was in the back of all our minds. Even though London had three or four good galleries, contemporary art was, as always, a weak point in Britain; there was no way to follow current art in sequence. London dealers like Kasmin or Robert Fraser were giving us a glimpse or two of what was going on, but we knew that seeing the whole picture meant a trip to New York.

My family claims that at the age of seven I was already making plans to go to New York. I am of Armenian extraction, but grew up in Abadan, an oil city between the desert and the Persian Gulf. It had been built by the British in the thirties, so it had a vaguely early-Hollywood look. In fact, we saw a great deal of American popular culture; young people all wore Lee jeans and went to see James Dean in *East of Eden* and Paul Newman in *Somebody Up There Likes Me.*

I finally made it to New York in June 1965. One of my first stops was Warhol's factory, which was operating around the clock in those days – silver pillow sculptures everywhere and records blasting nonstop on a phonograph. Another unforgettable visit was to Roy Lichtenstein's studio. He was such a gentleman. I had simply called him, out of the blue, and he invited me to come and have lunch. He had to go see his dealer afterward, so I tagged along. As we waited for Castelli to appear, Lichtenstein pointed to a canvas and said, "Isn't that a great painting." I looked, and the only thing I saw was a blank white canvas with numbers. Finally, all I could find to say was, "Do you really think so?" It was a Jasper Johns.

I also made it cross-country by Greyhound bus. As if the trip itself weren't enough, there was the experience of Los Angeles – meeting people on the scene like Dennis Hopper, and artists like Billy Al Bengston and Larry Bell made me all the more reluctant to leave. It had to end eventually, and when I returned to England I settled down to teaching jobs

at Manchester College of Art and a few other places. I also
continued my own work as an artist.

By the time I did manage to break away to New York
again, the atmosphere had changed drastically since my
first trip. It was 1969: an attempt had been made on Warhol's life; Bobby Kennedy had been assassinated; the Viet-
nam War was raging. Shortly after my arrival, the School of
Visual Arts gave me a teaching job, and then I found myself
taking part in things like the Artists' Strike and the Art
Workers' Coalition. Looking back, I can say that I did get
carried away with it all; yet it was a dream we all believed
in, almost religiously, and some positive effects may in fact
have come out of our protests. But in retrospect, they were
lonely, frustrating years of conflict for everyone.

The premature death in 1973 of the great American
sculptor Robert Smithson was a turning point in my life. I
had grown very close to him, and he had invited me to
Amarillo, Texas, where he was doing a project. It was there
that his fatal airplane accident occurred. Smithson was a
very clear-minded artist, a lucid writer full of awareness,
and a great person to be around. And in a way, his death did
not seem tragic because the work he left was so awesome
and extraordinary. But I knew that my way of thinking
about the art world had been changed for good. Coming
back into Manhattan from the airport that week, the first
thing I saw was a large graffito on an Upper West Side wall:
"FIGHT BACK."

One artist whom I met in that period is part of my gallery today. The sculptor Richard Serra introduced me to
Zadik Zadikian in 1973, and I was impressed by Zadik's fantastic visionary power and by his feeling for life. Richard
and I both got excited just watching him work. For one
thing, he decided to transform the whole interior of his
house and studio into a magical space by gilding every inch
of it. The result was electrifying. It was a good example of
the abhorrence of "angst" and any expression of life in pain
that has always characterized Zadik's view of art. This kind
of single-minded dedication to everything that's glorious and
heroic in art was very moving for me.

I began to find my own work as an artist more and more
frustrating; for the most part the art world appeared to be at
a standstill. Then in 1976, word came to me that a major
museum of contemporary art was being created in Teheran.
I had always dreamed of such a cultural exchange, an

Zadik Zadikian

Aram

1 9 8 2

opportunity to bring artists from America to the land where I was born. The idea inspired me. I was awakened by the thought of what I could contribute to the project. Such a museum could be the perfect bridge to the West; I plunged in wholeheartedly.

As the museum project got underway, the word "work" took on a new meaning for me: it came to signify the ability to touch important works of art, a new kind of contact with living artists. The responsibility of choosing these works was exhilarating in itself. It was the first time that I had worked with dealers. I now went back to artists who had been my friends to choose examples that would epitomize the art of our time, what had gone on in the immediate past. It was a question of recognizing the major artists of the past twenty years. One lesson I learned then has served me well today: choosing works should not be a matter of likes and dislikes, but rather a natural reflex, a shutting off of the esthetic principles that we all carry around with us. It's very hard to keep an open mind, but only in taking that larger view can we transcend our own expectations and really surprise ourselves.

In a very short time we acquired excellent works by Rauschenberg, Johns, Warhol, Lichtenstein, Oldenburg, Stella; later on, Robert Morris, Sol LeWitt, Keith Sonnier, and others. One of the best museum collections anywhere in the world was coming together under the auspices of the empress and her museum director, Kamran Diba. Then, in 1979, impulsively and without foreseeing the consequences, I went ahead and opened a gallery in Teheran. No one had any idea of how suddenly and disastrously the political climate of Iran would change. Within a few weeks the country was in chaos, and that was the end of another chapter, another dream. Fighting my disappointment, I came back to New York and put together a semiprivate gallery on Lexington Avenue, a portfolio in a sense, a place to experiment.

Those last days of the seventies saw many changes in the art world. New artists fresh off the street were beginning to offer the public a new kind of metropolitan view. The routines of the old guard were beginning to falter; a whole new world of possibilities in art making suddenly opened up to anyone who had the drive to take advantage of it.

One day a young man named Keith Haring came to help me install exhibitions, and he worked like a wizard, quickly and efficiently. I knew he was a student of Keith Sonnier at

Keith Haring

Untitled

1 9 8 2

the School of Visual Arts, but I hadn't yet seen any of Haring's work. My first exposure came when he showed at a couple of spaces in New York, P. S. 122 in the East Village and in Westbeth, where I was confronted by hundreds of drawings pinned to the wall. Immediately I felt that I was witnessing something incredibly powerful.

Inspired by the graffiti he saw in the subways when he first came to New York, Keith had begun formulating his own world of imaginary people and events by drawing with white chalk on the empty advertising spaces in subway stations all over Manhattan. These drawings were seen by millions of people every day of the week, and Keith was using this public forum to cultivate a vast vocabulary. In just a few years it has already become an immediately recognizable part of our urban culture. This unique talent for direct expression has given us a memorable and haunting experience. Out of nowhere, it became a part of our lives.

Around 1980, I first saw the work of Donald Baechler, and I was struck by the feeling for paradox and irony that his painting displayed. He had come back from studying in Germany not long before and was holding down a job at the Dia Art Foundation while doing his own work. The illustrations he found in the Yellow Pages and in cheap magazines served as the basis for intentionally banal images in his drawings and paintings, which were done with thick applications of enamel house paint. There was a certain throw-

Donald Baechler

The Zabreg Picture

1 9 8 2 – 8 3

away quality about it all, but I knew he wasn't kidding when he told me that "a painting must have the right degree of indecipherability in order to work." He certainly had that. Then at a certain point Baechler began treating the themes in his own drawings as if they were images found somewhere else, and these motifs became the source of paintings.

Sooner or later my Lexington Avenue space had to give way to a more public scene, and in 1981 I managed to open up a shoestring gallery on Mercer Street. I wanted the youthful, spontaneous quality of the artists I was meeting to carry over to the new space, and, to be frank, I was tired of the old ideas that were weighing down the art scene. I wanted to rejuvenate myself by confronting my own prejudices: I didn't want to represent art that I myself already knew thoroughly.

Ronnie Cutone was typical of the tremendous vitality coming from new artists. I'd known him since 1977 when he was still working for Andy Warhol, and I was struck by his zany sense of humor. Wearing a loud sport jacket, with shaving cream all over his face, he would let me into his studio full of toys, comics, souvenir items, and thousands of records. It was a playland. At the time, he was doing beautiful, witty drawings with subject matter from television commercials, then pictures that came directly from coloring books, cartoons, scientific illustrations, and biblical scenes. Eventually there came the series of paintings using real flags from around the world as canvases. Ronnie is like a child who has grown up unattended in the wildest circles of New York life. He had survived on his native strength, and I felt that he had the pulse of his generation.

When I was still organizing the opening show of the Soho gallery, I kept trying to get in touch with Jean Michel Basquiat, an artist who was highly thought of on the street at the time and whose work I wanted very much to show. He was nowhere to be found that summer. Jean Michel started making a very strong showing on the scene soon after.

Meanwhile, I was fortunate to be able to show the painter Kenny Scharf. The first things of his I saw were works made from broken appliances, painted and glued all over with small figurines. From the minute Keith Haring introduced us, I was amazed by Kenny's world of dayglow and black light, a sort of technicolor cartoon paradise. Despite this sense of fun, the paintings obviously meant business; there was a deep identity with the early Renaissance in his use of color and form, and there was an interest in things like dream interpretation. He has a great ease and confidence, a deliberately unconscious knack for inventing shapes and bizarre characters as he goes along.

Sometimes, although rarely, a discovery can arrive in a packet of slides. When I looked at James Brown's slides in the winter of 1981, the work I saw brought back the kick and excitement I first had felt years before from the early Hockney paintings, which were primitive but at the same time refined. That definition fit Brown's work, too. When I met the artist, I was surprised to see a very sophisticated, tall, elegant young man in his late twenties, fresh from eight years in Paris. He has a great line and a very loose, festive feeling for paint. Tribal arts – American Indian, African, Hawaiian – are important sources of inspiration in his work.

All during this time the street scene was warming up rapidly with a broad range of phenomena in music, dance, style, graffiti. Again, it was Keith Haring who tipped me off about an artist calling himself Futura 2000. Keith showed me pictures of his work done directly on subway cars, and months later Futura (who took his sobriquet from the typeface of the same name) came to see me in the summer of 1982, bringing a book of drawings with him. I took one look at his incredible "handwriting" and that was it. One of the earliest stars of the graffiti scene, he had painted insignia onto jet fighters while in the Navy as a troubleshooter on an aircraft carrier. All this space-age experience had helped him create a fantastic vision. He used the spray can like magic, drawing perfect circles and ovals in a completely original style that shows a sophisticated color sense.

I had to wait until 1982 finally to get a look at the paintings of the reclusive Brett De Palma, which were shown at Documenta that year. De Palma consistently comes up with striking imagery – a totemic Easter Island head done in a heavy-handed, comic-book manner with thick paint build-up is a typical example. I was immediately struck by the way he infuses various jarring languages with Cubist or Futurist structures. It showed a real knowledge and a lot of nerve,

James Brown

Horse Shoes and Crosses

That's Good Luck

1 9 8 2

Futura 2000

Letter to Myself

1 9 8 3

both of which appeal to me.

Each of the artists in my gallery bears witness to the diversity of expression in art today. Extreme opposites in style and clashing methods have turned the art world upside down, and art history along with it. Artists today are drawing upon the whole of art history just as freely as they use the stimuli of the inner-city world they live in.

One of the saving graces of not having had much money when I started my gallery was that I had to work doubly hard. That, in addition to insisting on totally new art, kept me so preoccupied that I overcame any temptation to look over my shoulder, to try to see what other dealers were doing. I just wasn't comparing myself to anyone and wasn't even thinking of myself as an art dealer.

I wanted to leap further ahead into the area where no one had been before, bringing in things that were not even considered art, the unknown elements of the art world. Above all I did not want to be around things I already knew about, things that had been thoroughly digested by other galleries before my time. I wanted something that I would have to learn from. And that meant, as it always does, starting from scratch. Those lessons are an art dealer's best reward.

LIST OF ILLUSTRATIONS

p. 22 **Adolph Gottlieb,** *Untitled,* 1942. Ink on paper, 29½ x 20¾ in. Betty Parsons Estate.
p. 23 **Barnett Newman,** *Concord,* 1949. Oil on canvas, 89¾ x 53⅜ in. The Metropolitan Museum of Art, George A. Hearn Fund, 1968 (68.178).
Jackson Pollock, *#2,* 1951. Oil on paper, 42 x 26 in. Betty Parsons Estate.
p. 24 **Ellsworth Kelly,** *Cowboy,* 1958. Oil on canvas, 45 x 43 in. Collection of Neubauer, Paris. Courtesy Leo Castelli Gallery.
p. 25 **Clyfford Still,** *Untitled,* 1945. Oil on canvas, 42½ x 33½ in. Collection of the Whitney Museum of American Art. Gift of Mr. and Mrs. B. H. Friedman.
p. 26 **Jan Groth,** *Sign,* 1981–82. Unique tapestry, 87 x 207 in., woven by Benedikte and Jan Groth. Courtesy Marian Goodman Gallery, New York.
p. 28 **Ad Reinhardt,** *#38,* 1949. Oil on canvas, 50 x 20 in. Private Collection.
p. 29 **Saul Steinberg,** *Drawing of Betty Parsons,* 1958. Ink on paper. Betty Parsons Estate.
p. 30 **Betty Parsons,** *Eyes of the Sea,* 1981. Acrylic on wood, 18 x 39½ x ¾ in. Betty Parsons Estate.
Betty Parsons, *Village Shop,* 1981. Acrylic on wood, 18 x 12½ x 4 in. Betty Parsons Estate.
p. 33 **Constantin Brancusi,** *Fish,* ca. 1926. Bronze and stainless steel: sculpture 16½ x 5 in., base 19½ in. diameter. Collection Sidney Janis Gallery.
p. 34 **Matta,** *To Cover the Earth with a New Dew,* 1953. Oil on canvas, 79½ x 114 in. Collection, The Museum of Modern Art, New York
Piet Mondrian, *New York City, New York,* ca. 1942. Oil, pencil, charcoal, and painted tape on canvas, 46 x 43½ in. Thyssen-Bornemisza Collection, Lugano, Switzerland.
p. 35 **Fernand Leger,** *Deux Plongeurs,* 1942. Oil on canvas, 50 x 58 in. Collection Sidney Janis Gallery.
Jackson Pollock, *The She-Wolf,* 1943. Oil on gouache and plaster on canvas, 41⅞ x 67 in. Collection, The Museum of Modern Art, New York. Purchase.
p. 36 **Pablo Picasso,** *Femme à la Mandoline,* 1911. Oil on canvas, 15 x 9½ in. Courtesy Sidney Janis Gallery.
p. 37 **Jackson Pollock,** *Autumn Rhythm,* 1950. Oil on canvas, 105 x 207 in. The Metropolitan Museum of Art, George A. Hearn Fund 1957. (57.92) All rights reserved, The Metropolitan Museum of Art.
p. 38 **Willem de Kooning,** *Woman I,* 1950–52. Oil on canvas, 75⅞ x 58 in. Collection, The Museum of Modern Art, New York. Purchase.
p. 39 **Franz Kline,** *Turbin (Black & White),* 1958–59. Oil on canvas, 112 x 86 in. Courtesy Sidney Janis Gallery.
Mark Rothko, *Light Over Grey,* 1956. Oil on canvas, 67 x 50 in. McCrory Collection, New York.
p. 40 **Tom Wesselmann,** *Great American Nude #73,* 1965. Acrylic on canvas, 72 x 88 in. Private collection.
p. 41 **George Segal,** *The Hustle: The Four Hand Pass,* 1980. Plaster, wood, plastic, metal, videotape, and sound: soundstudio, 96 x 144 x 192 in., figures 68 x 38 x 38 in. Collection of the artist.
p. 44 Announcement for exhibition of paintings and drawings by **"George Hartigan,"** March 25–April 12, 1952. Courtesy Tibor de Nagy Gallery.
Red Grooms, *Tibor de Nagy Presents,* 1963. Painted cardboard, 20 x 30 x 5½ in. Collection of Tibor de Nagy.
p. 45 **Fairfield Porter,** *Portrait of Tibor de Nagy,* 1958. Oil on canvas, 40 x 30 in. Courtesy Tibor de Nagy Gallery.
Larry Rivers, *Frank O'Hara Double Portrait,* 1955. Oil on canvas, 15 x 25 in. Courtesy Tibor de Nagy Gallery.
p. 46 **Kenneth Noland,** *Curious Course,* 1975. Acrylic on canvas, 70 x 70 in. (diamond). Courtesy Tibor de Nagy Gallery.
p. 47 **Robert Goodnough,** *Excursion,* 1963–64. Oil on canvas 96 x 216 in. Courtesy Tibor de Nagy Gallery.
p. 50 **Man Ray,** *Untitled,* 1959. Oil on masonite, 14½ x 17½ in. Courtesy Brooks Jackson–Iolas Gallery.
p. 51 **Victor Brauner,** *Fish,* 1959. Plaster and oil on canvas, stretched on board, 24 x 32 in. Courtesy Brooks Jackson–Iolas Gallery.
p. 52 **Jean Cocteau,** *Scene from the ballet* Orpheus, no date. Collage of photomontage and crayon, sheet 13¼ x 16½ in. Collection, The Museum of Modern Art, New York. Gift of John Pratt.
p. 53 **Magritte,** *Madame Recamier de David,* 1967. Bronze, 41¼" height. Courtesy Brooks Jackson–Iolas Gallery.
p. 54 **Joseph Cornell,** *Taglioni's Jewel Casket,* 1940. Wood box containing glass ice cubes, jewelry, etc., 4¾ x 11⅞ x 8¼ in. Collection, The Museum of Modern Art, New York. Gift of James Thrall Soby.
p. 55 **William Copley** (CPLY), *The Champ,* 1970. Acrylic on canvas, 58 x 45½ in. Courtesy Brooks Jackson–Iolas Gallery.
p. 56 **David Hockney,** *Andre Emmerich, Los Angeles,* 1982. Polaroid assemblage, 14½ x 10 in. Courtesy Andre Emmerich Gallery, New York.
p. 57 Gold bird pendant with double crocodile headdress. Diquis Delta, Costa Rica, A.D. 800–1500, 3¼ x 3½ in. Private collection. Courtesy Andre Emmerich Gallery, New York.
p. 58 **Sam Francis,** *Muted No. 2,* 1957. Oil on canvas, 71½ x 40¾ in. Courtesy Andre Emmerich Gallery, New York.
p. 59 **Morris Louis,** *Moving In,* 1961. Acrylic on canvas, 87½ x 41½ in. Private collection. Courtesy Andre Emmerich Gallery, New York.
p. 60 **Helen Frankenthaler,** *Tangerine,* 1964. Acrylic on canvas, 76 x 66 in. Private collection.

Courtesy Andre Emmerich Gallery, New York.
Hans Hofmann, *Ora Pro Nobis,* 1964. Oil on canvas, 60 x 48 in. Private collection. Courtesy Andre Emmerich Gallery, New York.

p. 61 Kenneth Noland, *Saturday Night,* 1965. Acrylic resin on canvas, 60 x 60 in. (diamond). Private collection. Courtesy Andre Emmerich Gallery, New York.

p. 62 Jules Olitski, *Nathalie Type – 3,* 1976. Waterbase on canvas, 110 x 146 in. Private collection. Courtesy Andre Emmerich Gallery, New York.

p. 63 Al Held, *Inversion XII,* 1977. Acrylic on canvas, 60 x 60 in. Private collection. Courtesy Andre Emmerich Gallery, New York.

David Hockney, *Paper Pool #10 "Midnight Pool,"* 1978. Colored and pressed pulp, 72 x 85½ in. Private collection. Courtesy Andre Emmerich Gallery, New York.

p. 67 Ilya Bolotowsky, *Blue Rhomb,* 1981. Acrylic on canvas, 83 x 48 in. Courtesy Washburn Gallery.

p. 69 Leon Polk Smith, *Form Space – Black Red,* 1981. Acrylic on canvas, 2 panels: 108 x 55 in., 60 x 54 in. Courtesy Washburn Gallery.

p. 70 Jack Youngerman, *Huracan,* 1981. Oil and gesso over epoxy resin on carved polystyrene, 105 x 72 x 6 in. Courtesy Washburn Gallery.

p. 71 Marsden Hartley, *Abstraction (Military Symbols),* 1914–15. Oil on canvas, 39 x 32 in. The Toledo Museum of Art: Gift of Edward Drummond Libbey.

p. 74 Jules Olitski, *Thales Enthralled 1,* 1978. Acrylic on canvas, 81 x 48 in. Courtesy M. Knoedler & Company, Inc. New York.

Friedel Dzubas, *Agmont,* 1981. Acrylic (magna) on canvas, 55 x 160 in. Courtesy M. Knoedler & Company, Inc., New York.

p. 75 Richard Diebenkorn, *Ocean Park #117,* 1979. Oil on canvas, 45 x 45 in. Courtesy M. Knoedler & Company, Inc., New York.

p. 76 John Walker, *In Truth I,* 1981–82. Oil on canvas, 96¼ x 84 in. Courtesy M. Knoedler & Company, Inc.

p. 78 Robert Motherwell, *Portal,* 1982. Oil and acrylic on canvas, 60 x 44 in. Courtesy M. Knoedler & Company, Inc., New York.

p. 79 Frank Stella, *Talladega,* 1981. Mixed media on etched magnesium, 108 x 125½ x 17¼ in. Private collection, New York. Courtesy M. Knoedler & Company, Inc., New York.

Nancy Graves, *Fanne Figura,* 1982. Bronze with polychrome patina, 54½ x 28 x 21½ in. Private collection, New York. Courtesy M. Knoedler & Company, Inc., New York.

p. 89 Jasper Johns, *Small Numbers in Color,* 1959. Encaustic on wood, 10³⁄₁₆ x 7³⁄₁₆ in. Collection of the artist.

Jasper Johns, *Target with Plaster Casts,* 1955. Encaustic and collage on canvas with plaster casts, 51 x 44 x 3½ in. Collection of Mr. and Mrs. Leo Castelli.

p. 90 Robert Rauschenberg, *Bed,* 1955. Combine painting, 75¼ x 31½ x 6½ in. Collection of Mr. and Mrs. Leo Castelli.

p. 92 Cy Twombly, *Untitled,* 1968. Oil, crayon, and pencil on canvas, 68 x 86 in. Courtesy Leo Castelli Gallery.

p. 93 Frank Stella, *Gezira,* 1960. Enamel on canvas, 122 x 73 in. Private collection, New York. Courtesy Leo Castelli Gallery.

p. 94 Lee Bontecou, *Untitled,* 1962. Metal and canvas, 76 x 70½ x 27 in. Courtesy Leo Castelli Gallery.

p. 95 Roy Lichtenstein, *Girl with Ball,* 1961. Oil and synthetic polymer paint on canvas, 60¼ x 36¼ in. Collection, The Museum of Modern Art, New York. Gift of Philip Johnson.

Andy Warhol, *Coca Cola Bottles,* 1962. Oil on canvas, 82 x 105 in. Harry N. Abrams Family Collection. Courtesy Leo Castelli Gallery.

p. 96 James Rosenquist, *F–111,* 1965. Oil on canvas with aluminum, 10 x 86 ft. Courtesy Leo Castelli Gallery.

Claes Oldenburg, *Three-Way Plug – Scale A, Soft, Brown,* 1970. Naugahyde, 144 x 77 x 59 in. Collection of Walker Art Center.

p. 97 Ellsworth Kelly, View of exhibition, March 8– April 5, 1975. Courtesy Leo Castelli Gallery.

p. 98 John Chamberlain, *Mr. Press,* 1961. Welded auto metal with fabric, 95 x 90 x 50 in. Collection of Mr. and Mrs. Leo Castelli.

p. 99 Robert Rauschenberg, *Rebus,* 1955. Combine painting, 96 x 130½ x 1¾ in. Courtesy Leo Castelli Gallery.

p. 100 Robert Morris, *Untitled,* 1961. Fir, 10½ x 25 x 74 in. Courtesy Leo Castelli Gallery.

p. 101 Donald Judd, *Untitled,* 1965. Painted galvanized iron, 5 x 69 x 8¾ in. Collection of Mr. and Mrs. Leo Castelli.

Dan Flavin, *Monument for V. Tatlin, No. 1,* 1964. Cool white fluorescent light, 96 x 23 x 4 in. Courtesy Leo Castelli Gallery.

p. 102 Richard Serra, *St. John's Rotary Arc,* 1980. Corten steel, 12 ft. x 200 ft. x 2½ in. Courtesy Leo Castelli Gallery.

Joseph Kosuth, *One and Three Brooms (English),* 1965. Broom, photos of broom, and definition of broom, 59⅞ x 75¾ x 3 in. Courtesy Leo Castelli Gallery.

p. 103 Bruce Nauman, *Henry Moore Bound to Fail (Back View),* 1967. Wax over plaster, 26 x 24 x 3½ in. Collection of Mr. and Mrs. Leo Castelli.

p. 104 Keith Sonnier, *BA-O-BA, Number 3,* 1969. Glass and neon, 91¼ x 122¾ x 24 in. Collection of

Whitney Museum of American Art. Gift of the Howard and Jean Lipman Foundation, Inc. Acq #69.126.

p. 105 Jan Dibbets, *Dutch Mountains – Big Sea A*, 1971. Eleven color photographs mounted on aluminum panels, overall 33⅞ in. x 14 ft. 10⅛ in.; eleven color photographs and pencil on paper, 29½ x 39⅜ in. Collection, The Museum of Modern Art, New York. Purchase.

p. 107 Julian Schnabel, *Portrait of a Girl*, 1980. Oil, plates on wood, 96 x 84 in. Collection of Mr. and Mrs. Leo Castelli.

p. 108 Roy Lichtenstein, *Two Paintings: Craig*, 1983. Oil and magna on canvas, 48 x 36 in. Collection of the artist.

p. 111 Jasper Johns, *Flag*, 1955. Encaustic, oil, and collage on fabric, 42½ x 60⅝ in. Collection, The Museum of Modern Art, Gift of Philip Johnson.

p. 112 Robert Rauschenberg, *Shortshop*, 1962. Oil on canvas, 60¼ x 60¼ in. Courtesy Sonnabend Gallery.

Andy Warhol, *Gold Marilyn*, 1962. Oil, acrylic and silkscreen ink on canvas, 83¼ x 57 in. Courtesy Leo Castelli Gallery.

p. 113 Arman, *Infinity of Typewriters and Infinity of Monkeys and Infinity of Time – Hamlet*, 1962. Typewriters in wood encasement, 72 x 69 x 12 in. Courtesy Sonnabend Gallery.

p. 115 Gilbert and George, *The Alcoholic*, 1978. Black and white photographs, 16 panels, 23¾ x 19¾ in. each, overall 95¼ x 79⅜ in. Courtesy Sonnabend Gallery.

p. 116 Jannis Kounellis, *Untitled*, 1972. Installation. Courtesy Sonnabend Gallery.

p. 117 A. R. Penck, *Am Fluss (Hypothese 3)*, 1982. Acrylic on canvas, 102⅜ x 137½ in. Courtesy Sonnabend Gallery.

p. 118 Vito Acconci, *Installation*, 1979. Courtesy Sonnabend Gallery.

Anne and Patrick Poirier, *The Temple of One Hundred Columns*, 1980. Plaster on wood base, 34½ x 109 x 109 in. Courtesy Sonnabend Gallery.

p. 119 Mel Bochner, *Syncline*, 1978–79. Caselin on wall, 114 x 139 in. Courtesy Sonnabend Gallery.

p. 123 James Rosenquist, *Marilyn Monroe I*, 1962. Oil on canvas, 93 x 72 in. Collection, The Museum of Modern Art, New York.

p. 124 Donald Judd, Untitled, 1961. Galvanized iron and plywood, 52 x 43 x 5 in. Collection of Mr. and Mrs. Lewis Winter, Courtesy Leo Castelli Gallery.

p. 127 Myron Stout, *Untitled*, 1955–68. Oil on canvas, 25 x 19 in. Richard Brown Baker Collection. Courtesy Oil and Steel Gallery.

p. 128 Jo Baer, *Untitled Diptych*, 1968. Oil on canvas, 42 x 98 in. Courtesy Oil and Steel Gallery.

David Rabinowitch, *Metrical (Romanesque)*

Construction in Eleven Masses and Two Scales, 1980. Steel, 3 x 82 x 69 in. Courtesy Oil and Steel Gallery.

p. 129 Alfred Leslie, *First Four*, 1955. Oil on canvas, 10 x 12 ft. Courtesy Oil and Steel Gallery.

p. 130 Mark di Suvero, *Mon Père, Mon Père*, 1974. Steel, approximately 36 ft. wide x 42 ft. high. *Etoile Polare*, 1973. Steel, approximately 90 ft. wide x 120 ft. high. Courtesy Oil and Steel Gallery.

p. 131 Michael Heizer, *Dissipate: Number Eight of Nine Nevada Depressions*, 1968. Liner with wooden sleeves, 45 x 50 ft. area. Courtesy Oil & Steel Gallery.

p. 132 William Crozier, *Marilyn*, 1975–80. Plaster state, 44¼ x 34¾ x 38⅛ in. Courtesy Oil and Steel Gallery.

p. 137 Roy Lichtenstein, *Masterpiece*, 1962. Oil on canvas, 54 x 54 in. Collection of Mr. and Mrs. Albrecht Saalfield, New York.

p. 140 Andy Warhol, *Flowers (Installation View)*, 1964. Courtesy Leo Castelli Gallery.

p. 144 Deborah Butterfield, *Armor-Plated Horse*, 1979. Aluminum sheet, mud, sticks, wire and steel, 31 x 48 x 14 in. Courtesy O.K. Harris.

Aris Koutroulis, *Untitled #4*, 1981. Acrylic on linen and cotton, 72 x 96 in. Courtesy O.K. Harris.

p. 145 Ilan Averbach, *Installation, October 17– November 7, 1981.* Mixed media. Courtesy of O.K. Harris.

Kenneth Morgan, *Night Flight*, 1982. Oil on canvas, 65½ x 77¾ in. Courtesy O.K. Harris.

p. 146 Ralph Goings, *Still Life with Coffee*, 1982. Oil on canvas, 38 x 52 in. Courtesy O.K. Harris.

p. 147 Robert Rohm, *Untitled*, 1975. Wood and rope, 62 x 99 x 34 in. Courtesy O.K. Harris.

p. 148 Peter Saari, *Bust with Shells*, 1981. Caselin and gouache with plaster on canvas and wood, 74 x 51 x 6 in. Courtesy O.K. Harris.

John DeAndrea, *Model in Repose*, 1981. Polyvinyl ploychromed on oil, lifesize. Courtesy O.K. Harris.

p. 149 John Kacere, *Ileana – 82*, 1982. Oil on canvas, 48 x 72 in. Courtesy O.K. Harris.

p. 152 Edward Kienholz, *Little Eagle Rock Incident*, 1958. Mixed media construction on wood, 61¼ x 48⅞ in. Courtesy Brooks Jackson–Iolas Gallery.

p. 154 Joseph Cornell, *Central Park Carrousel, in Memorium*, 1950. Construction in wood, mirror, wire netting, and paper, 20¼ x 14½ x 6¾ in. Collection, The Museum of Modern Art, New York. Katherine Cornell Fund.

p. 155 Andy Warhol, *32 Soup Cans*, 1961–62. Acrylic on canvas, each painting 20 x 16 in. Collection of Irving Blum, New York.

p. 156 Robert Moskowitz, *Thinker*, 1982. Pastel on paper, 108 x 63 in. Courtesy Blum-Helman Gallery.

p. 157 Andrew Lord, *Two Teapots in Morning Light/Grey/Angled*, 1981. Unglazed earthenware, left: 7½ x 7½ x 6 in.; right: 9½ x 11½ x 7 in. Courtesy Blum-Helman Gallery.

Roy Lichtenstein, *Compositions III*, 1965. Magna on canvas, 56 x 48 in. Courtesy Blum-Helman Gallery.

p. 160 Roy Lichtenstein, *Baseball Manager*, 1963. Magna on canvas, 68 x 58 in. Collection of Joseph Helman, New York.

p. 161 Richard Serra, *Around the Corner*, 1982. Cor-Ten steel, 50¼ x 480 x 1 in., 50¼ x 437 x 94 in. as installed. Courtesy Blum-Helman Gallery.

p. 162 Bryan Hunt, *Arch Falls*, 1980–81. Cast bronze with limestone base, 94 x 42 x 18 in. Courtesy Blum-Helman Gallery.

Claes Oldenburg, *Giant Loaf of Raisin Bread, Sliced (Raisin Bread: Five Slices and End, 42 Raisins)*, 1967. Liquitex, glue, and graphite on canvas filled with kapok. Collection of Joseph Helman, New York.

p. 163 Donald Sultan, *Rain, July 8, 1982*. Oil, charcoal, and encaustic on vinyl tile over wood, 86 x 48 in. Courtesy Blum-Helman Gallery.

Steve Keister, *USO #64*, 1980. Acrylic, fluorescent plexiglass, and metallic leather on wood, 15 x 30 x 30 in. Courtesy Blum-Helman Gallery.

p. 164 Chuck Close, *Arnold*, 1979. Conte crayon on paper, 29 x 21¾ in. Courtesy The Pace Gallery.

p. 166 Louise Nevelson, *Sky Cathedral – Moon Garden Plus One*, 1957–60. Black-painted wood, 109 x 130 x 19 in. Courtesy The Pace Gallery.

p. 167 Agnes Martin, *Untitled*, 1977. Watercolor, graphite, and ink on paper, 9 x 9 in. Courtesy The Pace Gallery.

p. 168 Jasper Johns, *Three Flags*, 1958. Encaustic on canvas, 30⅞ x 45½ x 5 in. Collection of Whitney Museum of American Art. 50th Anniversary Gift of the Gilman Foundation, Inc., the Lauder Foundation, A. Alfred Taubman, and anonymous donor (and purchase). Acq #80.32.

p. 169 Mark Rothko, *Untitled*, 1958. Oil on canvas, 105 x 149 in. Estate of Mark Rothko.

p. 171 Pablo Picasso, *La femme au Jardin*, 1929–30. Unique bronze (after the original in painted forged iron), 82½ x 46 x 32 in. Courtesy The Pace Gallery.

p. 172 Brice Marden, *Card Drawings (Counting) #17*, 1982. Ink on card, 6 x 5⅞ in. Courtesy The Pace Gallery.

Jim Dine, *Two Mighty Robes at Night in Jerusalem*, 1980. Two panels, overall 89½ x 106 in., each panel 89½ x 53¾ in. Courtesy The Pace Gallery.

p. 173 Lucas Samaras, *Sittings 20x24 (7G)*, 1980. Polaroid, 20 x 24 in. Courtesy The Pace Gallery.

p. 176 Claes Oldenburg, *Screwarch Bridge, State II*, 1980. Etching, 31½ x 58 in. Courtesy Multiples, Inc./Marian Goodman Gallery.

Larry Rivers, *Cigar Box*, 1966. Silkcreen and wood construction. Numbered edition of 20, published by Multiples, Inc./Marian Goodman Gallery.

p. 177 Roy Lichtenstein, *Huh?*, 1976. Silkscreen, 41½ x 29½ in. Edition of 100. Courtesy Multiples, Inc./Marian Goodman Gallery.

View of exhibition "Banners," ca. 1970. Courtesy Multiples, Inc./Marian Goodman Gallery.

p. 178 Marcel Broodthaers, *"Portraits,"* 1983. A portfolio of 17 photographs: 16 photographs and one self-portrait. Numbered edition of 50. Courtesy Multiples, Inc./Marian Goodman Gallery.

Ger Van Elk, *Sketch for the Last Adieu*, 1975. Acrylic on photograph, 39 x 39 in. Courtesy Multiples Inc./Marian Goodman Gallery.

p. 179 Anselm Kiefer, *Ein Schwert Verhiss mir der Vater (My Father Promised Me a Sword)*, 1981. Oil on canvas with straw, 67 x 75 in. Courtesy Multiples, Inc./Marian Goodman Gallery.

p. 182 Michael Heizer, *45°, 90°, 180° (#2)*, 1982. Quarzite and aluminum, 45°: 4 x 4 x 5 ft., 1250 lbs.; 90°: 3½ x 4 x 7 ft., 1400 lbs.; 180°: 4 x 5 x 5 ft., 1350 lbs. Courtesy Xavier Fourcade, Inc., New York.

Malcolm Morley, *The Palms of Vai*, 1982. Oil on canvas, 48½ x 38 in. Private collection. Courtesy Xavier Fourcade, Inc., New York.

p. 183 Willem de Kooning, *Untitled III*, 1982. Oil on canvas, 88 x 77 in. Courtesy Xavier Fourcade, Inc., New York.

p. 184 Henry Moore, *Working Model for a Stone Memorial*, 1961–71. Bronze, 23 x 23 x 22 in. Private collection. Courtesy Xavier Fourcade, Inc., New York.

p. 185 Georg Baselitz, *Glastrinker (Glass Drinker)*, 1981. Oil on canvas, 63¾ x 51¼ in. Private collection. Courtesy Xavier Fourcade, Inc., New York.

p. 188 Elizabeth Murray, *Keyhole*, 1982. Oil on canvas, 99½ x 110½ in. Private collection. Courtesy Paula Cooper Gallery.

p. 189 Lynda Benglis, *Bijlee*, 1981. Brass screen, hydrocal, gesso, and gold leaf, 27¼ x 33½ x 12 in. Collection of the artist. Courtesy Paula Cooper Gallery.

p. 190 Jackie Winsor, *Glass Piece*, 1978–79. Glass, wood, and tar, 31⅜ x 31 x 31 in. Art Gallery of Ontario, Toronto. Purchased with assistance of Wintario 1979.

Robert Grosvenor, *Untitled*, 1980–81. Wood (pine) and paint, 67 x 133 x 74 in. Courtesy Paula Cooper Gallery.

p. 191 Alan Shields, *Mt. Saint Helens*, 1980. Acrylic and stitching on canvas, 71 x 104 in. Courtesy Paula Cooper Gallery.

Carl Andre, *Shiloh, New York*, 1980. Sixty-four redwood timbers, 12 x 12 x 36 in. each, 36 x 216 x 216 in. overall. Private collection. Courtesy Paula Cooper Gallery.

p. 192 Joel Shapiro, *Untitled*, 1980–81. Bronze, 52⅞ x 64 x 45½ in. *Untitled*, 1980–82. Bronze, 23¾ x 13 x 8⅛ in. Courtesy Paula Cooper Gallery.

p. 193 Jonathan Borofsky, View of exhibition, Museum Boymans van Beuningen, Rotterdam, Holland, February 20–April 4, 1982. Courtesy Paula Cooper Gallery.

p. 194 Jennifer Bartlett, *At Sea*, 1979. Enamel, silkscreen grid, and baked enamel on steel plates (107 plate), oil on canvas (2 ellipses), measurements variable. Private collection. Courtesy Paula Cooper Gallery.

p. 195 Michael Hurson, *Study for a Portrait (William)*, 1981. Pencil, pastel, ink, conte crayon on paper, 26¼ x 40½ in. Private collection. Courtesy Paula Cooper Gallery.

p. 198 Sol Le Witt, *Six Geometric Figures in Three Colors*, 1980. Installation John Weber Gallery.

p. 199 Alighiero e Boetti, *Map of the World*, 1972. Canvas and thread, 61¼ x 93¼ in. Courtesy John Weber Gallery.

Daniel Buren, *Photo-souvenir: "Exit" work* in situ, Installation John Weber Gallery, New York, November 1980. © Buren.

p. 200 Robert Smithson, *Spiral Jetty, April 1970, Great Salt Lake Utah*. Courtesy Gianfranco Gorgoni.

p. 201 Jeremy Gilbert-Rolfe, *Masurian Lakes*, 1981–82. Oil on linen, 110 x 302 in. Courtesy John Weber Gallery.

Lucio Pozzi, *The Picture Plane*, 1981. Oil on canvas, 124 x 108 in. Courtesy John Weber Gallery.

p. 202 James Biederman, *Untitled*, 1980. Gouache, pastel, and charcoal on paper, 91 x 47½ in. Courtesy John Weber Gallery.

p. 203 Alice Aycock, *The Savage Sparkler*, 1981. Installation John Weber Gallery. Steel, sheet metal, electric heating elements, motors, and fluorescent lights, 10 x 14 x 8 ft. Courtesy John Weber Gallery.

Mel Kendrick, *Hucklebuck*, 1981. Painted wood, 76 x 55½ x 20½ in. Courtesy John Weber Gallery.

p. 206 Christo, *Wrapped Coast, Little Bay, Australia*, 1969. Photograph, 36 x 48 in. One million square feet. Courtesy John Gibson Gallery, Inc.

p. 207 View of exhibition, *Anti-form*, John Gibson Gallery. October–November 1968. Left to right: Alan Sarat, Keith Sonnier, Richard Serra, Bob Ryman, Richard Tuttle, Eva Hesse. Courtesy John Gibson Gallery, Inc.

p. 208 Dennis Oppenheim, *Annual Rings*, 1968. Frozen river (St. John River at Fort Kent, Maine), 150 x 200 ft. Courtesy John Gibson Gallery, Inc.

p. 209 Dennis Oppenheim, *Parallel Stress*, 1970. Documentation (a 10-minute performance piece on collapsed concrete pier between Brooklyn Bridge and Manhattan Bridge). The photo was taken at the body's point of extreme stress, 39 x 39 in. Courtesy John Gibson Gallery, Inc.

p. 210 Peter Hutchinson, *January (from "Year" series)*, 1978. Black and white photograph, 20 x 24

in. Courtesy John Gibson Gallery, Inc.

p. 211 Marcel Broodthaers, *Museum*, 1968. Colored plastic impression, 32½ x 46¾ in., seven examples. Courtesy John Gibson Gallery, Inc.

p. 212 Joseph Beuys, *Felt Suits (Installation view)*, 1970. Courtesy John Gibson Gallery, Inc.

Ben Vautier, *I reserve the right to consider this text as interesting in the future as it is in the present*, 1971. Acrylic on canvas, 29 x 35 in. Courtesy John Gibson Gallery, Inc.

p. 213 Bill Lundberg, *Detail from "Charades,"* 1976. Film sculpture (Super-8 color film projection onto vinyl card placed in glass of water). Courtesy John Gibson Gallery, Inc.

p. 216 Joseph Beuys, *Evervess*, 1968. Box containing two bottles and felt, 11 x 6½ x 3½ in. Edition of 40. Courtesy Ronald Feldman Fine Arts, New York.

Joseph Beuys, *Without the Rose, It Doesn't Matter*, 1972. Lithograph, 33⅞ x 24 in. Signed, numbered edition of 80 with 20 artist's proofs. Courtesy Ronald Feldman Fine Arts, New York.

p. 217 Buckminster Fuller sitting with his work, *Tetrascroll*, at Ronald Feldman Fine Arts, Inc., New York. Photo © Peggy Jarrell Kaplan.

p. 218 Thomas Shannon, *Compass of Love*, 1981. Twenty-four-foot magnesium needle floating over a 12-foot dome. Courtesy Ronald Feldman Fine Arts, New York.

Conrad Atkinson, *Northern Ireland 1968–May Day 1975 (detail)*, 1974. Seventy-five color photographs mounted on board, each 5 x 7 in. Sixty-four typewritten sheets mounted on board, each 8¼ x 5¾ in. Courtesy Ronald Feldman Fine Arts, New York.

p. 219 Eleanor Antin, *Eleanora Antinova reminiscing about her life with Diaghilev at Ronald Feldman Fine Arts, Inc., New York, 1980*. Courtesy Ronald Feldman Fine Arts, New York.

p. 222 Harold Edgerton, *Shock Waves from Impact*, 1965. Silverprint, 20 x 24 in. Copyright Harold Edgerton. Courtesy Daniel Wolf, Inc.

p. 223 John Coplans, *Mummers' Parade, Philadelphia, 1982*, 1982. Silverprint, 25 x 31 in. Copyright John Coplans 1982. Courtesy Daniel Wolf, Inc.

p. 224 Sheila Metzner, *Turquoise Vase – Painted Gladiola*, 1980. Color fresson print. Copyright Sheila Metzner. Courtesy Daniel Wolf, Inc.

p. 225 Jed Devine, *Untitled*, 1978. Palladium print, 8 x 10 in. Copyright Jed Devine. Courtesy Daniel Wolf, Inc.

p. 229 Michael Graves, *Garden Facade, Plocek House, Warren, New Jersey*, 1977–79. Pencil on tracing paper. Courtesy Max Protetch Gallery.

Michael Graves, *Preliminary Street Facade, Plocek House, Warren, New Jersey*, 1977–79. Pencil and prismacolor on tracing paper. Courtesy Max Protetch Gallery.

p. 230 Richard Fleischner, *Untitled*, 1981. Modular block construction, 48 x 60 x 60 in. Courtesy Max Protetch Gallery.

p. 231 Siah Armajani, *Closed Door-Open Door*, 1981. Redwood, aluminum, and plexiglass, 54¼ x 79 x 38 in. Courtesy Max Protetch Gallery.

Scott Burton, *Concrete Tables*, 1981. (Installation) Courtesy Max Protetch Gallery.

p. 232 Jackie Ferrara, *Gray Gazebo*, 1982. Pine and poplar, 28 x 18 x 18 in. Courtesy Max Protetch Gallery.

p. 233 Mary Miss, *Veiled Landscape*, 1979. Wood and wire mesh, 400-ft. long. Courtesy Max Protetch Gallery.

p. 235 Andy Warhol, *Holly*, 1966. Silkscreen painting, 81 x 81 in. (in 9 panels). Collection of Holly and Horace Solomon, New York.

p. 237 Thomas Lanigan-Schmidt, *The Siberian Monk and the Philokalia*, 1978. Mixed media, 17 x 12 in. Courtesy Holly Solomon Gallery, New York.

p. 238 Ned Smyth, *Study for floor mosaic, Prudential Insurance Company West Coast Headquarters, West Lake, California*, 1981. 35-ft. diameter. Courtesy Holly Solomon Gallery, New York.

p. 239 Robert Kushner, *Mixed Emotions*, 1979. Acrylic on paper, 44½ x 60 in. (2 panels). Courtesy Holly Solomon Gallery, New York.

Kim MacConnel, *Greek*, 1980. Acrylic on cotton, 98 x 128 in. Courtesy Holly Solomon Gallery, New York.

p. 240 Judy Pfaff, *Magic*, 1981. Contact paper collage on mylar, 89 x 45 in. Courtesy Holly Solomon Gallery, New York.

Nicholas Africano. *The Body and Soul II (from Dr. Jekyll and Mr. Hyde)*, 1981. Acrylic, oil, and wax on canvas with frame, 38 x 32 in. Courtesy Holly Solomon Gallery, New York.

p. 241 Joe Zucker, *Ivan Koloff vs. Executioner One*, 1981. Acrylic, rhoplex, and cotton on canvas, 99 x 99½ in. Courtesy Holly Solomon Gallery, New York.

p. 244 Manuel Neri, *Penance #3*, 1982. Bronze, 46½ x 17 x 22 in. Courtesy Charles Cowles Gallery, Inc.

p. 246 Peter Voulkos, *Untitled*, 1981. Ceramic, 36 x 18 in. Courtesy Charles Cowles Gallery, Inc.

p. 247 Nathan Olivera, *Figure Six*, 1983. Bronze, 45½ x 35½ x 35 in. Courtesy Charles Cowles Gallery, Inc.

p. 248 Dale Chihuly, *Untitled*, 1981. Six glass pieces, approximate 20 in. diameter for largest piece. Courtesy Charles Cowles Gallery, Inc.

p. 249 Nino Longobardi, *Untitled*, 1981. Mixed media on canvas, 140 x 220 cm. Courtesy Charles Cowles Gallery, Inc.

David Bates, *The Dream*, 1983. Oil on canvas, 90 x 72 in. Courtesy Charles Cowles, Inc.

p. 251 Alex Katz, *Self-Portrait*, 1978. Aquatint, 36 x 30 in. Edition of 32. Courtesy Brooke Alexander, Inc.

p. 252 Fairfield Porter, *Rocks and Shore Growth*, 1975. Watercolor, 211 x 30½ in. Courtesy Brooke Alexander, Inc.

Martha Diamond, *Façade*, 1982. Oil on canvas, 84 x 56 in. Courtesy Brooke Alexander, Inc.

p. 253 Judy Rifka, *A Museum Piece*, 1982. Oil on two linen panels, 66 x 48 in. Courtesy Brooke Alexander, Inc.

p. 255 Richard Bosman, *The Kick*, 1982. Oil on canvas, 54 x 42 in. Courtesy Brooke Alexander, Inc.

p. 256 John Ahearn, *Louis with Bite in Forehead*, 1980. Painted plaster cast, 24 x 21 x 6 in. Courtesy Brooke Alexander, Inc.

p. 260 Auste, *I Look at You*, 1981. Acrylic on canvas, 72 x 27 in. Courtesy Hamilton Gallery of Contemporary Art.

p. 261 David Hare, *Elephants and Violets No. 5*, 1979. Acrylic on canvas, 69 x 53 in. Courtesy Hamilton Gallery of Contemporary Art.

p. 262 Richard Hennessy, *Stay of Execution*, 1981. Oil on canvas, 66 x 69 in. Courtesy Hamilton Gallery of Contemporary Art.

p. 263 Joan Snyder, *Symphony V*, 1982. Mixed media on canvas, 72 x 96 in. Courtesy Hamilton Gallery of Contemporary Art.

p. 264 Martin Silverman, *Passion*, 1981. Cast bronze, 36 x 19 x 17 in. Edition of 6. Courtesy Hamilton Gallery of Contemporary Art.

p. 265 Michael David, *Between Seduction and Subversion*, 1982. Wax, pigment, and wood, 72½ x 33½ x 6½ in. Courtesy Hamilton Gallery of Contemporary Art.

p. 267 Morris Graves, *Bird Masking*, 1953. Tempera and gold, 20 x 30 in. Courtesy Willard Gallery.

p. 268 Susan Rothenberg, *Untitled #147*, 1980–81. Acrylic and flashe on canvas, 111 x 114 in. Courtesy Willard Gallery.

p. 269 Lois Lane, *Untitled, WG #122*, 1981. Oil and graphite on canvas, 75 x 120 in. Courtesy Willard Gallery.

Judith Shea, *Young One*, 1981. Wool felt, 19 x 28 x 8½ in. Courtesy Willard Gallery.

p. 270 Bob Lobe, *Trees*, 1981. Hammered aluminum, 87 x 56 x 69 in. Courtesy Willard Gallery.

Tod Wizon, *Gradient*, 1980. Acrylic on wood, 40 x 30 in. Courtesy Willard Gallery.

p. 271 Ralph Humphrey, *Ground Control*, 1981. Acrylic and modeling paste on wood, 54 x 54 in. Courtesy Willard Gallery.

Joan Thorne, *Zamba*, 1982. Oil on canvas, 108 x 240 in. (triptych). Courtesy Willard Gallery.

p. 274 Anselm Kiefer, *Ikarus I*, 1976. Oil on canvas, 46 x 57½ in. Courtesy Mary Boone Gallery.

p. 275 Julian Schnabel, *St. Francis in Ecstasy*, 1980. Oil and plates on wood, 96 x 84 in. Courtesy Mary Boone Gallery.

p. 276 David Salle, *Cut Out the Beggar*, 1981.

Acrylic on canvas, 86 x 56 in. Courtesy Mary Boone Gallery.

p. 277 Gary Stephan, *Century*, 1983. Acrylic on canvas, 106 x 144 in. Courtesy Mary Boone Gallery.

p. 279 Troy Brauntuch, *Untitled*, 1982. Pencil on cotton, 96 x 68 in. (two panels). Courtesy Mary Boone Gallery.

p. 281 Francesco Clemente, *Sound Point*, 1983. Oil on canvas, 63 x 83 in. Courtesy Mary Boone Gallery.

p. 284 Sandro Chia, *Kangaroo Boxing Match*, 1977. Oil, collage on canvas, 31 x 31 in. Courtesy Annina Nosei Gallery.

Mimmo Paladino, *Porta (Door)*, 1980. Papier-mâché, handmade paper, powders, glue, and acrylic, 84 x 36 x 3 in. Courtesy Annina Nosei Gallery.

p. 285 Donald Newman, *The Drummer*, 1981. Acrylic on photograph and paper, 60 x 56 in. Courtesy Annina Nosei Gallery.

p. 286 Mike Glier, *The Glory of Crispus Attacks (Monuments Lie)*, 1980. Oil on paper, 60 x 55 in. Courtesy Annina Nosei Gallery.

K. H. Hodicke, *Potsdamer Strasse*, 1979. Oil on canvas, 74½ x 61 in. Courtesy Annina Nosei Gallery.

p. 287 Berndt Koberling, *Wingspan*, 1981. Oil and kunstcharz on jute, 77½ x 108 in. Courtesy Annina Nosei Gallery.

David Deutsch, *Untitled*, 1979. Ink on paper, 66 x 106 in. Courtesy Annina Nosei Gallery.

p. 288 Jean Michel Basquiat, *Mater*, 1982. Acrylic and oilstick on canvas, 72 x 84 in. Courtesy Annina Nosei Gallery.

Jack Goldstein, *Untitled*, 1983. Acrylic on canvas, 84 x 144 in. Collection of Mr. and Mrs. Robert Kaye. Photo courtesy of Metro Pictures.

p. 293 Cindy Sherman, *Untitled*, 1983. Color photograph, 57½ x 106 in. Courtesy Metro Pictures.

p. 294 John Miller, *Untitled*, 1983. Acrylic on canvas, 28 x 22 in. Collection of Martin Sklar. Courtesy Metro Pictures.

Richard Prince, *Untitled*, 1982. Color photograph, 30 x 44 in. Courtesy Metro Pictures.

p. 295 Mike Kelley, *Cross-Cultural Development*, 1983. Ink on paper, 24 x 35 in. Courtesy Metro Pictures.

p. 296 Robert Longo, *Ornamental Love*, 1983. Mixed media, 96 x 228 in. Collection of Mr. and Mrs. Richard Black. Courtesy Metro Pictures.

Walter Robinson, *Willie's Girl*, 1982. Acrylic on canvas, 48 x 36 in. Collection of Doris and Robert Hillman. Courtesy Metro Pictures.

p. 297 Thomas Lawson, *To Those Who Follow After*, 1983. Oil on canvas, 60 x 168 in. Courtesy Metro Pictures.

p. 300 Zadik Zadikian, *Aram*, 1982. Cast plaster, burlap support, and 24-karat-gold gilded tip, 66 x 96 x 6 in. Courtesy Tony Shafrazi Gallery.

p. 302 Keith Haring, *Untitled*, May 1982. Vinyl ink on vinyl tarpaulin, 12 x 12 ft. Collection of Tony Shafrazi.

Donald Baechler, *The Zagreb Picture*, 1982–83. Acrylic on canvas, 96 x 68 in. Courtesy Tony Shafrazi Gallery.

p. 303 Ronnie Cutrone, *A Little Knowledge*, 1982. Acrylic on American flag, 10 x 15 ft. Courtesy Tony Shafrazi Gallery.

Kenny Sharf, *Plasmospace*, November 1982. Oil and spray paint on canvas, 103 x 114 in. (framed). The Morton N. Neumann Family Collection.

p. 304 James Brown, *Horse Shoes and Crosses That's Good Luck*, 1982. Pencil and enamel on canvas, 78 x 84 in. Collection of Tony Shafrazi.

Futura 2000, *Letter to Myself*, 1983. Spray enamel on canvas, 96 x 69 in. Collection of Ara Arslanian, New York.

p. 305 Brett De Palma, *Incognito*, 1982. Acrylic and collage on canvas, 115 x 84 in. Courtesy Tony Shafrazi Gallery.

INDEX

Page numbers in *italics* refer to illustrations; those in **boldface** refer to page spans of interviews.

Abstract and Surrealist Art
  (Janis), 32, 35
Abstract Expressionism, 23, 32,
  39, 58, 59, 86, 87–88, 93, 96,
  98, 111, 121, 125, 135, 136, 138,
  147, 171, 197, 221, 229, 231,
  271
"Abstract Images," 268
Académie Royale de la Peinture,
  13
Acconci, Vito, *118*, 210
action painting, 58, 121
Africano, Nicholas, 239–240, *240*
Agnetti, 219
Ahearn, John, 250, 253, *256*, 256–
  257
Albers, Josef, 151, 175
Alexander, Brooke, **250–257**
Alexander, Carolyn, 251, 252
American Place, 23
Anderson, Laurie, 241
Andre, Carl, 44, 101, 131–133,
  188, 191, *191*, 199, 284
Andrejevic, Milet, 124
Andrew Dickson White Museum,
  91
Angeli, Franco, 283
Annual Rings (Oppenheim), 207,
  208
"Anti-Form," 207, *207*
Antin, Eleanor, 219, *219*
Anxious Girl, The (Lichtenstein),
  236
Arakawa, Shusaku, 176, 216, 219
Archipenko, Alexander, 20, 21
architecture, 28, 227, 228–230
Armajani, Siah, 228, 231, *231*
Arman, 113, *113*
Armstrong, Tom, 169
Arp, Jean, 235
"Arp to Artschwager," 133
Art Dealers' Association, 246, 248
Art Deco, 82
Art Deco Gallery, 110
Arte Povera, 99, 199, 200, 207,
  274
Artforum, 238, 242, 243, 244
Art in America, 258, 259
Artists and Photographs, 176
Artists Space, 253, 267, 276, 279,
  292
Artists' Strike (1969), 300
Art Museum Directors' Associa-
  tion, 244

Art News, 90
Art of this Century Gallery, 17, 23
Art-Rite, 254
Arts, 124
Artschwager, Richard, 174
Art Students League, 187
Art Workers Coalition, 190, 300
Ashbery, John, 45
Ash-Can School, 66
"Aspects of New Realism," 251
Ast, Patty, 237
Atkinson, Conrad, 218, *218*
auction houses, 29–30, 67–68, 78,
  116, 202, 223
Austé, *260*, 262
Avery, Milton, 175
Avignon paintings (Picasso), 171
Aycock, Alice, 203, *203*

Baechler, Donald, *302*, 302–303
Baer, Jo, *128*, 129, 188
Balanchine, George, 51
"Banners," *176*
Barnes, Edward Larrabee, 231
Barr, Alfred, 26–27, 41, 47, 84,
  90, 91, 93
Barry, Robert, 101
Bartlett, Jennifer, 193–194, *194*
Basel Art Fair, 238
Baselitz, Georg, 116, 184–185, *185*
Basquiat, Jean Michel, 287–288,
  288, 303
Bates, David, *249*
Battered Woman, The (Africano),
  239–240
Baynard, Ed, 237
Bed (Rauschenberg), *90*, 91
Bell, Clive, 82
Bell, Larry, 167, 299
Bellamy, Richard, 96, 100–101,
  120–133, 134, 135, 144, 236,
  275
"Below Zero," 207
Benglis, Lynda, 188, 189, *189*
Bengston, Billy Al, 299
Berman, Eugene, 82
Betsy Ross Banner Co., 175
Beuys, Joseph, 178, 211, 212, *212*,
  215–216, *216*, 219, 269
Beyeler, Ernst, 170
Biederman, James, 202, *202*
Bing, Alexander, 46
Birch, Walter, 22
Bird in Space (Brancusi), 33

Bitter Box, The (Clark), 131
Bleckner, Ross, 273, 275, 277, 279
Block, René, 179
Blue Poles (Pollock), 39
Blum, Irving, 71, 100, **150–158,**
  161, 243
Blum-Helman Gallery, 150, 156,
  159, 161
Bochner, Mel, *119*
Boetti, *199*, 201
Bolotowsky, Ilya, *67*, 71
Bonnard, Pierre, 44
Bontecou, Lee, 93, *94*
Boone, Mary, 107, 265, **272–
  281,** 289
Borofsky, Jonathan, 192, *193*
Bosman, Richard, 253, 254, 255,
  255
Bourdelle, Anton, 20, 21
Bowness, Alan, 114
Boyle, Mark, 245
Brancusi, Constantin, 12, 33, *33*
Brandt, Mortimer, 16, 22
Braque, Georges, 50, 85, 273
Brauner, Victor, 17, 50, *51*
Brauntuch, Troy, 279, *279*, 284
Brecht, Bertolt, 50
Breton, André, 113
Brillo boxes (Warhol), 236
Broadway Boogie-Woogie
  (Mondrian), 35
Broodthaers, Marcel, 174, *178*,
  178–179, 211, *211*, 212
Brown, Helen Gurley, 57
Brown, James, 304, *304*
Burchfield, Charles, 259
Burden, Chris, 219
Buren, Daniel, *199*, 201, 202
Burgin, Victor, 202
Burton, Scott, 228, 231, *231*
Butterfield, Deborah, *144*
Byers, James Lee, 179
Bykert Gallery, 272, 273, 274, 275

Cage, John, 90, 283
Calder, Alexander, 67, 257
Cameron, Julia Margaret, 221
Canberra Museum, 39
Castelli, Leo, 12, 29, 45, 46, 52,
  57, 71, **80–109,** 125–126, 127,
  134, 136–144, 154, 157, 160,
  241, 243, 273, 274, 275, 281,
  292, 297
Castelli, Toiny, 105

Castelli Gallery, 73, 110, 124, 136, 143, 144, 149, 160, 166, 190, 199, 236, 246, 257, 279–280
Castelli Graphics, 105
Cézanne, Paul, 15, 50, 59
Chamberlain, John *98*, 123, 140, 197, 283
Chia, Sandro, 107, 284, *284*, 286, 288, 289
Chicago Art Institute, 27, 224
Chihuly, Dale, 248, *248*
Childress, William, *213*
Christie's, 58, 168
Christo, 205–206, *206*
Cicero, Marcus Tullius, 13
Clark, Eleanor, 131
Clemente, Francesco, *281*, 284
Clert, Iris, 208
Close, Chuck, 172, 273
Club, The, 34
Cocteau, Jean, 52, *52*
Collage with Red (Rauschenberg), 91
collectors, 47, 70, 77, 78, 103–105, 148–149, 157–158, 162, 177, 217–218, 239, 247, 248, 255–256, 263, 265, 273, 280, 287
"Color and Structure," 261
Color Field painters, 56, 59, 109
color intervals, 122–123
Colt, Tom, 197
combine paintings (Rauschenberg), 89, 123
Compass of Love (Shannon), 217, *218*
Conceptual Art, 101, 102–103, 105, 186, 191, 199, 200, 201, 238, 285, 286
Contemporary Museum, 201
Cooper, Paula, 29, **186–195,** 255, 257, 265
Coplans, John, *223*, 224
Copley, William, *55*
Cordier-Ekstrom Gallery, 66
Cornell, Joseph, 12, 54–55, *54*, 69, 150, 153–154, *154*
Corot, Jean Baptiste Camille, 60
Courbet, Gustave, 60
Cowles, Charles, **242–249**
Cowles, Gardner, 243
Crispo, Andrew, 259
critics, art, 26, 60–61, 62, 68–69, 141–142, 246
Cozier, William, *132*, 184
Cubism, 33, 37, 40, 58, 171, 304
Cutone, Ronnie, 303, *303*

Dada, 86, 90, 113
Dali, Salvador, 34, 51, 82, 84, 181, 184
Damasippus, 13
Danese, Renato, 167
Darboven, Hanne, 101
Daughters of the American Revolution, 90
d'Autremont, Phillipe, 74
David, Jacques Louis, 60
David, Michael, *264*
Davis, Brad, 238
Davis, Doug, 210, 219
Davis, Stuart, 34
de Ak, Edit, 254
De Andrea, John, *148*
de Chirico, Giorgio, 17, 49–50, 51
de Cuevas, Marquis, 51
de Kooning, Willem, 16, 23, 37, *38*, 39, 40, 43, 84, 85, 86, 121, 123, 182–184, *183*, 288
Delacroix, Eugène, 60
della Palla, Giovanni, 13
del Sarto, Andrea, 13
de Maria, Walter, 188, 198, 284
de Nagy, Tibor, 42–47
de Nagy Gallery, 188
de Noailles, Countess, 52
De Palma, Brett, 304, *305*
de Pompadour, Madame, 13
de Rossi, Bernardino, 13
de Saint-Phalle, Niki, 113
Descamp, Gérard, 113
Deutsch, David, 287, *287*
Device Circle (Johns), 103
Devine, Jed, 224, 225, *225*
Dewey, John, 228
de Wilde, Edi, 114
Diamond, Martha, 251, *252*
Diba, Kamran, 301
Dibbets, Jan, 101, *105*, 176
Diderot, Denis, 14
Diebenkorn, Richard, 75, *75*
Dietrich, Marlene, 50
Dine, Jim, 143, 172, *172*, 197
Directed Seeding/Cancelled Crop (Oppenheim), 209
Disaster paintings (Warhol), 125
di Suvero, Mark, 120, 124, 127–128, 130, *130*, 197
"Documenta," 178, 199, 205, 211, 297, 304
Doty, Robert, 259
Dove, Arthur, 23, 270
Downtown Gallery, 34
Droll, Donald, 294
Drovin, René, 82, 83

Dubuffet, Jean, 36, 85, 136
"Duchamp, Anti-artist" (Janis and Janis), 34
Duchamp, Marcel, 12, 17, 34, 50, 86, 90, 211, 219, 283
Dudensing, Valentine, 33
Duff, John, 267
Dufy, Raoul, 50
Durand-Ruel, Paul, 14, 15–16
Dutch Master series (Rivers), 176–177
Duthuit, 85
Duvaux, Lazare, 13
Duveen, Joseph, 273
Dwan, Virginia, 17, 100, 197, 198, 199, 208
Dwan Gallery, 196, 199, 207, 283
Dzubas, Friedel, 74, *74*, 101

earthworks, 198, 199, 207, 284
"Earthworks," 207
East River Gallery, 267
École de Nice, 212
École de Paris, 37, 111, 197
Edgerton, Harold, *222*
Editions Alecto, 250
Editions Mat, 176
Egan, Charles, 16, 23, 65, 85
Egan Gallery, 87, 88
"Eight Contemporary Artists," 201
Elkon, Robert, 139, 188
Ellin, Everett, 100
Elmslie, Kenward, 45
Élvard, Paul, 50
Emmerich, André, 12, 46, **56–63,** 68, 128, 245, 274
Ernst, Max, 50, 54, 73, 82, 84
Exotic Birds (Stella), 146
Expressionism, 269, 271, 286

Farber, Manny, 130
Fauve Movement, 40, 85
Feldman, Ronald, **214–219**
Ferrara, Jackie, 231, *232*
Ferrer, Rafael, 261, 265
Ferus Gallery, 100, 150, 151–153, 243
figurative painting, 12, 45, 108, 262, 276, 277
Filliou, Robert, 212
Fini, Leonor, 50, 82
First Landing Jump (Rauschenberg), 91
Flannery, Vaughan, 68
Flavin, Dan, 100, *101*, 143, 200, 236

Fleischner, Richard, 228, *230*, 231
Fluxus movement, 197, 212
F-111 (Rosenquist), *96*, 103
Ford, Charles Henri, 43
Fourcade, Xavier, **180–185**
Fox, Terry, 219
Frampton, Hollis, 191
Francis, Sam, *58*, 135
François I, king of France, 13
Frankenthaler, Helen, 46, 56, 59, *60*, 61–62
Fraser, Robert, 299
Freilicher, Jane, 44
French & Co. Gallery, 46
Friedrich, Caspar David, 60
Friedrich, Heiner, 198
"From Matisse to American Abstract Painting," 71
Fuller, Buckminster, 216–217, *217*
Fuller Collection of Asian Art, 244
Futura 2000, 304, *304*
Futurists, 286, 304

Gainsborough, Thomas, 60
Galerie du Dragon, 73
Galerie J. Led, 113
Galerie Neufville, 72, 73
Galerie Rive Gauche, 111
Garouste, Gérard, 107
Gatch, Lee and Elsie, 187
Gauguin, Paul, 15
Gehry, Frank, 228
Geiger, Michael, 224
Geldzahler, Henry, 125, 139
Gemini G.E.L., 105, 251
Genauer, Emily, 93
geometrical art, 55
Gerber, Ann, 244
Gersaint, Edme-Francois, 14
Gibson, John, 179, 188, **204–213**
Gilbert & George, 111, 114, *115*
Gilbert-Rolfe, Jeremy, 200, *201*
Ginsburg, Allen, 188
Girouard, Tina, 237
Giurgola, Aldo, 231
Glass, Philip, 188, 278
Glier, Mike, *286*
Glimcher, Arnold, **164–173,** 273, 280
Gloria (Rauschenberg), 89
Goings, Ralph, *146*
Goldin, Amy, 238
Goldowsky, Noah, 127, 128, 129
Goldstein, Jack, 292, *293*
Goodman, James, 67

Goodman, Marian, **174–179,** 289
Goodman Gallery, 178
Goodnough, Robert, 45, *47*
Gorchov, Ron, 44, 261
Gorky, Arshile, 22, 37, 38, 70, 85
Gorney, Jay, 259
Gottlieb, Adolph, 16, 22, *22*
Goupil, Frederic Auguste Antoine, 16
Goya, Francisco, 60
graffiti, 304
Graham, Dan, 176
Graham, Robert, 66, 175
Graham Gallery, 66, 67
Graves, Michael, 229, *229*
Graves, Morris, 244, 267, *267*
Graves, Nancy, *79*
Green Gallery, 96, 120, 124–127, 129, 144, 166, 190, 236
Greenberg, Clement, 37, 46, 61, 73, 84, 109, 121, 200, 274
Greenberg, Ronald, 161, 284
Greenwald, Ted, 236
"Grids," 167
Gris, Juan, 25
Grisi, Laura, 101
Grooms, Red, 44, *44*
Groover, Jan, 225
Grosman, Tatyana, 105, 175, 251
Grosvenor, Robert, *190*, 192
Groth, Jan, *26*, 27
Grushkin, Alan, 21
Guggenheim, Peggy, 17, 22, 23, 46, 83, 154, 244
Guggenheim, Solomon, 36, 83
Guggenheim Museum, 27, 200–201
Gussow, Alan, 66
Guston, Philip, 39, 175

Hague Art Deliveries, 199
Hall, Susan, 237
Hamilton, Patricia, **258–265**
Hamilton, Richard, 177, 247
Hammer, Armand, 72, 76
"Hanging, Floating, Cantilevered Show, The," 205
Hansa Gallery, 120, 121–122, 124, 127, 133, 134, 135
"happenings," 122, 236, 283
Happy's Curios (Price), 269–270
Hare, David, 260, *261*
Haring, Keith, 301–302, *302*, 304
Harrison, Helen and Newton, 219
Harrison, Margaret, 219
Hartigan, Grace, 44, *44*, 46, 47

Hartley, Marsden, 71, *71*, 270
Harvey, James, 69
Heade, Martin Johnson, 64
Hearst, William Randolph, 57
Hedreen, Richard, 244
Hefner, Hugh, 57
Heizer, Michael, 120, *131*, 181, *182*, 198, 206–207, 284
Held, Al, *63*
Helman, Joe, 150, 156, **159–163,** 289
Helman Gallery, 159
Hennessy, Richard, *262*, 262–263
Herald Tribune, 68
Herbert F. Johnson Museum of Art, 91
Hess, Tom, 90
Hesse, Eva, 294
Heubler, Doug, 176
Hirshfield, Morris, 34
Hirshhorn, Joseph, 46–47
History of the Universe (Bartlett), 193
Hockney, David, *63*, 299, 304
Hödicke, K. H., 286, *286*
Hofmann, Hans, 35, 36, 59, *60*, 61, 121, 122–123
Hogarth, William, 60
Holtzman, Harry, 87
Hopper, Dennis, 156, 299
Hopps, Walter, 151, 153
Huebler, Douglas, 101
Hugo, Jean and Maria, 16–17
Hugo Gallery, 16–17, 48
Hulten, Pontus, 114
Humphrey, Ralph, 271, *271*
Hunt, Bryan, *162*
Hunter, Sam 265
Huot, Bob, 191
Hurok, Sol, 18
Hurson, Michael, 194–195, *195*
Hutchinson, Peter, 207, 208–209, *210*

"Illustration and Allegory," 254
Impressionists, 14, 280
Indiana, Robert, 166, 197
"Information," 101
Ingres, Jean-Auguste-Dominique, 60
Institute for Art and Urban Resources, 238
Iolas, Alexandre, 12, 17, **48–55**
Irwin, Robert, 167
"Is Not Lichtenstein the Worst Painter of Our Time?" 141
"It's Not the Bullet that Kills You, It's the Hole" (Anderson), 241

Jackson, Brooks, 48, 51
Jackson, Martha, 29, 122, 125, 134, 135–136, 139, 140, 155, 165, 197, 204
Jackson-Iolas Gallery, 48
Janis, Sidney, 12, 29, **32–41,** 52, 65, 68, 69, 73, 85, 87, 98–99, 136, 151, 158
Janis Gallery, 86, 97, 190, 235
Jenney, Neil, 268
Jewish Museum, 88, 200
John Gibson Commissions, 205
Johns, Jasper, 12, 74, 88–91, *89,* 92, 94, 95, 103, 104, 105, 108, 111, *111,* 113, 124, 136, 141, 142, 147, 160, *168,* 168–169, 177, 254, 278, 299
Johnson, James P., 34
Johnson, Joshua, 67
Johnson, Miani, **266–271**
Johnson, Philip, 27, 90, 91, 108
Judd, Donald, 100, *101,* 102, 106, *122,* 124, 127, 129, 143, 160, 191, 200, 205, 255, 257

Kacere, John, *149*
Kahnweiler, Daniel-Henry, 11, 16, 79, 238–239, 273, 274
Kalish, Ursula, 175
Kandinsky, Vasily, 83
Kaprow, Allan, 122, 137, 188, 197
Karp, Ivan, 45, 93–94, 122, 124, 125, 127, **134–150,** 154, 160–161, 275
Kasmin, John, 299
Kasmin Gallery, 74
Katz, Alex, *251*
Keister, Steve, *163*
Kelley, Mike, 294
Kelly, Ellsworth, 24, *24,* 71, 74, 97, *97,* 156
Kelly, Leon, 70
Kelly, Mike, *295*
Kendrick, Mel, *203*
Kennedy, John F., 198
Kennedy, Robert F., 300
Kertess, Klaus, 17, 272, 273
Kiefer, Anselm, 174, *179, 274*
Kienholz, Ed, 150, 151, *152*
Kiesler, Frederick, 187
Kitaj, R. B., 30
Klee, Paul, 25, 41, 58, 83, 114, 244
Klein, Yves, 113
Kline, Franz, 23, 39, *39,* 40, 43, 58, 73, 84, 85, 86, 131
Knoedler, Michel, 16, 33

Knoedler & Co., 72, 76, 77, 79, 180, 181, 183
Knoedler Contemporary Art, 76
Knoedler's, 65, 85
Knoll, Hans, 151
Knoll Associates, 151
Koberling, Berndt, 286, *287*
Koch, Kenneth, 45
Komar, Vitaly, 219
Koolhaas, Rem, 230
Kootz, Sam, 16, 22, 36, 85, 151
Korman, Harriet, 271
Kornblee Gallery, 143
Kosuth, Joseph, 101, *102,* 176, 285
Kounellis, Jannis, 116, *116*
Kowalski, Peter, 216
Kramer, Hilton, 141, 184, 200
Krasner, Lee, 35, 37
Kraushaar, Antoinette, 64, 65–66, 68
Krier, Leon, 230
Kruger, Barbara, 232
Kulick, Barbara, 175
Kushner, Robert, 237, *238*

Lam, Wilfredo, 73
Lambert, Yvonne, 198
Landscape with Noses (Oldenberg), 176
Lane, Lois, 268–269, *269,* 270–271
Lang, Mr. and Mrs. Richard, 244
Lanier, Mary, 265
Lanigan-Schmidt, Thomas, 237, *237*
Lannan, Patrick, 256–257
Lannan Foundation Museum, 256
Larcade, Jean, 111
Larcade Gallery, 74, 111
Lawson, Thomas, *297*
Leavin, Margo, 281
Le Corbusier, 229
Ledoux, Barry, 269
le Gac, Jean, 212
Léger, Fernand, 35, *35,* 36, 67, 114, 157, 273
Leider, Phil, 192–193
Leslie, Alfred, 45, 129, *129*
Levin, Raoul, 50
Levine, Les, 219
Levy, Julien, 16, 17, 71, 83, 154
LeWitt, Sol, 101, 198, *198,* 202, 205, 232, 274
Lichtenstein, Roy, 93–95, *95,* 105, *108,* 111, 137–138, *137,* 140, 141, 147, 148, 154, 157, *157,*

160, 177, *177,* 236, 243, 246, 299
Lieder, Phil, 243
Lindner, Richard 29
Lippard, Lucy, 192
List, Vera, 205–206, 208
Lloyd, Frank, 169–170, 250
Lloyd, Mrs. Gates, 22
Lobe, Robert, 269, *270*
Long, Richard, 208
Longo, Robert, 278, 292, *296,* 296–297
Longobardi, Nino, *249*
Lord, Andrew, *156*
Louis, Morris, 56, *59,* 61, 257
Luce, Henry, 57
Ludwig, Peter, 105, 129
Lumberg, Bill, *213*
Luminists, 60, 64

Mabou Mines, 191
MacConnel, Kim, *239*
Machine Show, 201
McShine, Kynaston, 100, 101
Magritte, René, *52,* 95
Malcolm, Janet, 216
Malraux, André, 113
Mangold, Robert, 232, 274, 281
Manzoni, Piero, 283
Marden, Brice, 172, *172,* 273, 275–276
Margolis, Margo, 251
Marilyn paintings (Warhol), 112, 125
Marin, John, 23
Marlborough Gallery, 75, 128, 169–170, 204, 250
Marquis de Cuevas Ballet, 51
Marriage of Squalor and Reason (Stella), 93
Martin, Agnes, *167*
Martha Jackson Gallery, 122, 196
Masson, André, 36
Matisse, Henri, 33, 58, 171
Matisse, Pierre, 136
Matta, *34,* 38, 73, 85, 259
Matta-Clark, Gordon, 236, 237
Maximillien Fur Storage, 260
Max's Kansas City, 200
Meadmore, Clement, 260
Meeting Garden (Armajani), 228
Meier, Richard, 229
Melamid, Alexander, 219
Mellon, Paul, 21
Memoir of an Art Dealer (Levy), 11
Merz, Mario, 201

Metro Pictures, 290, 291, 292, 293, 295, 297
Metropolitan Museum, 70
Metzner, Sheila, 224, *224*
Michelangelo Buonarroti, 13
Midtown Gallery, 21
Miller, Dorothy, 26, 27, 47, 92–93
Miller, John, 294, *294*
Millet, Jean François, 53
Minimalism, 100–101, 102–103, 105, 143, 186, 198, 199, 200, 203, 238, 257, 271, 274, 278, 283, 284, 286
Miró, Joan, 25, 33, 113
Miss, Mary, 228, 231, *233*
Mitchell, Joan, 88
Modigliani, Amedeo, 21
Mondrian, Piet, 12, *34*, 34–35, 36, 55, 58, 83, 87, 123, 168
Monet, Claude, 58
Monti, Beatrice, 74
Moore, Henry, 183, *184*
Morgan, Kenneth, *145*
Morley, Malcolm, 181, *182*
Morris, Robert, 100, *100*, 143, 176, 200, 207
Mortimer Brandt Contemporary Gallery, 20
Moskowitz, Robert, *156*
Mosset, Olivier, 284
Motherwell, Robert, 39, 46, *78*, 121
Moynihan, Daniel Patrick, 59
Mueller, Fred, 166
Müller, Jan, 133, 135
Mullican, Matt, 279
multiples, 209, 212
Multiples, Inc., 174, 175, 176
Murray, Elizabeth, *188*, 189
Murray, Robert, 260
Museum of Modern Art, 21, 26–27, 34, 36, 39, 58, 66, *78*, 84, 90, 92–93, 101, 108, 161, 167, 187, 201, 243, 281
museums, 27, 41, 70, 71, 77–78, 109, 244–245, 281
Myers, Frosty, 199
Myers, John Bernard, 42, 43, 45, 46

Nam June Paik, 188
Namuth, Hans, 84
"Narrative Art," 212–213
"Narrative II," 213
Nauman, Bruce, 101, *103*, 207, 213
Negatives Show, 284

Neiman, LeRoy, 63
Neri, Manuel, *244*
Neuhaus, Max, 188
Neuman, Morton, 138–139, 255
Nevelson, Louise, 165, *166*, 168, 169
New Dada, 283
"New Forms, New Media," 125
Newhouse, Si, 104
New Image group, 106–107
Newman, Barnett, 16, 22, *23*, 25, 26, 73, 175, 181
Newman, Donald, 284, 285, *285*
"New Realists, The," 39
"New Spirit in Painting," 184–185
"New Work," 89
New York City, as art center, 17–18, 33–34, 35, 51, 74, 98, 100, 114, 158, 190, 199, 215, 245, 273, 281, 299, 300
New York School, 37
New York Times, 18, 26, 61, 68, 141, 149, 200, 263
Nine Evenings of Experiments in Art and Technology, 188
98.5, 236–237
Ninth Street Show, 86
Nivola, Constantino, 44
Noland, Kenneth, 44, 46, *46*, 56, *62*
Nonas, Richard, 130, 237
Nosei, Annina, 200, 277, 279, 281, **282–289**
Nouveau Réalisme, 113, 197

Oeuvre, L' (Zola), 14
O'Hara, Frank, 45
Oil & Steel Gallery, 120, 129
O'Keeffe, Georgia, 23
O. K. Harris Gallery, 134, 144–150
Oldenburg, Claes, *96*, 96–97, 111, 114, 121, 129, 141, *162*, 166, 174, 175, 176, *176*, 177, 188, 197, 200
Olitski, Jules, 59, *61*, 62, 74, *74*
Oliveira, Nathan, 246, 247, *247*
Once group, 283
One (Pollock), 39
One-Hour Run (Oppenheim), 207
Opalka, Roman, 199, 201
Op Art, 29
Oppenheim, Dennis, 206–207, *208*, *209*, 209–210
Oppenheim, Meret, 82
Ordover, Jerry, 129

Pace Editions, 166
Pace Gallery, 28, 164, 165, 166–167, 169, 202
Painting with Ruler and "Gray" (Johns), 160
Paladino, Mimmo, 284, *284*, 287, 288
Palais de Beaux Arts, 213
Panza, Guiseppa, 101, 104–105, 114, 200
papiers découpages, 171
Paracutin volcano, 208–209
Paris as art center, 73–74, 111, 112, 118
Parke-Bernet Galleries, 67, 218
Park Place Gallery, 188, 192, 204
Parsons, Betty, 11, **20–31**, *30*, 37, 65, 69, 89, 151, 265
Parsons Gallery, 20, 86
Partisan Review, 121
Pattern and Decoration Movement, 234, 238
"Pattern Painting," 238
Pavlova, Anna, 49
Pei, I. M., 231
Penck, A. R., 111, 116, *117*
Peridot Gallery, 66–67
Perreault, John, 199, 238
Perugino (Pietro Vannuci), 13
Petersburg Press, 105
Pfaff, Judy, *240*
Phenomena (Tchelitchew), 82
Phillips, Duncan, 27
Phillips Gallery, 27, 267
photography, 208, 220–227
Picasso, Claude, 170–171
Picasso, Pablo, 15, 16, 22, 33, *36*, 50, 51, 164, *170*, 170–172, 255, 273, 281
Picasso: The Recent Years (Janis), 32
Pillows (Warhol). 125
Pisis, Filippo de, 286
Pissarro, Camille, 14, 15
Pistoletto, Michelangelo, 283
Poirier, Anne and Patrick, *118*
Polke, Sigmar, 287
Pollack, Lou, 66, 67
Pollock, Jackson, 12, 22, 23, *35*, 35–36, 37, *37*, 38, 39, 40, 43, 58, 61, 84–85, 86, 104, 121, 123, 244
Poons, Larry, 121, 125
Pop Art, 29, 39–40, 45, 58–59, 96, 97, 100, 118, 124, 125, 134, 137–141, 157, 160, 165–166, 197, 198, 221, 231, 235, 251, 274,

278, 279
Porter, Eliot, 223
Porter, Fairfield, 45, *45*, 47, 252, *252*
Pound, Ezra, 45
Pozzi, Lucio, *201*
pre-Columbian art, 56, 57, *57*, 58
Prendergast, Maurice, 66, 68
Preston, Stuart, 26
Price, Ken, 267, 269–270
"Primary Structures," 100
Prince, Richard, 285, *294*
prints, 175–177, 251
"Procedure and Process," 207
Projects Show, 201
Protetch, Max, **227–233**
Provincetown, Mass. as art center, 121, 122
P.S. 1, 238, 253, 292

Rabinowitch, David, *128*, 129, 130
Racetrack (Stella), 106
Raphael Sanzio, 13
Rauh, Emmy, 160
Rauschenberg, Robert, 12, 54, 86, 89, 90, *90*, 91–92, 99, *99*, 104, 111, *112*, 113, 114, 123, 140, 142, 147, 208, 219
Ray, Man, 50, *50*, 226
Ray Gun Rifle (Oldenberg), 129
Raysse, Martial, 113
Realists, 135, 147
Rebay, Hilla, 36, 83
red paintings (Rauschenberg), 87, 88, 91
Reich, Steve, 188
Reinhardt, Ad, 22, *28*, 131, 198, 285
Reiring, Janelle, 290, **291–297**
Reis, Bernard, 169
Relais Bisson, Le, 112–113
Remington, Deborah, 260
Renoir, Auguste, 15
Revolutions per Minute (The Art Record), 217, 219
Rifka, Judy, 250, *253*, 253–254
Ripley, Dwight, 43–44
Ripps, Rodney, 251
Rivers, Larry, 44, 45, *45*, 46, 88, 174, 175, 176, *176*
"Robert Kushner and His Friends Eat Their Clothes," 237
Robertson, Bryan, 114
Robinson, Walter, 254, *297*
Rochas, Marcel 50
Rockburne, Dorothea, 273
Rockefeller, David, 47

Rockefeller, Nelson, 47
Rohm, Robert, 147, *147*
Romney, George, 60
Root, Edward, 22
Rorem, Ned, 43
Rosai, Ottone, 286
Rose, Barbara, 143
Rosenberg, Harold, 58, 61, 84, 200
Rosenblum, Robert, 171–172
Rosenquist, James, 95–96, *96*, 103, 106, 113, *123*, 125, 139–140
Ross, Ed, 170
Rossi, Aldo, 230
Rothenberg, Susan, 267, 268, *268*, 271, 278
Rothko, Kate, 169–170
Rothko, Mark, 16, 23, 25, 27, 35, 39, *39*, 73, 85, 164, *169*, 169–170, 280
Rubin, Bill, 172
Rubin, Lawrence, **72–80**, 142
Rubin, William, 61
Rubin Gallery, 72, 74
Ruscha, Ed, 54, 243
Russell, John, 18, 114, 200, 260
Ryman, Robert, 101, 198, 241

Saalfield, Agnes, 108
Saari, Peter, *148*
St. Luke, Guild of, 13
Salle, David, 107, 231, 262, *276*, 276–277, 278, 279, 281, 284, 285, 286
Samaras, Lucas, 121, 122, 124, 167, 172, *173*, 259, 281
Sand, George, 44
Sander, Ludwig, 84
Saret, Alan, 193
Scarpitta, Salvatore, 138
Scharf, Kenny, 303–304
Schjeldahl, Peter, 199, 236
Schlossberg, Ed, 217
Schmela, Alfred, 74
Schnabel, Julian, 53, 106–107, *107*, 118, 231, 252–253, 275, *275*, 276, 277, 278, 279, 281, 286–287
Schneeman, George, 236
Schoenberg, Arnold, 51
School of Visual Arts, 300
Schum, Gerry, 207
Schuyler, Jimmy, 45
Schwartz, Alexandra, 167
Schwarz, Arturo, 18
Screwarch Bridge (Oldenburg), 176

Scull, Ethel, 103–104, 126
Scull, Robert, 46, 103–104, 120, 124, 126, 140–141, 144, 148
sculpture, 184, 230–231, 236
"Sculpture in the Constructivist Tradition," 260
Seated Woman on Bench (de Kooning), 184
Seattle Art Museum, 242, 244–245
Segal, George, *41*, 111, 124, 135, 166, 173
Segal, Helen, 173
Seligman, Kurt, 43
Serra, Richard, 101, *102*, 106, 161, *161*, 162, 199, 300
Shafrazi, Tony, **298–305**
Shannon, Thomas, 217, *218*
Shapiro, Joel, *192*, 192–193, 257, 268, 269
Shea, Judith, 269, *269*
Sherman, Cindy, 292, *293*, 297
Shields, Alan, 191, 192
Siler, Todd, 216
Silverman, Martin, *265*
Simonds, Charles, 236–237
Since Cézanne (Bell), 82
Sinsabaugh, Art, 224
"Sixteen Americans," 92–93
Sloan, John, 65
Sloan, Sunny, 175
"Smashing Beauty" (Shannon), 217
Smith, David, 71, 87, 121, 123, 230
Smith, Leon Polk, *69*
Smith, Tony, 28
Smithson, Robert, 198, 199, *200*, 300
Smyth, Ned, *238*
Snow, Michael, 191
Snyder, Joan, *263*, 264
Soho as art center, 190, 199, 245
Solomon, Alan, 91, 200
Solomon, Holly, **234–242**, 265, 279
Solomon, Horace, 234, 235, 236, 237, 241
Solomon, Richard, 166
Solomon Gallery, 234, 237
Sonnabend, Ileana, 12, 81, 82, 98, 99, **110–119**, 136, 141, 144, 179, 198, 202, 274, 282, 283, 292
Sonnabend, Michael, 111
Sonnabend Gallery, 98, 225
Sonnier, Keith, 101, *104*, 301

Soulages, Pierre, 85
Soutine, Chaim, 58
Sperone, Gian Enzo, 101
Sperone Westwater Gallery, 107
Spielvogel, Burt, 236
Stable Gallery, 69, 95, 127, 153, 166
Stable Pieces (Cornell), 153
Standing Broadjump (Oppenheim), 210
Star Thief (Rosenquist), 106
Stearn, Robert, 237
Stedelijk Museum, 297
Stein, Gertrude, 181, 281
Steinberg, Leo, 171
Steinberg, Saul, 22, *29*, 172
Stella, Frank, 55, 59, 79, *79*, 92–93, *93*, 97, 100, 106, 132, 139, 142–143, 146, 154, 160, 257
Stephan, Gary, 277, *277*, 279, 281
Stern, Hedda, 22
Stieglitz, Alfred, 16, 23
Stieglitz group, 66, 67, 223
Still, Clyfford, 21, 23, *25*, 26
"Stock Up for the Holidays," 165–166
Stoller, Ezra, 230
Stone, Allan, 155
Stones (O'Hara and Rivers), 45
Store (Oldenburg), 96
"Story Art," 213
Stout, Myron, 127, *127*, 130
Strasberg, Lee, 236
Stravinski, Igor, 51
Structure group, 213
Sullivan, Mrs. Cornelius J., 21
Sultan, Donald, *163*
Surrealism, 35, 37, 48, 73, 82, 83, 95, 113, 262

Tamarind Lithography Workshop, 251
Tanglewood Press, 176
Tanguy, Père, 15
Target with Plaster Casts (Johns), *89*, 91
Tatransky, Valentin, 213
Tchelitchew, Pavel, 82
"Ten American Masters of Watercolor," 259
They Taught Themselves (Janis), 32
Thomas, Dylan, 43
Thompson, Bob, 188
Thorne, Joan, 271, *271*
Three Flags (Johns), *168*, 168–169
Time, 208, 209

Time Line (Oppenheim), 207
Times Square Show, 253, 254, 256
Tinguely, Jean, 113
Tobey, Mark, 244, 267
Tremaine, Burton and Emily, 103, 168–169, 235
Turandot (Ashbery), 45
Twombly, Cy, 54, 88, 92, *92*, 141
Tyler, Ken, 105

Ukele, Mierle, 219
ultimate paintings (Reinhardt), 198
Universal Limited Art Editions, 105, 175
Utrillo, Maurice, 65

Valentin, Curt, 16, 25, 40–41, 65
Vanderbilt, Alfred G., 68
Vanderbilt, Gloria, 44
Van Elk, Ger, *178*, *179*
Van Gogh, Theo, 15
Van Gogh, Vincent, 15, 65
Vanity Fair, 67
Vasari, Giorgio, 13
Vautier, Ben, 212, *212*
Velásquez, Diego, 59
Venice Bienale, 91–92, 99, 114, 123, 184, 199, 243
Venturi, Robert, 228
Victory Boogie-Woogie (Mondrian), 35, 168
View, 34, 43
Village Voice, 135, 184
Vlaminck, Maurice de, 65
Vollard, Ambroise, 15, 21, 79, 119
Voulkos, Peter, 246, *246*

Wadsworth Atheneum, 66
Wakefield Bookshop, 22
Wakefield Gallery, 21, 22
Walker, John, *76*
Wallace, Mr. and Mrs. Dewitt, 57
Ward, Eleanor, 17, 69, 95, 96, 153
Warhol, Andy, 54, 69–70, 95, *95*, 111, 112, *112*, 125, 138–139, *140*, 144, 150, 155–156, *155*, 157, 205, 235, 236, 299, 300
Washburn, Joan, **64–71**
Washington Crossing the Delaware (Rivers), 44
Watteau, Antoine, 14
Waxman, Dr., 247–248
Weber, John, **196–203**, 274, 283, 289
Weber Gallery, 196
Wegman, Bill, 287

Weill, Kurt, 50
Weiner, Larry, 101
Wesley, John, 188
Wesselmann, Tom, *40*, 166
White, Minor, 220, 221
White Columns, 253, 292
"White on White" (Anderson), 241
Whitman, Bob, 121, 122, 188
Whitney, David, 108
Whitney Museum, 27, 168–169, 201, 207, 259
Wilder, Nicholas, 243
Wilke, Hannah, 219
Willard, Marian, 23, 29, 65, 121, 267
Willard Gallery, 266, 267
Wilson, Robert, 278
Winer, Helene, 279, 290, 291, 292
Winsor, Jackie, *190*, 190–191
Wizon, Tod, 270, *270*
Wolf, Daniel, **220–227**
Women (de Kooning), 37, 39
World House Galleries, 187
World-Telegram, 68
WPA (Works Progress Administration), 67, 71, 175
Wrapped Coast (Christo), 205, *206*
Wright, Frank Lloyd, 229
Wright, Mrs. Bagley, 235

X (Long), 208

Youngerman, Jack, 25, 64, *70*, 71

Zabriskie, Virginia, 29, 265
Zadikian, Zadik, 300, *300*
Zadkine, Ossip, 20, 21
Zen Movement, 197
Zola, Emile, 14
Zucker, Joe, *241*, 278

PHOTO CREDITS

Abbott, Jon, 198, 199 bottom, 203 top
Baker, Oliver, 25, 27, 34 top, 37
Barker, Grant, 60 bottom, 63 bottom
Beard, Peter, 159
Blell, Dianne, 120
Burckhardt, Rudolph, 44 bottom, 89 right, 90, 92, 94, 96 top, 98, 101 top, 103, 111, 122, 137, 176 bottom, 250
Clements, Geoffrey, 23, 33, 35 top, 38, 40, 60 top, 67, 69, 188, 189, 190 top, 191 bottom, 194, 195, 267
Cohen, Ken, 74 bottom, 76, 78, 79 bottom
Conway, Alexandria, 46
Coplans, Jon, 223
Dalla-Tana, Ivan, 182 top, 300, 302, 303, 304, 305
Davenport, Linda, 201 bottom, 203 bottom
Davies, Bevan, 275
Dee, D. James, 148, 149, 237, 238, 239, 240 bottom, 241, 282, 284 top, 285, 286, 287, 288
Delsol, Michel, 110
DeStaffen, Deborah, 258
Devine, Jed, 225
Edgerton, Harold, 223
eeva-inkeri, 36, 48, 50 bottom, 152, 191, 192, 216, 218, 244, 246, 261
Elkind, Roy M., 232, 268, 269, 270, 271
Finkelman, Allan, 264, 265
Freund, Gisele, 32
Gibson, Susan, 204
Groover, Jan, 196
Gorgoni, Gianfranco, 200, 272
Heins, Greg, 96
Hockney, David, 56
Hoheb, Bruce, 180
Horton, David, 134
Incandela, Gerald, 242
Jones, Bruce C., 99, 183, 185
Kaplan, Peggy Jarrell, 217
Kayafas, Guy, 220
Kent, Karen, 186
Liberman, Alexander, 20
Longo, Robert, 290, 291
Mapplethorpe, Robert, 80
Mates, Robert E., 128 top, 150
Meneeley, Edward, 39 bottom
Metz, Gwyn, 22
Metzner, Sheila, 224

Moynehan, Barbara, 174
Mozell, Al, 70, 164, 166, 169, 170, 172, 173
Muller, Paula, 64
Namuth, Hans, 214
Nelson, Otto E., 29, 30, 34 bottom, 39 bottom
Noble, Kevin, 262
Pelka/Noble, 253, 260
Pollitzer, Eric, 47, 59, 102 bottom, 119, 252, 256
Reens, Louis, 177 bottom
Rose, T., 45 top
Rubin, Nathan, 51, 55
Scherr, Helen, 42
Schiff, John D., 112 bottom
Schinz, Marina, 72
Sheidy, Nick, 112 top
Skunk-Kender, 206, 207
Sloman, Steven, 129, 263
Strongwater, Peter, 298
Sulzer, Bettina, 63 top
Swift, Mary, 219
Wegman, William, 234
Westenberger, Theo, 227
Wirtz, David, 266
Zindman/Fremont, 117